Praise for Elizabeth's first book *The Retu*
into Inka Initiation Rites & their Prophecι
in sixteen countries (first published as *1*
venture in the Heart of the Andes, Putnam, 1997:

"For more than twenty years, dozens of candidates for the position of female Carlos Castenada has annually claimed… to have been initiated into a secret Native American tradition…Lynn Andrews is certainly the most successfull…well, move over Lynn! Jenkins is going to put you out of a job. Jenkins' record of her explorations of Andean, especially Incan, spirituality has the ring of truth and is crafted in compelling prose. By definition, it is difficult to express the ineffable, yet Jenkins brings to life not only the Andean landscape and its people but also the mysterious spirits that dwell in those snowy mountains. This is a riveting book with a powerful spiritual message."

— PATRICIA MONAGHAN, Booklist, September 1, 1997

"Her experiences are exciting, portrayed here with a great deal of honor and respect, and her writing is compelling. The result is a fine addition to the growing genre exploring indigenous spirituality. Highly recommended."

— *Library Journal,* September 1, 1997

"In a unique guide to the region of Cuzco and Machu Picchu, Jenkins describes her arduous 12-day pilgrimage to Incan temple sites where, under the tutelage of a Q'ero priest, she perceived powerful transformative energies and encountered the spirits that bring to mind nature-based deities of the pre-Christian era.

"…she concedes that silencing the critical mind and allowing intuition to guide her were prerequisites for entry into the spirit word, in this well-written account of her adventure, filled with recreations of her dialogues with her guides and the spirit world she employs her rationalist, academic background to evaluate her paranormal experiences."

— *Publisher's Weekly,* August 18, 1997

Journey to Q'eros:

GOLDEN
CRADLE
of the INKA

International Bestselling Author

Elizabeth B. Jenkins

Note: All Quechua spellings are taken from the 1995
edition of the Quechua dictionary published by the
Higher Academy of the Quechua Language, Cuzco, Peru.

Published in English by
Pu'umaka'a Press
PO Box 500
Naalehu, Hawaii 96772 USA

www.inka-online.com

ISBN 0-9762387-5-6

FOREWORD

*(The Q'ero) ... live nourished by their traditions,
legends and myths that explain the world that surrounds
them, the origins of corn, coca, and animals that are
the genesis of their music and dance ...*

*Their poetry, supremely beautiful, takes as a
fundamental theme, the magnificence of nature ...*

—Oscar Nuñez del Prado,
Q'eros, 1955

CONTENTS

ACKNOWLEDGMENTS

FIRST AND FOREMOST I must give thanks to a few of my non-human colleagues—the host of Nature Beings that I have had the honor to come to know and call my friends. Without you this book would never have been. To the *Nust'a* of the Hudson River, my *paqarina,* the most gorgeous female spirit of my birthplace, a thousand thank-you's for your wisdom and lessons. May you glide on silvery and endless, stunning New Yorkers with your power and beauty. To *Pachamama* Hollywood, you surprised me completely with what you had to say. Never again will I assume anything about anything. To the waterfall spirit of Hanakapei, on the Garden Island of Kauai, thank you for your generosity, your laughter, and the gift of your living energy. May more people come to understand and make *ayni* with you. To the *Santa Tierra* of Waimea Canyon, Kauai, thank you for your excellent and effective instructions on how to formulate the Wiraqocha Foundation. May the power of this gift return to you a thousand-fold.

To all the European *Pachamama's* with whom I have had the privilege to converse, especially *Pachamama* Italia, beyond your incredible wisdom and guidance, your love and welcome has made my life a far richer and place. To my Californian *Apu* Mount Diablo and the Lady Tamalpais, thank you for making life beautiful with your presence. For Madame Pele my unending respect and gratitude for the call to your land and for your power and presence in my family's daily life. To all our Peruvian *Apus* and *Nust'as, Phausi Runa's,* and *Santa Tierra's* too numerous to name, I give great gratitude. And to you all, from the Great Mother Ocean to the largest *Apu,* to the lake *Nusta's,* the flowering trees, and down to the spirit of the tiniest flower, thank you for not giving up on us humans. Thank you for still being willing to share with us after we have ignored and mistreated you, after we have murdered certain of your species, after we

[viii]

have abused the law of *ayni* with you in the extreme. Thank you for seeing us as the ignorant fools that we are, and continuing to give your soul-sustaining beauty to us. I pray that we humans learn from your incredible compassion and generosity.

For the dear human souls without whose love I would wither and die, first I must thank my nearest and dearest *yanantin*, my mate Barney. Thank you sweetie pie for your deep integrity, your nectar-like love, your strength, and for being different than me. And thanks especially for those two little sperm that were strong enough to make it through, cracking the barrier of possibility to bring forth on a tidal wave of love, sensuality, spiritual power, and deliciousness our sons Sammy and Gabriel. Thank you darling Gabriel, my Archangel, for choosing to leave the vastness and come down here to be with us. Thank you for cooking in my womb during the entire writing of this book, for reminding me to get up more often, to stay away from cell phones, to go swimming, and to feel and enjoy the holiness in every living moment. Thank you Sammy Whammy for insisting we move to Hawaii, and for your vast being, your brilliant two-year old mind, and your "joker" smile.

To all my students and friends everywhere around the world, especially those of you dedicated enough to create Wiraqocha Foundation Italy—my most gorgeous *Nusta's* Paola & Concetta, Wiraqocha Foundation Denmark—Anita and Jens Peter, Wiraqocha Foundation Sweden—Jan, Susanna and Ana. Anton & Gundhild "danke" for translating our entire website into German, and "gracias" Margarita for the Spanish version. Thank you Valerie and Stephen in Eugene for your incredible organizational and human beings skills.

For Doug Childers, my editor, there cannot be enough thanks for your encouragement, humor, writing talent, and for being unafraid to whack the weeds in this manuscript where you saw them growing. To my dear friend Carol Adrienne you are a world of inspiration, a rare and precious gem. Thanks to everyone at Sonzogno for the Italian version of this book, including Alessandra, my delightful translator, and especially that "tough little geisha" Ornella, my beloved and beautiful-spirited publisher. Thanks Dutch publishers for the cool color photos! To Linda

Michaels, again, you are a wonder. Candice not only are you a genius literary agent, you are a good egg and my beloved friend. Thanks for your help getting this book published.

Finally, to Juan Nuñez del Prado, Lida, Ivan, and Juan Murillo, my deepest heartfelt thanks. Juan your generosity knows no bounds. May the fire in your gingerbread-man eyes remain forever unquenched. And if you make to the fifth-level first you'll have to share that with me too. HA! And at last to the entire Q'ero nation and my particular teachers in Q'eros, Don Juan Pauqar Espinoza, Don Augustin Pauqar Qapa, Don Manuel Q'espi, Don Mariano & Doña Augustina Apaza, Don Julian Flores, and Don Humberto Sonqo, and everyone else in Q'eros, thank you for keeping the spiritual nectar of your tradition alive and well throughout so much adversity. I am honored to know you. I, and the entire world, thank you for remaining the true Keepers of the Spirit of the Inka! *URPI CHAI SONQOLLAY Q'EROS!**

**Urpi chai sonqollay* is Quechua for 'thank you'
Translated literally it means 'doves fly in my heart.'

In Loving Memory of
Leoncio Juan Pauqar Espinoza

*An Andean priest from choa choa, initiated by lightning, he died
suddenly in the fall of 2000 in Q'eros. He is survived by his wife and several
daughters to whom he was avidly teaching the Andean Mystical Path.*

DON JUAN PAUQAR removed his hat, signifying for an
Andean Priest that what he was about to say was sacred knowledge.
Abruptly, he began to speak.

"The Inka from the mountains had traveled all the way to the jungle.
And so Inkarri came with a golden cradle in his hand. Inkarri came
from the mountains and Qoyari, his wife, came out of the rivers. They
went together up to the Mountains and made an encampment near
the jungle. This was Q'eros. But finally they couldn't stay in Q'eros,
and Inkarri and Qoyari went back into the jungle, leaving their golden
cradle behind them."

This mysterious utterance was recorded at Juan Pauqar's Marin County, California appearance in October of 1996. Since then, I have come to understand that this unique speech may be a kind of metaphor for *Q'ero* historical knowledge. Q'eros was the first place founded by Inkarri—or Manqo Qhapaq—the first Inka, sometime in the early 1200's. Don Benito Qoriwaman was an Andean master from the Cuzco Valley in the lineage of Waskar—the last Inka. Don Benito's teachings represent certain advents in Andean mystical knowledge and practices that don't exist in Q'eros, and must have developed between the time of Pachacuti, in 1428, and the time of the last Inkas, Waskar and Atawalpa in 1532. For example, the practice of eating *hoocha* was, until recently, unknown in Q'eros. The *Q'ero* priests were fascinated to learn about it. So it may well be that Q'eros, the last modern bastion of Inka culture, was indeed the "golden cradle" of the illustrious Inka civilization.

*"Manqo Qhapaq, Sinchi Roq'a, Lloq'e Yupanki,
Mayta Qhapaq, Qhapaq Yupanki,*

*Inka Roq'a, Yawar Waqaq, Wiraqocha, Pachacuteq,
Topa Inka Yupanki,*

Wayna Qhapaq, Waskar, and Atawallpa"

$\mathcal{T}$hey were thirteen names of power, chanted almost as a song any ten-year-old Peruvian school child might know by heart. Names of the ancient Inkas who ruled the largest sub-continental empire on earth. Names recited to this day that conduct lines of living energy through time, lines of communication between past and present, between the material and spirit worlds. All these names and lines link the ancient Inkas to their modern day descendants, the Q'ero Indians of Peru.

The Empire of the Inkas no longer exists, but the Inkas have vanished only in our history books. I have had the honor to visit the Q'ero in their original homeland, and to touch the lines of living power that still invigorate their culture. The Q'ero still perform the ancient ceremonies to the spirits of the earth and of the mountains. They still read the *khipus*, the knotted cords that kept the Inkas' accounts and history of their vast empire. And if you ask them who they are, they will tell you, "We are Inkas."

So you see the Inka's have not disappeared at all.

Qosqo, the original Inka name for Cuzco, Peru, means "navel of the earth." The city, rising to nearly twelve thousand feet altitude, is a shining jewel set in a towering snow-capped-mountain bevel. Here, in the most ancient continuously inhabited city in the Western Hemisphere, I lived in the *barrio* of San Cristobal, on land my Peruvian families' ancestors had occupied for a thousand years. In the house of *la familia Machicao*, nestled between the ancient palace of Manqo Qhapaq—first ruler of the Inka Empire—and a ruin called Sapantiana, meaning 'place to meditate alone,' I began my spiritual journey. Here, I dreamt, breathed, studied, sang, struggled, and wept myself ever deeper into the heart of the Andean landscape. Like a seed, my soul burrowed into her rich soil, took root, and began to grow. And here at last, on this great globe of untold grief and unexcelled beauty, I found myself unaccountably at home.

Cuzco, once proud capital of the Inka Empire, is a place of potent mystery and enthralling natural beauty. Its heartful people live at the raw edge of life. Yet even a meal away from starvation, they are generous beyond belief. They are a population in sync with the irrational pulse of nature. Their lives move in accordance with the changing colors of the landscape, the flavor of a dream, the language of fishes, or the shape of a lightning strike. Community news is heard not on television, but rather in the whispers of the winds careening down from the Great Mountain Spirit protectively watching over their village. For these people, Nature is intelligent, alive with meaning. Even now they scan the night skies for portents of life changing events; great floods, droughts, or cataclysms that are sewn into the fabric of the stars. Here, Nature speaks in her original voice, and the ears of the people open to hear her.

Ten years before, in this place, among these people, I underwent a spiritual initiation into the mysterious workings of the unseen world. Here, the implacable cage of thinking I called "my mind," the rational, over-planned, fear-driven event I called "my life," and the tiny socialized identity I called "myself" were slowly reduced to a pure, living self that thrilled and quivered to life's most delicate currents. This stripping away, at times ecstatic, at times terrifying, was only a beginning, preparing me for higher initiation into the Mystical Path of the Andes.

Surely, I was called. Eagerly I went. Bewildered, I endured the ordeal of my undoing to its inexpressible culmination in the Great Initiation the Inkas call *Hatun Karpay*. But I have told this story in my first book, *The Return of the Inka*. Now I will tell you what happened after...

I invite you to join me on my journey to Q'eros, golden cradle of the Inka. This is the story of a quest, not only to a land few feet have ever traveled, but also into the heart of real mysteries, called legends, that turn out to be true. We ascend along dirt roads where Geographic Survey maps read "insufficient data," into 15,000-foot mountain villages. There, smiling sacred brown-eyed people, living on the edge of time, invite you into their stone houses and serve you tea. And in their presence, you know you are in a place where the heart of the land and the heart of the people are still one.

 Dream

*One enormous craggy finger points, resolute. I cannot
refuse. Body shaking, my breath comes in ragged gasps as I
turn to see. There. The ancient stone bridge. The river
humming beneath, shining, shining. But Juan? Where is
Juan?*

*My eyes, magnetically drawn by the great silver ribbon of
water, are compelled to follow it's shining curves up and
up … to the source. Great Mountain. Ancient Being looms
proud. Imposing. Instantly, Mountain becomes finger again
and curves backward … beckoning me. Commanding.
Insistent. My bones ache and crack as my body dissolves
into a million particles, and still, the relentless finger
pulls me onward … toward the mountain.*

"*Y*ah!!" I lurched bolt upright in bed, startling myself
and my partner out of a dead sleep.

"Honey, what's wrong?" he asked, worry and concern all over his
sleepy face.

"Mountain … the mountain … it's … it's calling … calling me," was
all I could gasp out.

I wasn't the only one who heard it. One week later I telephoned Nina from our original group. On impulse, I simply picked up the phone and dialed. I wasn't sure what to say. As it turned out I didn't

Apu Ausangate

have to say a thing. "Elizabeth, I'm not surprised it's you," Nina said.

"You're not?" I asked, a little afraid of what was coming.

"The Mountain ... Elizabeth ... it's calling us back."

Her words, her certainty, ended my doubt and hesitation.

Two years before, in Cuzco, Peru, Nina, eleven others, and I had undergone the *Hatun Karpay*, the Great Initiation ritual of the Inkas, with anthropologist Juan Nuñez del Prado. This ancient ritual, springing out of the sixteen thousand-year-old tradition of nature mysticism in the Andes, was designed to bring the individual into direct, intimate and mystical relationship to the Divine through Great Nature herself. This encounter triggers a kind of melt-down of the "personality" into it's primordial origins, and if all goes well, a recovery of one's "original self" and knowledge of one's role as a player in the great creation. After this disintegration and (hopeful) reconstitution of the personality, it is up to the initiate to make their way back into society and forge a position of spiritual authority in their local community.

There are, of course, casualties. Traditional Andean Initiation happens in one of two ways: you chose the path of Great Nature, or Great Nature chooses you. In the first case, an individual decides they want to learn and begins by bothering an Andean priest enough to convince the priest they are worthy, and that they can afford to pay. In the second, the initiate survives grave illness by communion with supernatural beings at sacred sites, or the initiate is struck by lightning three times and survives. In any case, initiation is not easy, cheap, nor painless.

[2]

Historically, as today, Andean priests are paid well for their knowledge and all exact a fortune in chickens, cows, and sheep—whatever valuable the initiate may possess—as payment for an Initiation Rite. This is a safeguard, insuring that the initiate has the required living energy to undergo the Initiation in the first place. Being a strong and clever tender of sheep and cows is evidence of the development of their personal power, or "bubble of living energy" as the Andean priests term what we call the "aura" or "energy field" that surrounds the body. The initiates' willingness to part with material wealth is witness to his or her strong and sincere desire to learn, and to make sacrifices in order to follow the spiritual path.

My own call to initiation on the Andean path had come in 1988, when I sacrificed my career as a clinical psychologist to follow a deep spiritual urging to move to Peru. In Cuzco, I had a visionary experience, or what Andean priests would call a "direct encounter with a supernatural being." *Apu* Ausangate, their most powerful Mountain Spirit, spoke to me. This "encounter" allowed me to begin my training with a third-level priest. Five years later, in 1993, I was finally ready to receive the fourth-level initiation of *Hatun Karpay,* at the hands of Juan Nuñez del Prado, an initiated priest of the fourth level, and an anthropologist from Cuzco.

After my Andean initiation, I found my way back to the "land of the dead," as the United States is known in many indigenous cultures, to make the monumental effort at reintegration not only within myself, but also back into the Western culture from which I came. In the Andes, nature and particularly the mountains that dominate the landscape are as integral a part of the inhabitants' psyches as they are part of the physical terrain. These mountains are to the Andean Mystical tradition what the Himalayas are to Tibetan Buddhism. The human psyche, the pulse, breath and very heartbeat of the people, and thus their culture and spiritual tradition, are inextricably linked to and configured by the staggering environment in which they have organically grown over many centuries. The land is their ancestor, their deity, and their mother, a living pulsing being who is the sacred source of their own living energy. By comparison, perhaps it is not surprising that indigenous people call the U.S.A. the "land of the dead."

Having lived two years in the lap of that throbbing life force, my return to the U.S.A. felt like the worst kind of exile. Yet I knew "the Gods" wanted me back in the States. My job now was to forge a kind of bridge between 'there' and 'here,' between two cultures, two states of mind, two human perspectives as alien as if they had sprung from two different planets. But central to the work and perhaps most difficult of all, was to fashion the bridge between my old self and my new self.

My own culture, the culture into which I had been born and grown for more than 28 years—the only world I had ever known—felt cold and foreign to me now. Everywhere I turned I experienced the same difficulty in every aspect of my life, whether it was with the land, with people, or with my job and position in society. Compared to Peru, the spiritual aspect of life here in the States was suppressed; submerged so completely that it was nearly inaccessible.

Although I had taken a job as a psychotherapy intern, this return to my previous identity didn't completely fit anymore, either. I couldn't identify with many of my old friends, or with this position in my community, as I once had. Now my job as a psychotherapist felt like trying to help people fit into a culture that had no spiritual reference points. A modern psychotherapist with no spiritual perspective seemed little more than a "personality technician," trying to convince people to adapt to a soulless society. And this did not satisfy me.

However, I had a curious shift in perception regarding my internship. It now struck me that the period of internship and examination before licensure was our Western equivalent of an initiatory process. The odious written and oral exams, with a notorious passing rate of about thirty-percent, reminded me of my first encounter with the third level Andean Priest Ricardo and his group. His initiates had projected their spiritual authority outside themselves, giving it to Ricardo and the infamous "mountain spirits" he was so good at conjuring. This was a characteristic of the "third-level" in the Andean system of psycho-spiritual development. My empowerment, and graduation to the next level, came in the process of rejecting this set-up and internalizing my own spiritual authority.

[4]

Only then was I ready to meet Juan, and receive the fourth-level initiation of *Hatun Karpay* that I describe in my first book, *The Return of the Inka.*

In the same way, I and the room full of three hundred psychotherapy interns being tested by the California Board of Behavioral Science Examiners had projected our authority outside ourselves. We felt, and perhaps rightly so in some cases, that the Examiners knew how to be therapists and we didn't. The testing process forced us to study the laws, codes of ethics, therapeutic procedures, etc., thus taking the authority represented externally by the Board and internalizing it. When the Board deemed us ready, we passed over to the next level. We became licensed therapists with our own authority to practice.

Conceptualizing the process as initiation in this way made it easier for me to bear. I purchased my conservative dark blue suit with the same love and care I had felt at buying my *unkhu,* the black woven alpaca Inka initiation tunic. In many ways the Andean initiation had been much more arduous. Still, engaging in the Western equivalent didn't stop me from invoking the power of the wind spirit—guardian over sound and speech—before walking into my oral exams.

Now, with both cultures' initiations under my belt, I was more unsure than ever of my place in the United States. I was more than a psychotherapist, but I certainly wasn't a priest. The uncomfortable rubbing of these two states of mind was, I suppose, just the irritant I needed to force me to write, to produce my pearl. In fact, the activity of writing was the only way I could find solace. The priest in me felt compelled to affect a larger populace than my one-on-one office job allowed. By day, I looked and acted like a psychotherapist. By night I wrote; a mad artist possessed by the desire to communicate a unique spiritual vision to the world.

As my Peruvian initiation took root and blossomed in me, the mystery I had felt in the Andes Mountains began communicating itself through occurrences in my everyday North American life. Even in the "land of the dead" great nature began to speak to me. Meanwhile my disassembled, fragmented unconscious began to re-organize itself and my writing became more and more lucid. As a result, I wrote a book proposal that was accepted by a very good agent and sold to a large publishing house.

No good Andean priest would receive such news without offering something back in gratitude to the spirits for their unquestioned assistance. So, before leaving for a meeting with publishers in New York, I performed the ancient ritual Juan taught me by which Andean priests speak directly with the spirits of nature. I made a *desapcho,* an offering to the *Santa Tierra* (earth spirit) of Avenue of the Americas, New York City. Assuming that New York earth spirits must be suffocated under so much cement, I was caught of guard by the power of the response.

"YES! WHAT DO YOU WANT?" I felt this *Santa Tierra* thunder at me with her wordless power. The essence of the communication that followed on the heels of my astonishment was something like, "You are surprised that I am powerful? Why do you think there is so much life force and action, trade and creativity here in New York City? Why do you think humans from around the globe are attracted to come and live here on my land? Because we are weak? Think again little sister. The spirit of the land on which you humans choose to live is what attracts you. You come because of US, and *you* reflect *our* natures!"

Unusual experiences and perspective changes, signs and dreams reorganized my thinking and my being. As a "paqo," an initiate on the path of mother-earth wisdom, I listened to these messages and took direction from them. My ability to speak directly with the New York *Santa Tierra* was a sign that my fourth-level initiation was deepening. Life and the nature around me revealed truths I could not deny.

So, after my dream of the Mountain and phone call with Nina, I began making morning prayers and magnetization rituals to attract the "right" group of people to come to Peru. Then I sat back to watch what came in. One month and a few dozen long distance phone calls later, we had our new group assembled. Some had undergone the *Hatun Karpay* Initiation. Others had not. But almost all had been to Peru, and all felt a deep calling, an invitation from Ausangate Mountain and *Apu* Sinak'ara the great glacial snow peak that oversees the Qollorit'i Festival, the highest and most sacred pilgrimage an initiate of the Andean Path can make. And that was the determining factor, the sense of having been called by the Mountain that was the glue that bonded our unusual group together.

Our group included a writer, a body worker, a computer systems designer, an environmental engineer, a nursing home director, a church office manager, an Emmy award winning filmmaker, and me … a psychotherapist turned priest? Nina and I were the only ones from the original group of twelve who had undergone the *Hatun Karpay* with Juan several years before. On a sunny day in June, we boarded a plane bound for Cuzco and beyond, on a

Don Juan Nuñez del Prado

voyage into the outback of Peru, and deep into the wilderness of our own souls.

After landing in Cuzco and celebrating a joyous reunion with our guide and initiation master Juan Nuñez del Prado, we took off for Paucartambo, a potent combination of exultation, fear and longing in our hearts. Juan explained to us that in order to properly arrive at the festival of Qollorit'i and the *Apu* (mountain spirit) Sinak'ara, we first must pass through the ancient villages of Q'eros and receive the blessing of its high priest, Don Manuel Q'espi. The dual prospects of this trip were at once enthralling and sobering—the opportunity to meet and learn from a living Andean Q'ero master—or potential disaster, the worst being death through accident or exposure to the brutal elements of this forbidding terrain. Yet our entire journey might be made in vain if the fickle mountain weather blocked our entry into this remote mountainous region. On the other hand, assuming our group arrived in Q'eros intact, what if Don Manuel Q'espi, highest of Andean Priests, did not want to receive us?

I thought back to the first Andean priest I had worked with six years before … Ricardo, and his "third level" group of initiates. One of them had mentioned a village of pure Inkas who lived high in the altiplano and still practiced the ancient ways. I had fantasized about meeting these Inkas even then. Now, six years later, the fantasy had become my real-life adventure.

[7]

The very road on which our bus now traveled would take us to meet them!

My spiritual enthusiasm was equaled only by the harsh reality of third world travel that was literally being "driven" home to us. Cold steel and wooden plank seats pounded our buttocks as the bus leapt and jounced its way along what was loosely termed "the road" between Cuzco and Paucartambo. It was an unnerving ride. Beach ball sized potholes and a driver on a suicide mission combined to devastate the gluteus maximi of the most toned among us. Beat-up and panting, we arrived in a picturesque little Andean town of perhaps a thousand inhabitants. A conglomerate of little cracked white plaster houses and buildings with bright blue and green shutters lined the streets of this high altitude municipality. I had heard our bus driver say that most people went to work in the surrounding fields each day. This explained why, in the middle of the afternoon, there was almost no one in sight.

Paucartambo, roughly two hundred and twenty kilometers from Cuzco, borders the Amazon jungle. It stands ten thousand feet above sea level, just southeast of the large white area on our topographic maps marked "insufficient data." The Peruvian Geographic Institute's 1994 map stated there had been no official aerial photographs taken of the region. Our trip would be taking us, quite literally, into uncharted territory!

The heat and dust of the bus ride left us all parched, so I ventured off on my own to find a soda pop street vendor. I strode down a dusty street that seemed to be the main drag through town, straight toward the little brown door with an orange Fanta sign above it that I hoped was a gateway to an oasis of refreshing beverages, or at least a local watering hole. In Peru you can never tell from the outside what you will see on the inside.

I arrived to find the door securely fastened, and a tiny sign that read "*cerrado*," closed, stuck through with a small rusty nail. I didn't realize the whole group had descended from the bus and was traipsing along some little distance behind me. Now I turned back and saw them standing on a beautiful stone bridge, looking down at the shining river below. Bridge? I had been in such a hurry that I hadn't even noticed I'd crossed a bridge. In a split second, the image of the stone bridge from my dream neatly superimposed itself over this bridge. A perfect fit! A cold shudder passed through me, raising the hairs on the back of my neck. I looked upward toward the Mountain—there he loomed overhead, just as I had seen him in my dream. *Apu* Ausangate.

"Where's Juan?" asked Mollie, the writer of the group. Just as he had been in my dream, Juan was missing! In one surreal moment, the dream world and the physical world had become unmistakably linked. This magical intersection of worlds created a moment of raw power, and I knew I had to act quickly or lose it forever.

"Quick everyone. Come here!" My tone of voice cut all conversation, and the group gathered around me in an instant. "You know that you were all called here by that mountain," I said, pointing at the snow-peaked form that towered above us. "This river comes down from *Apu* Ausangate and therefore carries his power. You are all familiar with the fact that in the Andean tradition everything emits living energy, and that there is no negative or positive energy, only heavy and refined." Heads bobbed up and down around the circle in acknowledgement, as the group gazed up at the mountain in awe. No one knew that we would arrive so soon to stand at the foot of this sacred mountain being.

"You know that your bodies are surrounded by a "bubble" of living energy through which you can connect to the forces of nature. Close your eyes now and focus on your own bubble of living energy. Connect your bubble with the bubble of the river, the living energy and power of the river. Release your heavy energy to the river as a sacred offering, for in order to receive we must first give. It is the law of *ayni*, sacred reciprocity." I paused, giving them a chance to complete the process. "Now, receive the power of the river directly into your bubbles."

Audible gasps were heard around the group as we exercised our rights as Andean *paqos* to enter the sacred geography of the region by touching the "world of living energies." It was our first ritual and served two purposes. First it united our group bubble, or energy field. And second, it connected us to the living energy bubble of the river and the Holy Mountain Ausangate, effectively placing us in spiritual harmony with our surroundings. During these sorts of ceremonies *paqos* can have visions or receive instructions directly from the mountains or other nature spirits.

Juan had often told me it was very difficult to enter Q'eros. Many had tried but were repelled by weather or upon arriving, by the people of Q'eros themselves. Now, in this moment of my dream and reality coming together suddenly, I understood. *Apu* Ausangate was the mountain spirit who guarded the door, the entrance to Q'eros. Perhaps my dream had been an 'instruction' on how to properly enter this sacred land. But it seemed yet another synchronicity was brewing for just as we concluded the exercise, Juan reappeared, greatly excited. His face softened visibly as he sensed our group bubble.

"Good. I see you have been working too," Juan said, smiling broadly. "Excellent. Now come. We must hurry!" he commanded as he led us off in a mad rush. "Amazing," he added, his words fitting sporadically between gasps from our killing pace, "the keeper of the Cathedral … they told me he was across town and there was no way … but his assistant … just happens to be there cleaning … he agreed to let us in!"

"Keeper of what Cathedral, Juan? Let us into where?" I asked in gulping breaths, trying to keep up with him.

"The *Mamacha Carmen.*" He said. I gaped, stupidly.

"This is one of the places of the prophecy. Elizabeth, the Festival of the *Mamacha Carmen* is the place where one of the female fifth-level priests will arise! Don't you remember?" Juan looked crushed.

"Oh my Gosh!" was all I could reply. During the *Hatun Karpay* or Great Initiation ritual Juan described the enigmatic Inkan Prophecy he had been researching for more than twenty years, which tells of the emergence of the Inka Mallkus and Ñust'as. These were six men and six women of the fifth level of consciousness, priests who could heal any illness, every time, with just one single touch. We were standing near one of the Cathedrals named by the prophecy, the very place where one of the Nusta's would arise.

"Come. Hurry!" Juan commanded, cutting off further conversation.

We reached one of the white buildings, where a young be-spectacled Catholic priest-in-training awaited. He inserted a three-inch medieval-looking key into the side door and ushered us into a low ceilinged portico. Then he led Juan to the far end of the long rectangular room. There a glass jar rested atop a white pillar. There was something in the jar that I couldn't quite make out. The young priest spoke a few words to Juan that made him chuckle. Then he led us around a corner and down another long hallway, to the main attraction.

At the far end of a huge room with a vaulted ceiling, a figure sat on an enormous golden throne atop a large elaborate dais. Juan motioned for us to go stand in front of this most beautiful shrine. The figure, a white woman with curly auburn hair and a beatific smile, wore a garnet-colored velvet dress with a wide gold-embroidered hoop skirt. She looked rather like a giant doll, and needless to say, not at all Inkan. Her clothes and throne were decorated with silk flowers and play paper money was tied to her skirt. A long white cape flowed over her shoulders and trailed to the floor. The air in this room was tangibly different; soft, fresh, luminous, with the slightest scent of peach flowers.

"This is the Virgin of Paucartambo, known here as the *Mamacha Carmen*. *Mamacha* is a Quechua word that refers to a most sacred feminine being."

"Isn't there a Festival associated with her?" I asked.

"Yes," Juan said. "The Festival of Paucartambo in mid-July is the most important festival to the divine feminine - just as Qollorit'i is the festival in honor of the divine masculine." As Juan spoke, I remembered this was part of the prophecy, these ancient festivals engendered a gathering of human living energy together with the power of a scared site, creating enormous potential power.

Juan's voice continued, "Here we must try to 'have a touch' with the sacred feminine power of the Mamacha Carmen. As you stand before her, open your bubble to receive her blessing."

I closed my eyes, and the peach scent grew immediately stronger. I paused trying to gather my thoughts. Then I pictured the bubble of living energy surrounding my body. I could see, as well as feel, that it was vibrant, clean, pulsing and shining, from the exercise with the river. I extended my living energy toward the figure, opening my bubble to her.

A luminous blue-white pearly substance, like warm opalescent milk, pours forth from her and wraps itself around me, cradling me like a newborn babe. My heart pounds and softly bursts with a flood of tenderness toward everything; trees, grass, the sky, parking lots. Every image in my mind, no matter how mundane, appears exquisitely beautiful, and I yearn to stroke these things of life, the objects of this world. I ask to know where she emanates from. The question is strange to me, even as I ask it. The answer is instantaneous. "I emanate from this world—the three dimensional reality. This is where I have my being." She wraps her soft luminous cloak around me, and I am lost in exultation.

"Juan, this is quite a bit of good luck isn't it, because we'll be going to Qollorit'i next week." A scratchingly mundane voice jerked me out of my exalted state. It was Josh—Josh who loved making connect-the-dots statements. I tried to release my heavy energy.

"Precisely," Juan answered, as unperturbed as ever. "That is why are here. It is no accident, my meeting this man in the street," Juan gestured to the novitiate. We all thanked the man and noted the synchronicity of events that allowed us to come here. "We must carry this sacred feminine energy with us to Qollorit'i!" Juan pronounced as we started down the dusty street from which we had come. This was standard practice in the Inkan Art of living energy; male and female were complement, not opposite. So if one absorbed divine female energy from a sacred place, the purpose would naturally be to take it where it could merge with a divine masculine energy. In this spiritual art, human beings become the legs to transport and harmonize the energy between sacred places.

"Juan, what was in that glass jar in the other room?" I asked, my curiosity getting the better of me.

"They say the last priest of this church was a gifted orator," Juan informed the group. "They set up that shrine to honor his gift when he died," Juan stopped and regarded the group with a meaningful gaze. Naively, I supposed he had forgotten my question.

"But what was in the jar?" I asked again.

"That," said Juan, fixing me with his direct gaze, "was his tongue."

CHAPTER TWO

The Road to Choa Choa

We got back in our bus and left the town heading uniformly up, traveling over what was far and away the worst road yet. After a few hours the road simply ended, and we had to get out and walk through the rolling countryside. The temperature was much warmer here than in Cuzco and the atmosphere felt distinctly thicker in texture. Cuzco's air crackled with that high, dry, bug-less electricity of the altiplano. Paucartambo's air was richer and warmer, with an aromatic humidity that emanated from the nearby jungle.

We followed a path by a stream and crossed endless fields covered with tiny potatoes—they lay spread over the earth in a very deliberate manner. Juan explained that these were *chuño*, a kind of rock-hard, black, freeze-dried potato that I had oftentimes eaten in my soup at Señora Clemencia's house in Cuzco. "It is very delicious and so good for you!" the Señora always insisted. I thought it tasted nasty.

Now the process for conserving these potatoes, nature's own freeze-dry, lay revealed at our feet. The farmers simply spread their little potatoes evenly over the ground and let the hot, high-altitude sun and the freezing Andean nights do their work. By day the sun dried all moisture out of the potatoes. The frigid nights completed the other half of the freeze-dry process. Thus preserved, the *chuño* could last unspoiled for years. I heard how the Inkas' skills in preserving and redistributing food indirectly benefited the Spaniards who conquered them. As much as twenty years after the conquest, enough food remained in the Inka storehouses to feed thousands of Spanish soldiers. In fact, some say the *chuño* found in Inka graves are still good enough to eat; and they are almost five-hundred years old!

Soon we arrived at a camp, already set up, where our horses waited for us. This place, Juan informed us, was called Kallakancha. We slept that night beside a field of *"chuños* in process" and woke to see the morning sun sparkling in the tiny rainbow crystals that covered the newly frosted potatoes. I imagined how the Andean climate and the innate humor of these people had combined to create the *Cuzqueño's* unique complexions. They had a kind of dry, burnt-red, crinkled-at-the-corner-of-the-eyes-from-laughing, complexion. Perhaps it was because, like the *chuños*, their cheeks had freeze-dried into smiles.

We breakfasted on the locally grown black tea from Cuzco, some bread with jam, and oatmeal. We couldn't see a town from our camp; but we knew one was close by when about thirty exquisitely beautiful but dirty creatures with sparkling eyes, and the most ingenuous expressions, began swarming around us asking for *caramelos*.

After finishing breakfast and handing out all the candy we could spare to the local children, we headed over to a stand of trees where our small Andean horses were saddled up and waiting.

I saw 'Jack' immediately – the tawny colored bad-boy with the white blaze on his forehead. No one had to tell me he was my horse. I walked straight up to him and patted him on the forehead. I didn't even have to reach up. As my hand was resting on Jack's red-brown neck, my mind became absorbed in trying to fathom how we could climb thousands of feet in altitude and traverse dozens of kilometers on these oversized dogs. I was so distracted, I didn't notice the swarthy, black-garbed figure arrive, though he effortlessly commanded the attention of all, including Juan, and even the horses. This horse master had clearly mastered more than horses.

Don Julio, a thin wiry fellow in his mid-fifties with black leather chaps, spurred boots, a bandana, a broad-brimmed leather hat, and not very many teeth, looked the closest thing to a Peruvian cowboy you could find this side of the Amazon basin. He was our guide from here on, and we could not make another step along our journey without him and his expertise. The special reverence and humility with which Juan treated him apprised us that Don Julio would be at the center of our world for the next eight days. Without Don Julio's knowledge and guidance at this altitude and in this place, we could, to put it bluntly, end up like human *chuños*—freeze-dried!

Don Julio commanded two of his four-man team to help our group with the saddles and stirrup adjustments. Then he, Juan, and the other two fellows secured our provisions onto the packhorses. Mercifully, I did not know then how crucial their actions were. For in securing our provisions to the packhorses, they were literally securing our lives. We were about to enter Q'eros country, the uncharted zone, the white area marked on the Peruvian Geographic Institute's map with two deceptively harmless words: "insufficient data." These provisions were all that would keep our souls tethered to our bodies over the next eight high-altitude days while traversing dozens of miles on steep mountains trails, far from any form of "civilization." If those pack horses bolted, or our provisions were lost or stolen, we would not last two days in this harsh environment.

While knowing full well the danger, neither Don Julio nor Juan showed the least bit of concern or worry. Both possessed either the presence or absence of mind (I can't honestly say which) to not communicate the seriousness of this to any of us in any way. Perhaps a lifetime's familiarity with Andean perils allowed them to take danger into account and for granted, at the same time. They laughed and chatted blithely as they tied the packs and checked for stability, secure ropes, and even distribution of weight.

Once he was fully satisfied, Don Julio turned his attention to the human element of the expedition, checking and rechecking the saddles, bridles, and stirrups of each of the eight members of our group. Mounting a horse the size of a large greyhound was easy, and in no time we were all up and ready to go. At Don Julio's signal we began the single file march that would make up our traveling formation for the next four days as we ascended into this glorious region of the high Andes.

We headed due East of Paucartambo. Over the next two days, on a surface consisting mostly of dirt, shale, and solid rock, we covered a distance of about twenty miles and ascended more than four thousand feet. The first morning passed rather uneventfully, if you can call straddling a pint-sized herbivorous quadruped along a foot-wide dirt trail at the edge of a two thousand-foot precipice uneventful! What made it even more nerve-wracking were the passages across large fields of loose shale, where the horses, at times, seemed almost to be skating over the top. There was also the occasional clamber-up-and-over monolithic passes of solid rock. These small horses were sure-footed. But the bone-like clatter of hooves on stone, and their chalkboard scraping for footholds as they heaved us ever upwards, was profoundly unsettling. We eased our nerves with humor, joking about the fact that we were rock climbing on horseback, but without ropes or crampons!

By contrast, the vistas amidst which we traveled were magnificent; and at an altitude of thirteen-thousand feet and rising, literally, breathtak-

Road to Chña Chña

ing. The Andes Mountains thrust upwards around us in every direction. Glorious white snow peaks glinted in the sun, contrasting brilliantly with the deep brown and black velvet of the lower slopes and the gorgeous green mossy carpet that came up to meet our shale and rock path. Twice, in the course of the day, Juan turned to me and spoke passionately from the back of his horse, "I want to be buried on this land when I die!"

I was in seventh heaven. Riding on horseback through mysterious landscapes of spectacular beauty, on my way to meet the lineal descendant and inheritor of the mantle of the Inkas more than met my qualifications for high adventure. I comfortably straddled my horse, gazing at the beauty surrounding me, an enormous, self-satisfied grin on my face. Looking around, noting my companions' expressions, I saw that not everyone seemed to share my feelings. Only the beautiful Nina, her long legs dangling nearly to the ground over her horse's sides, looked as at home as I felt. Our eyes met, our faces lit up, and she returned my wide grin with one of her own.

The others looked as if it took all their concentration just to stay on their horses. Mollie, a young woman from the East coast with almost no horseback experience, was as taut as a drawn bow, and looked literally as if she were perched two inches above her horse. Her body was visibly tensed, disconnecting her from her horse's movements. I became quite concerned about her falling off, since she wasn't really "on" the horse to begin with.

Her posture struck me as a kind of grand metaphor for modern civilization. She was afraid and didn't trust her horse, the animal instinct beneath her civilized persona, the seat of her own power, connecting her to the earth. Maybe, ultimately, that was why she was here. So many of us are afraid of our intuitive, instinctual natures, our primal selves. And our efforts to separate from the "beast" within often invite disaster.

Mollie, so afraid of falling off the horse, was creating the perfect conditions for falling. Her tension transmitted itself directly to her horse, making the horse more nervous on already unsure ground; and her disharmony with it's movements cut off her feedback system so she couldn't adjust her posture. The result was inevitable. Her horse stumbled and...bam! Mollie was on the ground. How often the very thing we feared most was the thing we inadvertently caused to happen.

Jeanette, another group member who had only been on horseback once before, did not have Mollie's fear. Jeanette's body relaxed against the horse, establishing a comfortable communication between her body and the horse's body, so that even when her horse stumbled, she did not fall off. Fear is a curious and highly individualized matter, which we would meet in many forms on this trip. By the end of our journey, we would each encounter our own unique brand of fear, and learn the tailor-made lessons that came with it.

By about one in the afternoon the sun was high and the temperature was tropical. Lunch was a welcome break from (and surely for) the horses. We stopped to rest on a wonderful grassy meadow, where the cooks whipped up a warm, hearty, high altitude feast. I knew from my years of living in Cuzco that at this altitude it was best to eat large meals during the day and smaller meals at night so the food did not disturb one's sleep. The altitude and hard morning's ride had stimulated our appetites, and our ravenous group quickly devoured the delicious Peruvian camp food.

After lunch and a bit of lounging in the sunny meadow, we were so warm that we stripped down to our T-shirts and shorts or light cotton trousers. We wrapped our polartec jackets and warm-up pants into bundles to be tied onto the packhorses—they were already carrying our heavier clothes for after sundown, when temperatures could plummet in moments. It was rather annoying to try to carry anything in our hands while riding, and our bright colored jackets tied around our waists only served to spook the horses.

Don Julio, who had been loading up the packhorses since well before our lounging period, was still re-tying and re-balancing the loads as we took off again. Juan was concerned about him taking so long, since he should have left at least a half hour before the group. But he convinced Juan that he would overtake us and get to Choa Choa well before us, giving him and his men time to set up camp and make the dinner preparations for our arrival. This day was to be one of our longest rides. We would be cold, tired, and hungry by the time we pulled up to our first village of the Q'ero Nation, the home of Don Manuel Q'espi, eldest and most powerful of the Inka Priests. Before leaving, Juan had carefully explained to us that Don Manuel Q'espi was a very moody and unpredictable character.

"Don Manuel's personality is like mountain weather, he can change his mind at the drop of a hat. We may see him ... and then again ... he may not chose to receive us at all. On four separate occasions I walked from Cuzco to Choa Choa, hoping to receive teachings and the *karpay* of Don Manuel, sleeping by the side of the road as I went. All four times when I arrived to Choa Choa, Don Manuel completely ignored me." Juan was letting us know our chances of actually meeting Don Manuel were pretty slim.

"What do you mean by 'receiving his *karpay*'?" Mollie asked.

"Don Manuel is a very rare kind of fourth-level priest called *kamasqa*." Juan told us, pausing for the impact to sink in. "That means he received the fourth level initiation directly ... " he said, pointing upward to indicate the direction from whence this initiation came. Some puzzled looks caused Juan to spell it out for the *gringos*.

"Most *paqos* study with a master and receive the fourth-level from that master. Of course you must possess the level of initiation that you are to bestow onto another during a *karpay* ceremony. In Don Manuel's case he received the initiation directly from the *hanaq pacha* ... from *Wiraqocha* ... *God!*" Juan blurted out, trying to make us understand. This last pronunciation turned on light bulbs and provoked audible grunts of awestruck comprehension from the group.

"So, if you receive his *karpay*, you receive the power of *his* initiation," Josh said, rubbing his chin thoughtfully.

"Precisely," Juan confirmed, giving Josh a warm smile of acknowledgment. A short quick streak of anger and jealousy flared through me. I recognized its pettiness, and immediately employed the Andean technique of using my spiritual stomach to eat and digest the heavy energy from my bubble. Eating one's own anger was definitely one of the most practical of the Andean tools, I mused...tasting as I chewed.

◆ ◆ ◆

We traveled over an endless gray tundra-like scrub, now well above tree line. At times our ascents were so steep we had to lie nearly flat against our horses, stirrups at their haunches, clutching their manes or wrapping our arms around our their necks as they pressed ceaselessly up the slopes. I felt sorry for the horses, especially Josh's, who was a white and very pregnant filly. Yet they showed little signs of strain, as if they were quite accustomed to the process. Their hardiness amazed me. From time to time I glanced back, expecting to catch a glimpse of the packhorses coming up behind us.

By the late afternoon, even Juan was looking back more and more often and with a worried expression. The two or three people who passed us, farmers returning from their fields on their way home to the Inka town, had not seen Don Julio or the pack horses. Suddenly I knew why Juan was looking so concerned. A biting afternoon wind had begun to blow, raising large goose bumps on my arms. The sun would set within half an hour! The coldness of these mountain nights seemed to descend straight from the stellar depths. Our collective teeth had already begun to chatter. I zipped my thin windbreaker up to my chin and told myself that Don Julio was right behind us.

We descended from the final pass and came around a little hillside— as if we might have passed through a doorway between worlds. A strange and barren lunar landscape spread out before us. It was marked off by large irregular boulders forming low walls that surrounded fifteen or twenty little gray stone huts. Their gray thatched roofs were the same color as the surrounding scrub. These primitive structures filled the small valley before us. A few dotted the hillside up the opposite slope. The town was cut almost exactly in half with mountain shadow and after-noon sunlight. And the murmuring winds picked up to a low howling, warning us that night and cold were coming on fast. In the fifteen min-utes it took us to descend the slope and enter the town, the sun fully set.

"This is it?" I thought, "This is Choa Choa? I came all this way for this?"

We arrive at Choa Choa

Shivering violently, we dismounted. Juan told us to leave our horses there in the field, and then he started back up the slope, searching desperately for signs of Don Julio. I knew it was up to me now. I headed for a little broken down stone hut at the lower end of the village—it looked uninhabited—and the group ambled after me, stupid with altitude, cold, and plain old physical exhaustion. Choa Choa, the highest of the Inka villages, was perched at a imposing fourteen thousand feet.

I approached the door and looked in, caught between not wanting to be rude in an unfamiliar culture, and the need to protect my group from the extreme physical conditions. No one was home, so I turned to wave the group in—and that's when I saw Josh stumble. As he caught himself and straightened up, I gasped. His normally ruddy complexion had turned ashen, and his expression spoke volumes on the subject of fear.

"Hypothermia," he whispered to me as I wedged my shoulder under his armpit. Nina took Josh's other arm and we moved him as quickly as possible inside the shelter. His pulse was weak and his teeth were chattering uncontrollably. We placed Josh in the center of the tiny hut and gathered around him in a tight circle, trying to lend him the heat from our bodies. Juan came to the door smiling, took one look at Josh, and sped off without a word.

The stone hut had no door or window to close and the freezing wind whipped in through both openings. I dislodged myself from the group long enough to close the gap in the window with an old board that was lying on the floor. Jeanette made the ultimate sacrifice—she took off her plastic poncho and used it to cover the doorway. We huddled wordlessly around Josh, sobered by the gravity of the situation.

Our baleful vigil seemed to last an eternity, though it was probably no more than thirty-five or forty minutes. We were waiting, hoping Juan or Don Julio would reappear. I began to pray for some unexpected miracle, anything to end the ominous waiting. When I could no longer stand it, I begged God silently to save Josh. Even though we were out of the wind, the temperature continued to drop. We were all contemplating the prospect of a night with no tents, no sleeping bags, no warm clothes, no food, and the possibility that we might soon share Josh's fate. As leader, I was responsible for the safety and well-being of the group. My own thoughts began to feel alien as they went square and stiff with fear!

Suddenly, there was a rustling at the doorway. A little man burst through the plastic poncho and into our midst. About four and half feet tall, he wore a pale gray-green wool poncho and a hat pulled down over his eyes. He carried another poncho in his hands, which he extended out toward Josh. Nina took the poncho and wrapped Josh up tight. The little man darted from the hut, and before we could speak, he reappeared again, carrying a small woven bag. He reached into the bag and began rapidly began handing out some warm, soft lumps with steam coming off them. Potatoes! And they were hot!

We took the tiny hot potatoes and began stuffing them into Josh's socks and pockets. We put them down his shirt, into his hat everywhere we could. At last Josh stopped shivering. It was Jeanette who finally broke the silence, speaking what had been in all our minds.

"Hey Josh, you know what book I read just before coming on this trip?"

Josh shook his head.

"Alive!" Jeanette shrieked impishly. Her timing was perfect, and everyone, including Josh, burst out laughing. "So, if you're going down, you can be the first one that we eat!" She continued mercilessly.

"No, you should be the first one to go," Josh shot back.

"Why?" asked Jeanette, looking stricken.

"Because you're a vegetarian. So if I go first, a good meal would only be wasted." At this we all burst into gales of laughter, and the group's mood improved by a solid nine hundred percent.

Our savior, as it turned out, was Don Julian Flores, last year's President of Q'eros! This much I could glean from his sketchy Spanish and my impossible Quechua, and until Juan returned it would have to do. *El Presidente* sat with us in a perfectly contented silence—a gracious, one-man greeting committee for our motley crew of half-frozen North Americans. Only weeks later would the grandeur of his greeting, and the magnanimity of his offerings of hot potatoes and a poncho, finally sink in.

He had somehow located and brought to us what had to be the only extra poncho in the entire village, though I doubt "extra" would be an accurate term. And in this village whose people live in abject poverty and basic malnutrition, with barely enough food for themselves, those hot potatoes were worth their weight in gold. The Q'ero's life-saving gifts to us that night, generous in the extreme, would be like one of us offering half our bank account to a complete stranger who came to our door needing help. Yet the Q'ero did this as a matter of course, without thinking twice about it. This is how the Q'ero culture lives, by what they call the law of *ayni,* sacred reciprocity. Without knowing it, we had just borne witness to the Q'ero's faithfulness to their Inka ancestry. *Ayni,* giving and receiving, was the sacred mandate in the Andes since ancient Inka times, and it still remains the one law of the Andean mystical tradition.

Juan now poked his head in the doorway. Seeing us all jovial again, the color returned to his cheeks and he gave us a huge smile.

"I have been securing us lodging for the evening. We have a lovely offer from the community of Choa Choa. But first, I want to test your group intuition," he told us. "When do you think Don Julio will be arriving with the horses?" What a clever man, I thought. Rather than saying, "Don Julio isn't here yet and I have no idea if and when he ever will be," Juan turned uncertainty into a game instead.

"Six thirty," Mollie blurted out.

"That's just an hour from now," Juan said nodding. "I think that is about right. In the meantime we have been offered a truly grand accommodation. The governing committee of Q'eros has invited us to stay in their Community House. Come this way." Juan escorted us out of our little shelter, of which I had grown quite fond during our short stay. Who knows what negotiations Juan had been making on our behalf, as we shivered away in our little hut. For all we knew he was going hut to hut himself, begging for a poncho. I was certain that Juan was behind *El Presidente*'s appearance. Before we stepped out of the hut, Josh, now much improved, cleared his throat loudly.

"Please … I really want to say something here," the tone of his voice quickly got everyone's attention. "I just want to thank all of you," he spoke with real feeling and a little water rising to his eyes. "One of my biggest fears has always been that I would be in some kind of physical danger, and no one would be there to help me. Because of all of you, that belief inside me is changed now, forever." A raucous cheer went up from the group. After a brief group hug, we left the hut, warmed inside and out by simple human feeling. We all felt the power of the group, and how working together in these extreme conditions had brought out the best in us.

We stepped out of the little hut into the bitter chill of the night air. The spectacle we encountered, revealed in this pure night, was utterly surreal. Massive, fist-sized stars studded the jet-black firmament. There was no moon, but the stars were so multitudinous and bright that you could almost read by them. I had never seen stars so close, so brilliant, or in such vast number. More miraculous still was the giant herd of luminous white Alpaca scattered on and about the road up to the Community House. They sat unmoving on their haunches even when we passed within inches of them, their eyes like huge reflective pools. The beasts stared at us silently, curious, yet without a trace of fear, as if they were just so many more white furry villagers. They lit our way home.

CHAPTER THREE

Don Manuel Q'espi:
Crystal Priest

*W*e ascended several hundred yards in the thin mountain air and came to a large, rectangular ten by twenty foot stone structure, with a thatched roof and a heavy wooden door—the Community House of Choa Choa. The two windows on either side of the door boasted real, intact panes of glass. As we entered our new accommodations the temperature rose by twenty degrees and audible sighs of relief were heard as the door closed tightly behind us. The stone walls, sealed with mud, allowed not a breath of wind to enter. The dirt floor was covered with a thin layer of golden hay.

I glanced around the group at the shining smiles, and knew instantly that we were all thinking the same thing. At this moment and under these conditions, this primitive dwelling was to us, more beautiful and more luxurious than any five-star hotel!

Five or six Q'ero were seated along the far wall. I scanned their faces in the candlelight hoping, beyond reason, to recognize Don Manuel. Although I had no idea what he looked like, I knew almost instantly that he was not yet among us.

I felt grateful to be here, in relative comfort and security. I burrowed down into my soft golden-hay seat, heaving a huge sigh of relief. I was feeling exhausted by the altitude, cold, hunger, and the sheer stress of the last few hours. Josh's hypothermia episode had brought me to the edge of my own deepest fear. As the group leader I felt unbearably responsible for the group's well being. Now that all my chickens were tucked warm and safe into tonight's nest I could finally relax.

We fell into friendly banter with one another, savoring the moment, exulting in our group triumph over the extreme conditions, and sensing the deepening of our common journey. A feeling of wordless union came over us, the deep bond of trust and togetherness that pilgrims share on their journey to the Sacred. Suddenly, an uncanny sensation made me turn and look toward the door.

Two lights swept over me, sending chills up my spine, as I felt myself at once penetrated and revealed. It took me a few long seconds to realize that an exquisite little man stood there looking at me. His eyes—the lights—literally shining like beacons. He was less than five feet tall, and a mysterious energy radiated from the depths of his copper colored features. He appeared neither young nor old … but deeply wise. As I gazed into his face, time stopped, and the atmosphere took on a heavy gelatinous quality. The molecules of air in the room seemed to expand as I saw—hanging suspended above his head—a pulsating, brilliant, blue-white star. It was as if one of those fist-sizes stars had come loose from the night sky and fallen to rest over him. I closed my eyes and opened them again. The star was still there.

Without hesitation, the man walked across the room, directly toward me. I was transfixed. The star moved when he moved. He stood before me and began speaking urgently to me in Quechua. Instantly, Juan was at my side, translating.

"I am an Inka, come here with the power given to me by God. Who are you?" As he translated these words, Juan looked at me with raised eyebrows—he was as impressed as I was. There was no question in my mind that the man who now stood before me was none other than the famed Don Manuel Q'espi.

"Me ... I'm ... no one ... just a gringa ... a gringa trying to become an Inka," I stammered out. I felt desperate to say something meaningful, or sincere, to this extraordinary man. "My friends and I have come a long way from our homes in California just to meet you." I felt ridiculous, incapable of correctly addressing someone of Don Manuel's spiritual stature. To cover my embarrassment I quickly added a tangible request. "Would you please do a *despacho* ceremony for us?" I asked, overwhelmed by the implausibility of the event now unfolding before my eyes. Here stood the chief of the Inka Priests, talking to *me*, with a brilliant star glowing above his head.

Don Manuel nodded slowly, then responded. Juan translated.

"You must take me to your home in California."

At this pronouncement there was an almost audible click, as if his words had locked into place some future event. I caught Jeanette's gaze and she smiled and nodded at me. Now, the pact had been sealed. As I assured Don Manuel I would be honored to do this, I knew without doubt, that one day we would bring this Andean Master down from his mountain home, into another kind of wilderness.

Having clearly been dismissed by Don Manuel's turning on his heel and walking away, I was left staring into emptiness. Juan approached me. "Juan," I stammered. "I saw a star...a star over Don Manuel." Juan eyes grew suddenly huge.

"You saw Don Manuel's star?" he asked, incredulous. Juan's words, pricked open a bubble of meaning in my head. Not "a star," HIS star, his guiding star, the luminous guiding light or spiritual presence all Andean Masters carry. "You know his last name, Q'espi. It means crystal in Quechua," Juan added, unwittingly solidifying the meaning of my vision of Don Manuel's star. I could only nod in numb reply.

When I asked Don Manuel to do a *despacho* ceremony for us, he didn't say yes and he didn't say no. He informed us, after conferring with his chief disciple, Don Julian Flores, (our savior and former President of Q'eros) that Don Julian would perform the ceremony. He, Don Manuel, would simply be present to assist. To make it even more official, he insisted that we were to pay Don Julian, and not him. It was customary to pay an Andean Priest at the beginning of a *despacho* ceremony so that the money could be tucked under the ceremonial cloth and blessed by the *despacho*. The *ayni* had to be in place so that the ceremony could proceed correctly.

Just as the priests began clearing an area to perform the *despacho*, we heard shouting and a great commotion outside. A young Q'ero, probably in his late teens, entered and announced that Don Julio had arrived at last, with all his horses and provisions intact. A huge cheer went up from the entire group. Juan looked at his watch and winked at Mollie, "Six thirty, precisely!" he said.

The *despacho* ceremony was delayed while we rushed to the door to fetch our down jackets, warm-up pants, sleeping bags, and whatever else we could scrounge from poor Don Julio and his men. Apparently one of the horses had run off and they had spent several hours tracking it down. After finding the horse, they had taken a wrong turn on the trail, trying to make up time, and ended up having to back track for some distance. By now none of us really cared, because we had begun to see divine providence at work in these seemingly "unfortunate" occurrences. Had we not met with such difficulties we might not have ended up at the Community House, or encountered Don Manuel. Certainly Josh would not have been brought face to face with his greatest fear, and been transformed by the event.

One of Don Julio's men had already put some water on to boil, and shortly thereafter asked if we would like a special Peruvian "warm-me-up" drink. Juan respectfully informed us that it had just a touch of alcohol in it. We roared for them to bring it on, and were soon toasting each other with our orange plastic cups. The drink, a mild cherry flavored intoxicant, warmed our bones and put us all at ease. Don Manuel drank and toasted with the rest of us—his star had now vanished from sight as mysteriously as it had appeared.

Using the classic Andean form of divination, Don Julian Flores and Don Manuel did a coca leaf reading, to see if everyone in the group was ready and able to participate in the ceremony. Don Manuel, who was clearly in charge, picked up the coca leaves, blew on them, and then let them fall one by one onto his ceremonial *manta*, a colorful rectangle of finely woven alpaca.

Both men stared intently, pointing here and there at the fallen leaves, determining what auspicious or inauspicious meaning they held. Finally, after a quarter hour of deliberation, Don Manuel gave a hearty chuckle and nodded to Juan, saying that the *Apus* had accepted our group as a whole and that we could all participate in the ceremony.

They made the first *despacho* to the *Apus*, the mountain spirits, using twenty-four *kintu*, which are little groupings of three perfect coca leaves each. The reasoning behind this was that there were eight of us, and they wanted to commend us three times each to the *Apus*. They laid the *kintu* out in three neat rows, one above another, forming a rectangular shape, not the circular or mandala-like patterns I had seen before. Both priests bowed, swayed and prayed over each *kintu* with profound devotion. Kneeling, with their gray wool ponchos wrapped tightly around them, they looked one moment like priests, the next like human cocoons. I now understood why Juan had always insisted that they were priests and not shamans. There was at once a dignity of spirit, and deep humility in their bowed heads, their postures and their gestures, that epitomized the priest archetype.

The next *despacho* was made to *Pachamama*, Mother Earth. Don Manuel and Don Julian whispered and prayed fervently over all the items, blowing on them to imbue them with their own living energy before making the offering. After spreading the *despacho* paper on the ground, they placed the shell in the center to represent both the earthly feminine power and the cosmic feminine power. Next they placed the *kintu* around the shell in a circle, while Juan whispered translations of their prayers into my ear. The prayers were a long, complicated series of supplications, offered for our benefit. Paraphrasing Juan's translations, the prayers went roughly as follows:

"O Sacred Mother, Divine Mother, Holy Earth Spirit, Pachamama. I don't know why these people have come here from so far away. I don't know why they have gone so far away from their homes. I don't know what they want

[29]

from me. I don't know what they are seeking, but Pachamama, they have come so far, please help them. Help them find what they are looking for. Please guide them and protect them. O Pachamama, keep them safe while they are looking for whatever it is they are looking for. Thank you Pachamama, thank you."

Don Manuel's prayer floored me. I saw that he couldn't comprehend why anyone in their right mind would travel half way across the planet to visit his little village. He didn't seem to understand that his way of life held something precious, something rich that Westerners longed to recover for themselves.

As Don Manuel and Don Julian prayed, they blew on the coca leaves, then passed them to us. We blew on them as well, adding our living energy to the prayer and the *despacho*. As they worked, they whispered quietly, arguing over which ingredient would be placed next and where. There was much good humor and many spontaneous outbursts of laughter.

With amazing tenderness, they kept adding more and more items to *Pachamama's despacho*—little bits of colored wool, candies, precious sugar, magnetic rocks, seeds, starfish legs, small candles, colorful confetti, and tiny lead replicas of people and animals. Colorful dried flowers were added last, to make the *despacho* beautiful for *Pachamama*.

We were awed by the tremendous patience, and loving care both priests exhibited in making the *despacho*. They were utterly deliberate, yet not sanctimonious or pompous. All was Done with love—you could feel it. They were priests of love. The entire ceremony was suffused with an extraordinary reverence, yet still managed to stay light-hearted and playful. We all felt purified and profoundly moved by the three-hour ceremony. When it ended we thanked them for their beautiful blessing, and Juan secured Don Manuel's promise for early morning teachings as we headed for our sleeping bags. Sleep seemed a blissful prospect with the encounter of the morrow to dream on. In minutes we were whisked from the waking world, deep into the arms of Morpheous.

◆ ◆ ◆

We awoke to a sea of mischievous brown eyes and the irrepressible laughter of the village children who had burst into the Community House, unable to contain their curiosity. Kids, crowded at the doorway and along the inside walls, waited with great anticipation to see what would emerge from our brightly colored sleeping bags. For those who couldn't squeeze into the Community House without trampling us, there were window panes against which to press their squealing faces. We couldn't help but laugh as they peered at us, and giggled at our groggy countenances.

There was no concern for our privacy, so we didn't worry about it either. We dressed, as far as possible, inside our sleeping bags, then climbed out to continue the process. The children observed, fascinated, exploding into gales of laughter when a bare appendage or an undergarment accidentally extruded from a sleeping bag. Modesty seemed an unnecessary luxury, and we all felt like family after what we'd been through the night before. The kids' refreshingly ingenuous and candid expressions were a delight, and we reveled in our unusual wake-up call.

Soon breakfast was announced. As we prepared to go outside, an elderly woman little more than four feet tall, came rushing across the room right up to Nina who, unbeknownst to her, was nearly six feet tall. Nina was sitting up, still in her bag. This tiny woman, with very dark skin, long black braids, and a brilliant toothy smile, grabbed Nina's hand and began speaking excitedly in her native language. Nina commanded that someone go find Juan so that her words could be translated. Luckily, Juan was lounging just outside the door, smoking a cigarette. He was quickly hustled into the room, and after a moment of bewilderment, began translating her words for the rest of us.

"We are women. Although we live in different parts of the world, we all suffer the same sorrows. We all feel the same joys. We all walk the same walk. We are the same. We are women."

The women in the group exchanged long, knowing glances with one another. Suddenly Nina, in a burst of enthusiasm, leapt out of her sleeping bag and onto her feet, grabbing up the diminutive Q'ero woman in a huge bear hug. The woman shrieked in terror at Nina's height, and

Nina and Q'ero Woman inside Q'ero Community House, Chöa Chöa

struggled like a small child wanting to be put down. But Nina held her fast and rocked her like a baby until she began to weep. She wept in Nina's arms, allowing herself to be comforted by the strawberry blond giantess. No one had ever seen a more touching sight. Her grief spent, she turned to give us a smile that was sheer sun coming out from a rain cloud. We dissolved in a contagion of laughter, until tears of joy streamed unchecked, down all our faces. And it was all the same, our joys and our sorrows. We were the same. We were women.

Later that day, Nina showed us a large fresh egg the woman had given her as a gift. The generosity of the gift was alarming. Nina gave her a blue scarf in observance of the law of *ayni,* sacred reciprocity. But she was so moved by the woman's gesture that she carefully carried the egg with her for days until it was put into a birthday cake for one of our guides.

The whole village was fascinated by our presence, and everyone came out to gander at the *gringos* who had climbed their mountain to meet Don Manuel. More people kept appearing, seemingly from out of nowhere, and the town came alive in the morning sunshine. Apparently, the villagers took our presence as cause for celebration. They had exchanged their gray-green ponchos of the night before, in favor of their

[32]

best and brightest garments, reserved only for high ceremonial events. Even the children were dressed in the most marvelous clothing. *Llikllas,* small rectangular hand woven cloths worn over the shoulders by women, literally exploded with colors. There were brilliant pinks, rich blacks, deep reds, oranges, and blues; all woven in a stunning variety of intricate patterns. There were many hand-beaded *chullos,* the traditional Inka wool hat, with mandatory earflaps, finished with brightly colored tassels. And finally, there were the ponchos of the men—woven in mind-altering, brilliant, geometric designs—to add to this riot of color and pattern. We were overcome by the magnificence and creativity of their apparel!

Breakfast was almost over when the bad news arrived. Don Manuel had gone up the mountain at five-thirty that morning because of some mysterious problem with his sheep. No one had seen him since. Juan reminded us that we were lucky to have seen him at all. Yet disappointment was written all over our faces. We were crestfallen at the thought of missing the opportunity to spend more time with this extraordinary person.

The Q'ero, a highly sensitive people, were quite aware of the change in our emotional state and began discussing something amongst themselves. Then, one of the villagers shuffled up to Juan and began whispering in his ear. Juan turned to us and said, "It seems the villagers like you, and they have offered to show you their extra weavings."

"Juan … .you mean … .shopping?" I asked in anticipation.

"Precisely!" he replied.

This was just the distraction we needed. Yet, none of us could have anticipated that the shopping experience that would take place over the next hour would forever change our lives!

Word of our eagerness spread at lightning speed through the village, and it seemed people were coming out of the very boulders to show us their wares. Each poncho, we were told, took anywhere from six months to a year to complete. Everything was hand spun and hand woven, made with natural dyes, and truly breath-taking in the beauty and precision of the designs. Our eyes now beheld traditional Inka patterns and designs that had been passed down, generation to generation, for untold centuries. Along with their training as musicians and priests, we soon learned that everyone in Q'eros was also a weaver.

The men learned from an early age how to weave their own ponchos, *chullos*, and *unkhus* (the traditional black ceremonial shirt with one small red stripe along its seam.) The women made their *llikllas*, multi-petticoated skirts, and traditional Inka hats.

Because each piece was made with such love and attention, and was imbued with the artist's living energy, the selling and purchasing was likewise a ritual. Whenever one of us found something that we wanted to buy, the creator of that particular piece was located, and a long bargaining session ensued. After a price had been agreed upon, the owner took his or her work in their hands, and spoke into the cloth, saying a prayer or blessing. It almost felt like they were talking to their creation, explaining that it would be going with one of us now. The act of buying a Q'ero weaving felt something akin to adopting a child! After a final agreement had been reached, and payment made, the owner would take our hands while looking deeply into our eyes—sometimes for as much as several minutes—before, at last, surrendering the weaving. Their love and innocence were overwhelming. Here was a primal human ceremony: a genuine exchange of energy, love, and appreciation. Shopping as Sacred Ritual! Our own distant world of commerce, advertising and the profit-motive seemed barbaric by comparison.

As the last bargaining session was being completed, we received the good news that Don Manuel had taken care of his sheep and was coming back down the mountain. He sent word ahead, asking for us to join him at his house within the hour. I marveled at this inconceivable man of spirit, living in these windswept peaks where the average life expectancy was fifty; while he, nearly eighty, still tended his own sheep.

When we arrived at Don Manuel's house we had to stoop low to enter the doorway. Once inside, we found ourselves in a pitch-black room. It took several minutes for our eyes to adjust. A large beam ran across the ceiling of the rectangular room, apparently the main support for the roof. An array of fascinating objects hung from this beam: a saddle, buckets, old clothes, pots and pans, leather harnesses, farm implements, and old baskets, to name just a few. I enjoyed the practicality of the outlay; everything was in easy reach.

Don Manuel invited us to sit down on the floor and we gathered in a semi-circle around him. As we sat down I realized we weren't sitting on a traditional straw covered floor. The ground was lumpy. Fishing in the darkness beneath me, I brought up a *chuño*. We were seated on a carpet of tiny,

Home of Don Manuel Qespi, Chöa Chöa

freeze-dried potatoes in Don Manuel's storehouse! This was the room he used for teaching, and for ceremonies. We found out later that his actual living quarters were in another building. Looking around the room, it dawned on me that Don Manuel was rich by village standards. For a Q'ero, he sure had a lot of stuff!

In the darkened room Don Manuel began preparing a *despacho*. Juan sat next to him in the role of his assistant. As Juan watched Don Manuel's preparations he grew visibly excited. He kept looking at me as if he wanted to say something, but every time he was about to speak, Don Manuel would ask Juan to hand him something else. Finally, when there was a break in the proceedings, Juan managed to shout to me in a whisper, "it's a *karpay despacho!*"

"A what?" I whispered back.

"A *karpay despacho,*" he whispered in earnest.

I repeated to the others what I had heard, and they all nodded their heads in enthusiastic ignorance. None of us knew what to make of it, and further explanations were clearly out of the questions. We would have to wait and see …

[35]

Inside his house Don Manuel Prepares to give Nina his Karpay, Chöa Chöa

Only later, when Don Manuel went out to burn the *despacho*, did we have a chance to ask Juan what in the world was going on. He looked stunned and could only shake his head, "Be grateful for this. He has made a *karpay despacho* which means he is now going to give you his *karpay!*" Don Manuel was coming back, so Juan had only a moment to instruct us further. "One by one he will place his *mesa* on your head. Try to open your bubble as much as possible, he will pour his power, his knowledge, his living energy into you! You must try to receive it."

The way in which a *despacho* burns is a general indicator of whether or not the *Apus* are pleased with the *paqo's* actions and intentions. Don Manuel returned with a big grin on his face, so we presumed that his *despacho* had burned well. We were excited and energized, but still had no real way to gauge the significance of this powerful ceremony. We simply sat in our semi-circle before this luminous man, and one by one, we went up to kneel before him. He held his *mesa*, a sacred bundle filled with his most potent power objects, above our heads, and paused, as if listening to instructions. Then he shook the *mesa* over us, gently tapped, or even whacked some of us on the head, shoulders, or spine with it. With each one of us he reacted differently.

Don Manuel was considered *qawaq*, which means something akin to "clairvoyant," or "seer" of living energy. He is able see our energy body

[36]

and to perceive how living currents of force are conducted through it. His *karpay* was both an individually tailored healing, and an electric jolt of spiritual force that awakened one's spiritual nature. *Karpay* means initiation, or transmission of energy, in Quechua. Receiving such an initiation at the hands of Don Manuel was an experience none of us would ever forget.

Watching the others kneel before him, I couldn't help wondering what I would experience when my turn came. The rattling of his *mesa*, his softly whispered prayers, and finally the sound of it clanking against someone's skull or spine made an impact! But my moment, when it finally came, was unlike anything I could have foreseen.

"*Pachamama, Wiraqocha, Inti Tayta* … Elizabeth … .." was all I could make out of the prayers he said over me. Then, as Don Manuel brought the *mesa* down on my head, an overpowering jolt of electricity coursed through my body. My head seemed to burst open, and a cross of visionary light, brilliant, intense, and delicious, exploded in my skull. A door behind my eyes flung wide open and I could see it's dazzling shape. A Maltese cross! I gasped aloud, staring at this form that shone with sublime, unearthly beauty! It seemed to come directly from Don Manuel's *mesa*, searing into the top of skull like a brand of light. The physical sensation was overpowering. Yet his *mesa* had never physically touched me! Only now, did he briefly touch each of my shoulders with his *mesa*, before moving on to the next person. I felt as if I had been Knighted.

When the ceremony was over we all stumbled out of the little room, blinking in the bright light of day. We thanked Don Manuel profusely and he smiled his approval. Then he impatiently shooed us away, as if he were saying, "I've done all I can for you poor fools. Now go! You're on your own!"

It wasn't until we mounted our horses and were heading down the trail that I realized I felt completely drunk. I mentioned this to Juan who only nodded, laughing. The others all reported the same sensation and after a few more paces, Jeanette dismounted, declaring herself far too drunk to ride a horse. She walked for the next six hours, all the way to Hatun Q'eros.

It was only later that Juan revealed his shock, surprise, delight, and a tinge of jealousy that Don Manuel had given us so much more than a double *despacho* ceremony. He had bestowed on us his greatest gift—his *karpay*—the direct transmission of his personal power, knowledge, and energetic link to the Inka tradition. Juan confided in us that he had had to visit Don Manuel many times before he was deemed ready to receive his *karpay*. He explained that this kind of transmission might manifest itself immediately as uncanny knowledge and spiritual power. Or it would slowly permeate our bubbles, the more desirable outcome, so that in months, perhaps even years later, we might suddenly receive profound illumination, or the development of healing powers.

"One thing is for certain," Juan warned us, "your lives will change. You may lose old friends or gain new ones. People may become very attracted to you, or frightened, even repelled by you. Your bubble has been irrevocably changed, filled with power. But how that manifests in your lives? How you use that power? That remains to be seen."

CHAPTER FOUR

Hatun Q'eros: Descent to Paradise

*H*ard, dry, gray earth and dusty boulders gave way to soft mossy greens and velvet browns as we swayed, struggling to stay atop our horses as we continued our descent. Now we traveled down inclines so steep that we lay nearly supine with our stirrups at our horses' ears. At times we had to grab onto their tails just to stay on. The steepness of our descent coupled with the fact that we were all in a drunken *karpay* stupor from our final ceremony with Don Manuel made staying in the saddle a real effort. A soft fuzzy glow surrounded everything, despite the severity of the landscape, and my thoughts like young free eagles, ascended to heights of contemplation as lofty as the mountainscapes we now traversed.

Slowly, surely, the monochromatic landscape began to transform. More shades of green gradually appeared. The omnipresent ankle-high, dry, gray-green scrub and matching boulders that had pervaded our field of vision for the last two days were replaced by innumerable waist-high bushes in a variety of moist greens. They seemed almost to reach out of the landscape like soft hands to caress us as we traveled past.

Suddenly I recognized the sounds I had been hearing—one echoing pattern in a vast, joyous, multi-layered speech rising over the hills and valleys—as the warbling of small birds. It seemed a speech I could easily comprehend, until my ordinary consciousness labeled it "warbling birds." And yes, in fact, those long green sparkling air fishes zipping, buzzing, chirping and diving happily in the air around and over our heads *were* humming-birds. Words seemed so inadequate to describe the rich visual and spiritual reality I was perceiving as we continued our descent.

The air had grown thicker, warmer, and much more humid than the arid Choa Choa. As we descended further, the greens became ever more abundant. At last we rounded a curve and came upon a large bush that simply shouted it's unbelievable celebration of radiant color.

"Look at me! Pink! Blue! Purple! Orange! Yellow! See me! Smell me! Am I not fabulously fragrant? Adorned with petaled jewels? Am I not deliciously ripe? Eat me! Eat me!" the bush pleaded and moaned. Spontaneously, I opened my bubble, extending my energetic "self" out to encompass the bush. My senses were instantly flooded with sweet fragrances, soft textures, brilliant colors and a literal blast of life force. Now I further understood the Andean metaphor of "eating" or exchanging living energies with nature. Just like the "scientifically documented" exchange of carbon dioxide and oxygen between human and plant life, the bush was begging to be "eaten" so it could exchange living energies with me!

The exquisitely complex tapestry of sights, sounds, textures and smells woven together exploded, expanding my ordinary senses further still. It seemed life had fully incarnated in this world, or perhaps it was rather that I, at last, could perceive it. All of nature sang at once, each element with its' own rhythm and melody, each thing in its' own voice, a great and resonant symphony of life forms.

In awe, I sat wondering, how on earth—on this fabulous, magical earth—had I not heard, seen, and felt all this before? Was this the effect of Don Manuel's *Karpay?*

How many times I had seen flowers reaching out their beauty, not only toward the sun, but extending this beauty, their life force, to me as well, desiring their fragrance to be inhaled? Fruits ripened and begged to be eaten, then excreted to grow and continue their existence in another place. We were the feet for their seeds! The incredible, elegant simplicity of it stupefied me. This world, God's world—Nature—was perfectly designed and synchronized to work in glorious harmony not only within itself...but also with HUMANS! I experienced a profound spiritual "duh" as my mind registered this common sense fact! What if nature needed us just as much as we needed nature, to achieve a collective supreme evolutionary purpose?!

As I continued to muse on this possibility of cooperative evolution, we came to a long narrow valley where we decided to stop for lunch. The mountain's music continued, joined now by human voices. Juan told us the story of how a famous and very powerful Andean Priest had made history right here in this very valley, Wiraqocha Pampa, or God's field, where we now sat lunching.

"In the time of the conquest, the Spaniards actually came all the way up here to Q'eros. According to Inka oral tradition, Q'eros was one of the towns originally founded by the first Inka, Inkarri. It was said that a large squadron of Spanish soldiers chased the Inkas all the way up to this valley, Wiraqocha Pampa, where one mighty and charismatic priest named Garibilu Q'espi was tending his llamas. When Garibilu Q'espi saw the Spaniards, he ran all the way to the top of these hills and made a powerful prayer to the *Apus*, the spirits of the mountains, to help drive the conquistadors out of their sacred territory. The *Apus* immediately answered his prayers telling Garibilu to build a great *saiwa*—a giant column of stones—at the top of the mountain. Then, the *Apus* told him, they would kick down the stones upon the Spaniards. When Garibilu completed the *saiwa*, clouds gathered in the sky and produced great flashes of lightning, striking the *saiwa* and causing the stones, and indeed the whole hillside, to fall down upon the Spaniards. The Spanish soldiers were crushed and driven from this land. And they never returned after that," Juan completed his story with a triumphant smile. He was obviously proud of the spiritual feats of the Andean priests. In fact, he seemed to feel they were equally his ancestors, as much as the Spaniards who also formed a significant part of his bloodline. The group enjoyed hearing it as much as Juan enjoyed the telling. His story was food to our souls, the dessert to our lunch

After lunch we mounted our horses again. This time Don Julio had taken off well before us. By now, we were all so delighted with the warm air, the colorful, sub-tropical foliage and vibrant landscape, that we hardly remembered our grim escapade of a scant twenty four hours ago when we nearly froze to death in the arctic Andean nightfall.

Soon a young alpaca herder joined us, walking along the path next to the horses. He was on his way home to Hatun Q'eros. Each moment of the path was all-absorbing, revealing the mountain's abundant life in innumerable forms. More and more birds, insects, flowers and plants appeared. I assumed the others were experiencing the same heightened perceptions as was I, because in our normally chatty group, not one word was spoken.

Suddenly, a thick mist appeared out of nowhere and rose all around us. Juan explained that this mist traveled up the mountain from the jungle floor every afternoon at this same time. Juan told us how his master, Don Andres Espinoza, "parted this mattress of clouds with a movement of his hands," allowing the sun to shine directly over his *despacho* as he was giving Juan, then his young, impetuous student, a heart stopping display of the power of *munay* (the power of love and will). The Inkas believed humans had three basic powers: *munay* is the power of the heart, or more precisely, the combined power of love and will together. *Yachay* is the power of the mind, and *llanqay*, the power of the body. Juan, raised in a *yachay* culture, was seeking the illusive *munay* power from this great Master.

Don Andres Espinoza, by all accounts, had been a very powerful *kurak akulleq*, or fourth-level priest, an acknowledged master of *munay*. Born in the village of Q'eros Totorani, Juan told us he had possessed a large, wheel-shaped altar of immense power, nearly nine feet across and carved out of stone. This altar had mysteriously disappeared with the death of Don Andres, then in his early nineties. No one knew where it had gone. When I suggested that someone should try to solve this mystery and find the stone, Juan waved his hand and laughed.

"I have asked everyone myself, and either they truly don't know, or they are simply not telling. Why bother any further about it?" Then he added cryptically, "It will reappear on it's own, if and when the time is right."

We rode on in silence while I contemplated these people, their magical land, and it's uncanny effect on me. Their humble yet supernatural lives were as mysterious and impenetrable to my mind as the thick jungle mist surrounding us.

A few minutes later the mist parted as suddenly as it had arisen, and a stone wall about four feet high with a gate stood before us. We entered, dismounted our horses and walked down a lane into a shaded pasture of deep soft grass. Its velvet green tendrils reached up to embrace us. On the far side of the pasture stood a large wooden structure with a corrugated aluminum roof. I heard the sound of running water coming from above. Looking up, I saw that we were in the shadow of a large and beautiful mountain, its peak obscured by mist. Qorimoqo! It had to be the "golden Mountain" that watches over Hatun Q'eros. A stream ran down from the mountain alongside the pasture.

Small houses made of stone with thatched roofs dotted the hillside above us and to either side. Far below us was the emerald green out of which the thick mist issued. The scene was utterly charming, and the complete opposite of Choa Choa. But now before us appeared the most dazzling spectacle of all; dozens of pairs of shining, liquid brown eyes, somehow as sacred in their beauty as the hummingbirds and the flowers and the "symphony" that had enchanted me on the morning's ride. We were standing in a schoolyard, looking at thirty-three of the most angelic faces I had ever seen. These were the children of Q'eros.

"This is the school house," Juan informed us, gesturing toward the shanty and the students.

Children of Q'eros, Hatun Q'eros

[43]

The children, obviously informed of our arrival—perhaps by the young llamaherd—were lined up in a neat little row, like a receiving line, to meet us. They politely extended their hands to shake each one of ours; however, this formality didn't last long. Once the children got a glimpse of Nina, the beautiful strawberry blonde, blue-eyed giantess, they lost their composure completely. They stared, wide-eyed and slack-jawed. They had never seen anything like her.

Nina's response was immediate—she began chasing the children back and forth across the schoolyard in a wild, chaotic game of "tackle-tag." They responded with shrieks of pleasure and fright, both at narrowly escaping from her, and even more at getting caught. A few of us who still had some energy left also joined in the game. Now the real getting acquainted had begun. Soon a rag-tag jumble of Inka children and gringos lay, arms and legs inextricably enmeshed, in a laughing heap on the village green. The few adults present, including the school master, looked on with obvious delight at the spectacle. We already knew that the Q'ero were no strangers to gaming, and in fact, their word for ritual, *pujllay*, was literally the same word for play. The Q'ero knew how to have fun!

Once we had gotten ourselves untangled, we sat sipping hot tea and eating bread and jam prepared by our excellent guides. Juan pointed over the stone wall of the school yard and down the mountain to the valley below us; the direction from which the thick mist could still be seen crawling slowly up the mountain slopes.

"That green valley down there is the beginning of the Amazon Jungle," he informed us. We all gaped in amazement. "There is a legend amongst the people here about an esoteric city called *Miskayani*," he continued. Supposedly it is out there, somewhere," he gestured toward the mist, "lost in the jungle."

"What kind of city is it?" Jeff asked Juan, intrigued.

"It is said to be a place of very highly advanced female spiritual beings," Juan stated quietly.

"I thought it was called *Paititi*," I mentioned, having heard tell of this metaphysical city.

"Like everything Inka, there is a masculine and feminine esoteric city.

The masculine one is called *Paititi*, or *El Dorado*, as it was known by the Spanish, because it was said to be filled with vast quantities of gold. But more intriguing and much less well known is *Miskayani*. This myth is only found in Q'eros and was discovered by my father in the late fifties. In fact, some of the Q'eros say their grandfathers married women from *Miskayani*, who were not only beautiful beyond belief, but were also highly intelligent and very powerful. They knew how to do everything!"

"Wow!" I uttered in amazement. "But Juan, what does *Miskayani* mean?" I prodded.

"*Miska*, in Quechua, refers to the most tender first shoot of the newly germinated plant. So *Miskayani* means, one possessed with the quality of that new, sweet tenderness," Juan continued, enraptured in his own narrative. "This city could be considered something like the feminine counterpart to the lost Tibetan kingdom of Shambhala, because it is said to contain the most elevated female spiritual knowledge. The legend says that if you are very, very lucky in this life, or if you work very hard and are very, very good, you may have a chance to be reborn into *Miskayani!*"

At the mention of *Miskayani*, some of the adult Q'ero males who stood nearby smiled, raised their eyebrows, and nudged each other, imparting a distinctly sexual overtone to the idea of the esoteric city. But that made sense, for, as with everything Inka, what was spiritual was also sensual.

In the chronicles of his first expedition to Q'eros in 1955, Oscar Nuñez del Prado describes the Q'ero as having a very liberal attitude toward sex. In fact, young, unmarried teenagers were free to have more than one sexual partner and were also free of parental control in mate selection. Juan's father was a proud, strong-minded academician, yet with an obvious taste for adventure. He goes on to describe the people of Q'eros in one gloriously succinct paragraph.

"The Q'eros man is of a clear and vivacious mentality, at once ingenuous and frank, he speaks little and is mortified if asked to repeat himself. Although severe in conduct and laconic in speech, the Q'ero are supremely hospitable to travelers."

He further described their direct kinship to the Inka, expressed through their clothing and hairstyle, a custom that was only recently lost due to an evil *patron* (landowner). " … (the Q'ero report that) the men wore their hair proudly in long braids as symbol of their Inka heritage until 1940 when the landowner made them all cut their hair … " (Nuñez del Prado, 1955)

The history of the Q'ero was a rather complex and fascinating one. In recent centuries they had farmed their lands as more or less indentured servants to the Spanish landowner, the *patron*. Even so, due to their isolation in these extremely remote territories, the Q'ero were able to maintain many of their traditions of weaving, ritual, music, and dance. Even the training in coca leaf divinations and the making of *despachos* to the *Apu* and the *Pachamama* was part of most every Q'ero child's upbringing.

Oscar Nuñez del Prado himself, and three others, were the vital force behind freeing the Q'ero from these ruling landowners and re-establishing their rights to their own homeland. The Q'ero emerged victorious in 1958 from their fight over land rights with the Peruvian government. The eight villages of the region Choa Choa were proclaimed the "Q'ero Nation": Hatun Q'eros, Q'eros Totorani, Kiku, Japu, Markachea, Kolpakucho, and Qochamoqo.

There was something deeply moving in this beautiful place, some ineffable spirit-power in the landscape and in these people that even Oscar Nuñez del Prado had felt. According to Juan, he had spent a great deal of time here and even became a part of the village life himself. Although Juan knew his father's interest in Q'eros as primarily academic, only after his father's death did Juan discover that he too, had been a student of the Andean spiritual path.

I could easily understand Oscar Nuñez del Prado's transformation into social activist and Andean *paqo* under the impact of these extraordinary people and this timeless place. At times I felt so alive here that I wanted to run through the jungle hurling stones and screaming like a wild animal. Yet in one and the same moment I experienced the deepest contentment and feeling of at-home-ness. I now understood in the very fibers of my body why Juan wanted to die here, in Q'eros country.

As our industrious guides prepared our dinner, Juan continued our lessons in Andean mysticism. He took us down a little hill below the schoolyard, in the direction of the Amazon valley, to a local Q'ero shrine of great importance—the *Seqe Rumi*! Arriving, we observed a rather large rounded stone sitting in the middle of a field. Upon closer observation we noticed the stone was covered by a series of lines, hatch marks, stars and asterix-like shapes that criss-crossed the top. Clearly these were intentional markings. Was it some kind of language? A map? Did these symbolic or ritual markings have esoteric meaning? But whether they denoted jungle trails or the pathways of stars we could not tell. Yet the stone seemed alive; it emanated a soft glow.

After some minutes of silence, Juan spoke.

"The Q'ero call this stone *Seqe Rumi*. That means rock of the *seqes*. *Seqes*, as most of you already know, are the lines of vital force that run along the earth between sacred sites, what I think you call 'ley lines.' Let us do a ceremony of connection here at this sacred stone."

We quickly and easily formed a circle around the stone, joining hands. After a moment's concentration we erected our collective bubble around the *seqe* stone, by visualizing sinking our roots deep into *Pachamama*, enveloping the *seqe* stone, and raising our large group energy field up to meet the heavens or the *hanak pacha*. It was a lovely sensation to feel our individual bubbles melt together into one large powerful group energy field that could extend into the earth and all the way up into the sky. Thus we connected the three worlds of living energy through our collective bubble.

Seqe Rumi, Hatun Qeros

[47]

I was beginning to understand that in performing this kind of ceremony our group became one huge living *despacho*. By ritually focusing our collective attention and life-force, we both magnified our energy fields, and entered into complete harmony with our environment. As a result we experienced a timeless, unutterable sense of connection with each other, with the ancient past, and with the living, writhing power of nature here in the presence of this almost mythical place where the Amazon Jungle meets the towering Andes.

We returned in silence, profoundly moved by our communion in this sacred valley, beneath the mountain of gold, before the shrine of the *seqe rumi*. "According to Q'ero myth, Inkarri, the first Inka, together with his mate Qoyari, created the very first Inka village here at Hatun Q'eros, at the confluence between these two powerful aspects of nature, the Amazon Jungle and the high Andes, before going on to found the city of Cuzco." Juan now spoke again like the Anthropology professor that he was. As fascinating as his facts were, my mind and spirit drifted. Enthralled by the power and beauty of this place and its people, I experienced a delicious aching sensation in my chest, like the slow breaking open of my heart.

Later, after a hearty dinner and a good long walk near the foot of Qorimoqo—the "Golden Mountain" that watched over Hatun Q'eros— we went to bed. Then I fell into what has remained to this day, one of the deepest slumbers of my life.

I am on a street in New York City surrounded by enormous glass skyscrapers. I feel good, deeply spiritually rich and peaceful. Although I am on a crowded New York City Street, there is no inconsistency between the place and my peaceful inner state. I walk into the lobby of one of the skyscrapers and see it is the lobby of a magnificent hotel. I see a very attractive young man about my age across the lobby. His eyes are luminous–they shine with inner beauty, humor and light. He is so magnetically attractive. I can feel warm beams from him reaching out to me across the room, drawing me in. Quite naturally, with no shyness or embarrass-

ment, I walk right over to him. We began to chat about nothing,
and flirt. It doesn't matter what we say. The energy and excitement
between us is intoxicating. He asks me to sit down and have a
drink with him. We sit together, talking and flirting giddily. I feel
a deep, happy and serene love for him. I know he feels the same for
me. It is the most natural thing in the world. All at once I turn to
him and say, "Ah, but I know you now. You're John Lennon!"
"That's right," he responds in a very off-handed way, like he
doesn't want this to matter. Bb ... bb ... but ... you can't be the
real John Lennon," I stutter."Yes I can," he says mildly, "here let me
show you ... come with me." He takes me by the arm, leads me to
the elevators, and we ascend to and enter his penthouse apartment.
It is filled with Beatles paraphernalia: posters, album covers, etc;
all the things a young John Lennon would have in his apartment.
He takes me into the bedroom and picks up a picture of him and
Yoko Ono in a white, heart-shaped frame. Removing the picture
from the frame, he carefully tears Yoko out. From out of nowhere
he replaces it with a picture of me in exactly the right pose to be-
kissing him! Then he puts it back into the frame and hands it to
me. "You see," he tells me, "I really am John Lennon. And you
really are the girl for me."

I awoke to a flood of delicious love sensations coursing through my
body, pervading my senses with an intoxicating warmth. At the same I
felt completely grounded and uniquely whole. Upon first inspection, this
seemed to be a classic wish-fulfillment dream; however the thoughts and
feelings it evoked in me were far too profound. I experienced a new and
indescribable sensation of empowerment that was at once graceful, feminine, sensuous, ecstatic, and creatively intelligent. I felt like superwoman
... like I could do anything! But it wasn't the familiar "power over" anything or anyone, not even "power over" myself. It was like being part of
a great flowing tide of love in the ocean of creation. It was a power that
was completely right, and in it's place. Benevolent. Unstoppable.

I soon learned that some of the others in the group had experienced similarly profound, highly personal dreams on quite a variety of themes. Nina had dreamt of being teased in school for being so tall and strong, and the insights she gained from the dream, she said, "felt like five years of psychotherapy in one night!"

What my dream meant I could not say. The Beatles were "like young gods" for me in my impressionable youth. But I had always been "in love" with Paul, identifying more with the dreamy romantic. As I contemplated my dream and it's potential meanings, I realized that John was really the one who had applied his artistic power to create social change. And now, in my adult life, this was much more my interest. Also, my "apprenticeship" these past ten years now allowed me to see John Lennon, and the Beatles, as the spiritual force they truly were. All my life I had wanted to be a musician—not for fame or fortune, but to bring visceral joy, love and happiness into people's lives. And this is also spiritual work.

As a young girl I dreamt almost nightly of the Beatles, joining their games and music making in a red brick apartment building. (I was flabbergasted at the age of ten when I saw on a TV interview the Fab Four walking into the door of the exact red brick apartment building I had visited in my dreams!) The Beatles certainly communicated to me, and to millions of others, an overwhelming spiritual force bearing a message of love that manifested through human artistry, and culminated in mass ecstatic gatherings called "Beatles Concerts" whose societal impact is still being felt today.

Also interesting to me now is how their power to affect people vastly diminished after they split up. Clearly, their combined personal energies and talents, their collective energy bubble, generated a special power that drew masses along with them on their journey toward love and higher consciousness. Not surprisingly, many people instinctively equated the Beatles inspired musical abilities with the powers of healing! I recall seeing a videotape of parents bringing their crippled children to the Beatles to be touched and hopefully healed by their charismatic power.

Curiously, the atmosphere of the Beatles concerts recalled descriptions I'd read of the power unleashed in the Andean people by their charismatic priests who rose to lead the Inka National Movement that nearly overthrew the Spanish in the late 1700's. This movement was called the *Taki Ongoy*, a phrase used to describe a collective delirium brought about by singing or chanting. How did this all fit together?

I remembered Juan telling me that the psychological work of the third-level corresponded to Jung's theory of individuation. The third-level in the Andean tradition involved bringing the "shadow" aspects of the psyche from the unconscious to the conscious mind, and integrating these elements into the aware personality. For Jung, the "shadow" included all the discomforting aspects of ourselves, including the primal wisdom and power that we hold in the unconscious—often repressed through cultural training or the socialization process.

In our culture, that would include our aggressive and sexual impulses, our divine or sublime impulses, and our unclaimed authority. At the third-level we project our own authority, our spiritual and psychological power, outside ourselves. Certainly that had been my experience in working with Ricardo's group, the third-level priest of my first Peruvian adventure.

After the emergence and subsequent integration of the "shadow," or the unclaimed aspects of the self, the next step or fourth-level in Andean terms, is the work with the "royal couple." The integration of the inner masculine and feminine aspects of the self, the anima and animus, was, according to Jung, the next challenge in the process of individuation.

My psychological mind interpreted John Lennon as my animus—my inner male—with all the power and creativity that his archetype represents. John Lennon was the Artist/Priest who delivered messages of love and peace to the masses through his music. In my dream he was loving and respecting—in fact falling in love with—my female side, my anima, immediately following the fourth-level *Karpay* of Don Manuel Q'espi. I wondered...could this represent the beginning of the integration of my anima and animus, and augur my real entrance into the fourth level?

Don Manuel Q'espi was a very unusual kind of priest. He was called *kamasqa*, which meant he received his fourth-level initiation directly from the divine with no human intermediaries. Certainly, I had received the fourth-level initiation from Juan a few years earlier, but the fourth-level covered a wide range of psychological and spiritual ground. As Juan so often reminded us, "initiation" means only beginning. Perhaps my initiation at the hands of Don Manuel, and later that night my dream, symbolized a kind of passage. Perhaps my psyche was giving me a sign that I had now truly entered, with both feet, into the fourth-level.

Passage into the fourth level meant an expanded meta-perspective, and an ability to problem solve from a new horizon not available to the psychology of the previous level. If opposites can be integrated at the fourth level, a psychological impossibility at the third-level, this frees the energy of the psyche to take on new challenges. At a societal level, this psychological development would allow differences between people to be tolerated and accepted without fear.

I day-dreamed myself momentarily into a society of fourth-level individuals. With inner "seeming" opposites integrated in individuals, external conflicts and contradictions could then be easily and naturally resolved. As I contemplated this idea, the implications were literally stunning—it would organically abolish or significantly minimize the destructive effects of a host of societal ills, from the "war between the sexes," to the racial, religious, economic, and political conflicts on which most wars are based.

A fourth level society would view these diverse elements from a non-oppositional perspective, as complementary and therefore advantageous, rather than inherently divisive and threatening. Diverse religious symbols would no longer create fear or division, rather each human would be able to perceive divine living energy directly, no matter the symbol. The embrace of inclusivity as the simple, logical, common sense collective value would be an epochal psychological advent. No more war over religious differences. It would change the face of the world as we now know it.

I sat in awed delight, contemplating this exalted possibility for the human race. And more marvelous still, if such might be the fruits of a fourth-level society, what new possibilities would the fifth-level bring?

CHAPTER FIVE

The Phausi Runa: Spirits of the Water Vapors

We reached the waterfall of Hatun Q'eros, an hour up a steep trail from the meadow school. At the sound of splashing water, my mind wandered back a year in time, to Marin County. I'd been having a difficult time translating my multi-dimensional Peruvian experiences into words on two-dimensional paper. The experience and all it's accompanying feelings of frustration suddenly came flooding back to me.

◆ ◆ ◆

Writing ... I just didn't have much confidence in my writing. I had never taken a writing course, and although I had attended a highbrow Ivy League college, I had never gotten the straight A's the 'good writers' got.

My agent kept telling me I was doing a good job, but we'd been working on my book proposal now for three months and I was sure it was taking too long. Besides, I wasn't at all convinced I could actually write a book. I felt stuck, and this was unusual for me. Normally, I raced to the empty page, teeming with so many ideas that I could barely get them all down.

I needed a long walk. I slipped out the back door and took the trail behind my house, heading for open space, grateful for the sunshine, the thick clouds gathering in the blue sky, and the wild sage-perfumed breeze. At the last minute I chose the longest path, the one that led down to a beautiful little waterfall that had become home to my purest self.

On this early spring day I arrived to find a fantastic flame-colored lily in full bloom in the middle of the waterfalls' lower pool. As always, the pair of hummingbirds whose domain this was chirruped and dived over me in greeting. Out of breath, I sat at the pools' edge, hoping to release my ravaging insecurities.

I began the prayers that had by now, after my Peruvian Initiation, become second nature. Extending my love and my energy bubble out to the surrounding area, I released my heaviness into the absorptive stone of the waterfall pool. I relaxed, gazing at the beautiful reflections of water and sunlight dancing on the stone walls with the water itself cascading ever downward, and drew the waterfalls' refined energy into my bubble, breathing into its refreshing embrace.

Now my perceptions drifted with the sounds of the water as they became a faint and rhythmic music. The bush beside me stirred, yet there was no wind. Something shifted … a current began flowing toward me, around the reeds and water lilies soaking into my mind, soothing my frustration. Naturally, effortlessly, along with the flow of energy came insight after insight—all that I needed to rearrange and complete the chapter I had been stuck on. All that had eluded me now poured gracefully into my awareness.

"You see? I can help you," a soft melodious voice pronounced.

"Eh?" I said aloud, startled.

"I will help you. Whenever you are having trouble with your writing," the voice continued, "come to me."

It was the waterfall herself, speaking with unmistakable, liquid clarity. Large water droplets splashing my face and hands brought me out of my reverie. A heavy rain began to fall. And as the hummingbirds dove for cover, I too realized it was time to go. I raced back home up the trail, dancing like a child under the raindrops, full of fresh writing ideas…and full of wonder at what had just occurred.

◆ ◆ ◆

"*Phausi Runa*, that's what the spirits of the waterfalls are called," Juan pronounced, and the sound of his voice snapped my mind back to the present. "They are the little people of light that live in the waterfalls, streams, or creeks. They just love running water." Juan spoke slowly as people took notes or changed cassettes in their tape recorders.

"Oohs" of delight and surprise escaped from several group members at Juan's thoroughly charming description of the *Phausi Runa*. I knew that *phasiy* in Quechua meant "water vapor" so *Phausi Runa* literally meant 'water vapor people.'

That morning after breakfast we had taken a long hike around the base of Qorimoqo—the golden mountain—to this special waterfall of Hatun Q'eros. Juan said he had to introduce us to someone very important in this place. On our way up the steep trail to the waterfall, small golden eagles, unique to the area, landed near us on the ground. They watched us serenely, as though giving their blessing. A good omen, to be sure.

By sheer coincidence or some unfathomable communication system of the Q'ero, we had unexpectedly encountered Don Mariano Apaza, another high priest of Q'ero, as we were clearing away the dense brush covering the entrance to this special waterfall. Juan spoke to Don Mariano, who agreed to return later that evening and perform a despacho ceremony with his wife. I was certain we had met our "important person," but I soon discovered this was not so.

"Now to contact the *Phausi Runa* is very simple," continued Juan, "but at the same time, very delicate. First we make the coca leaf offering." He passed around the *kint'u*, or little collection of three perfect coca leaves. Each of us blew onto it three times, offering our living energy to the "waterfall spirits." Afterward, Juan took the *kint'u* and added a beautiful tiny pink flower that he had plucked from a nearby bush. He first held the offering close to his heart. Next he blew three times upon it and released it into the current of the stream. We watched the tiny offering move effortlessly from pool to pool, to be swept down the little falls.

"Now, as my master Don Benito taught me, first you must choose a place where you are comfortable to perform this ritual. Then sit down and connect your bubble to the stream, and give all your heavy energy as an offering to the stream. Once you are connected, listen to the sound of the water until you can hear the music behind it. Then if you are fortunate enough that the *Phausi Runa* appear to you, open yourself completely and let them run through your bubble." Juan finished and sat down to begin his waterfall meditation.

"But Juan, what do the *Phausi Runa* look like?" Nelda asked.

"They are made of light," he answered. "Just pure living energy, so they can appear in any form they want."

"Oh and one more thing," he added. "The *Phausi Runa* are the guardians of art and the written word."

"Juan, I can't believe it!" I positively exploded. Briefly, I described to Juan and the group my experience with the waterfall spirit in the hills behind my house the year before.

"WONDERFUL! WONDERFUL!" Juan exclaimed, his characteristic thousand-watt smile lighting his features. "You see Elizabeth, you always give confirmation to the teachings of Don Benito!" he chided me, kindly.

I marveled at how Juan and the Andean tradition provided such apt, if unconventional, explanations for my life-changing experiences with the unseen world. Thank God I had found this rich tradition to nourish my spirit, and found someone like Juan who could explain these mysteries so beautifully and simply.

The instruction complete, Juan waved us away to go and commune as we might with the *Phausi Runa*. We each went off alone, hopeful of making contact with these delightful beings.

It was an odd exercise for average North Americans, so used to having their five senses continuously pummeled into submission by a furious tidal wave of stimuli. It required us to shift our attention to a much more subtle, intuitive level of sensation and awareness. We then needed to be able to recognize and trust the information or experience received through these less developed intuitive faculties.

Certainly none of us denied the validity of intuition. But trusting our own intuition was a different matter. My intuitions were not always right. But come to think of it, neither could my left-brain always be counted on for accuracy. I could make mistakes in simple addition, let alone solving higher calculus problems. Why should I discount my intuition because it wasn't always right? Yet like most westerners I trusted the information-gathering skills of my left-brain because it was more familiar to me, and more culturally accepted. We never had Intuition Class in school. This line of thinking—that information gathering of any kind is a learned skill—encouraged me. For if you could learn one way, you could certainly learn another!

As I engaged in the *Phausi Runa* exercise on my own, I had to fight feeling responsible for the group's experience. I hoped everyone would succeed and 'get in touch' with the *Phausi Runa*. But I had learned that inevitably some would and others wouldn't. It wasn't up to me.

I closed my eyes feeling the soothing contact with the river. Ahh, the delightful play of the water over the rocks did make lovely music. Many times I caught my mind wandering, or worrying about what the others were experiencing. Each time I patiently directed my attention back to the sound of the water. Perhaps ten minutes or more had passed when, all at once, the world seemed to shudder.

One! Two! Three! Tiny *Phausi Runa* appeared in my inner vision, with the sounding of three distinct musical notes. All three were doubled over, laughing hysterically at their own joke, a visual gag. For they appeared to me as miniature Juans, complete with salt and pepper beards, and mushroom-like white felt hats pulled down over their faces. I couldn't help laughing out loud at their playful sense of humor. My heart expanded as they disappeared into my bubble with three little flashes of light and a slight tickling sensation.

When I opened my eyes again the whole group was shiny—especially Juan—with fresh, smooth, youthful looks on their faces. They were surrounded by a soft sparkling atmosphere that could only have been created by people who recently had *Phausi Runa* running through their bubbles. Juan, who appeared about fourteen, positively glowed, emanating an atmosphere that for me smoothly translated into information.

"You love the *Phausi Runa*, don't you Juan," I pronounced assuredly. A few years before I wouldn't have trusted that knowledge.

"I love them more than anything," Juan crooned with the almost wistful, vulnerable ardour of a teen-ager in love.

Juan meets the Phausi Runa of Hatun Qeros

Still, a few of our group reported that "nothing" had happened. They saw nothing, felt nothing, and reported no *Phausi Runa* in the vicinity. It seemed they had been meditating in a kind of inner vacuum rather than next to a waterfall, in magical mountains, at the top of the world. One who had the most trouble was a very sweet computer scientist. I wondered what he considered, or could acknowledge as, "information." If you believe knowledge or experience occurs in only one particular dimension, or can assume only one particular form—and it comes in another—you may miss it and conclude that it didn't come at all. Something in his "atmosphere" revealed to me the strange and contradictory impulses we humans feel toward the spiritual dimension. A part of him, and perhaps part of all of us, wants the spirit world to be real, while another part doesn't want inexplicable things to happen. We don't *really* want there to be *Phausi Runa*, to be confounded by the sudden intrusion of the ineffable into our lives. Yet at the very same time, we want it so very much.

Spirits are no less alive and mysterious, and no more "otherworldly" than plants, or amoebas, or germs, or us. Today, many deny the existence of Spirit in all its forms, just as in previous centuries the "flat earthers" denied a spherical planet. The trouble is that Western culture is based on a denial of the spirit world, so how can you (and why would you?) learn the rules of a world that doesn't even exist? And if you don't know the rules of the game with the spirit world, you just can't play. How many obstacles we Westerners have placed between ourselves and Spirit, making it almost impossible for us to play, or even to imagine, beyond the material plane. Yet I knew SO many people who wanted to play so badly. Like me, they hungered deeply for contact with the spiritual aspect of life, yet if contact arrived they feared or even denied it. Nonetheless this spiritual hunger was a fact; it was what had drawn our whole group here to Peru in the first place.

The main difficulty I believed our culture was having was one of good old psychological growing pains. If you change your beliefs you have to change your actions. So if we truly began to live from this higher paradigm of harmony with nature, respecting the sacredness of all life and setting the needs of the whole before those of ourselves or our particular group, we would have to endure an ordeal of growth, develop a generosity of spirit, that would test us at every level. I know that I was tested in the early phase of my initiation into the Inka tradition by experiences that were at times terrifying and extremely destabilizing to the configuration of my psyche at the time. And this had so much to do with the changes in the structure of my beliefs, and my actions that followed those changes! While I was impatient with our world, I did have compassion for the deep fears that this kind of spiritual challenge causes one to suffer.

But ahhh ... the benefits! Waking up HAPPY everyday with a sense of freedom and belonging, knowing I am part of a great and glorious creation, feeling a magnificent life force flowing through me, seeing the world from a perspective that at last made sense to my mind *and* satisfied my soul. What suffering wouldn't I undergo to arrive here? I would gladly do it all again. How blessed I was to be in this sacred place, receiving from these people such a priceless gift, the nectar of their spiritual culture.

I was becoming aware of how our psychological and even our physical health improved as our spiritual understanding deepened. If intimate relationships boosted our immune systems and improved our health, as modern scientific research showed, imagine the benefits to one who enjoyed intimate communion with their own life force, with the energies of nature and the world of spirits? The local proof of this theory was that while the average life expectancy in Q'eros was only about fifty years or so, truly talented Andean Priests like Don Manuel and Don Andres, even in such brutal and 'primitive' physical conditions, lived well into their eighties and nineties. Such were the practical benefits of living the spiritual laws of *Ayni*.

And with all of my heady philosophical reflections, there was Juan sitting before me, still glowing from his communion with the *Phausi Runa*! It was all so simple. He fed them with his life force, his love; and they fed him with theirs—*AYNI!* The one law of the Andean Tradition—the sacred law of reciprocity. We sat together, in a timeless harmony with our surroundings—this peaceful sense of belonging was one of the greatest blessings of the fourth-level. Once again I marveled at the simple, profound teachings of the Andean path, a most healing psychological perspective that over time dissolved that deep-seated, almost unconscious fear of others (be they human, spirit, or nature being), which is so much a part of our human condition.

After a deep-shared silence the group continued to discuss their experiences. Although a few had felt nothing, most had sensed the presence of the *Phausi Runa*. Some had felt a soft wind, others had heard faint music, and still others had seen strong visual images of light beings in various forms. Several also reported feeling a sense of warmth or well-being, and a feeling of deep connection with the water and the place itself. These intimate visceral experiences revealed the heart of the Andean path, which offers individuals a direct and personal connection with the invisible world of living energies. I was delighted by these sensory-based reports. So many people wanted to "see" the invisible world. I chuckled to myself contemplating that funny contradiction that revealed our cultural obsession with the visible.

At last, Juan smiled and nodded, signaling that it was time for us to go. We had more interesting things planned for the late evening. Somehow, through Juan, the *Phausi Runa* had charmed us all, whether we saw them or not. On our way back, I smiled to myself, noting that our computer programmer was walking with much more careful steps and glancing around as if worried that he might inadvertently step on a *Phausi Runa* at any moment. Well…it was certainly a beginning.

Hapu:
Sacred Couple

$\mathcal{A}$s I stood in the cook tent I saw three forms rise out of the earth and move toward us, casting shadows across our tent wall. Whipping aside the tent flap, the shadows entered. It was Don Mariano Apaza, his wife Doña Augustina, and their five-year old son, Gabriel. The dirt covering their hands, clothes and faces, from long hours of work in the fields, couldn't hide the shining spirits that crackled, sparked and spilled out through their black eyes. Without a word they sat down in a corner of the tent, took out their ceremonial paraphernalia, and began preparations for a *despacho*.

Juan had told us we would meet a powerful *yanantin*, a mated alchemical couple, priest and priestess, who served their community together, performing spiritual ceremonies, healings, and coca leaf divinations. The highest form of a *yanantin* was called a *hapu*.

This term referred to a couple who had each individually developed all three human powers of *munay* (love/will), *yachay* (intellect), and *llanqay* (industriousness) to their ultimate fullness and expression. When two individuals came together who were *tukuymunaniyoq, tukuyyachayniyaoq*, and *tukuyllanqayniqoy*, meaning fully developed in all three powers, these two would form a *hapu*—the most highly evolved and perfected form of a

A family of Priests

partnership that two human beings could achieve. I was enthralled by the idea and further impressed at the elaborated philosophy of psycho-spiritual development the Inkas possessed. Their very language held a host of specific terms to delineate the fascinating concept of a perfected sacred couple! I didn't know what it took to be a *yanantin*, let alone a *hapu*, but I was sure beyond any doubt, that this was the road I wanted to be on.

Juan ordered candles to be lit. The couple and their son spread their ritual *mantas* on the ground and began choosing coca leaves for the *k'intu*. Suddenly it dawned on me ... this would be the first time I had ever seen a woman perform a *despacho* ceremony.

I knew that women were considered innately powerful in their connection to the *Pachamama*, and therefore, experts in *Pachamama despachos*. Of course, men were naturally connected to the *Apus* and thus the experts in that spiritual art form of offering. Even so, that I had never, in all my years of training, seen a woman *altomisayoc* (high priestess) in action, suddenly struck me as ludicrous. Ludicrous that I hadn't even noticed until this moment, ludicrous that that's how it was. I decided to take advantage of the moment and observe carefully.

Doña Augustina looked very young. In fact, I later discovered, she was only in her early thirties! Her husband, one of the most powerful fourth-level priests in Q'eros, was nearly fifty. Her presence revealed quite

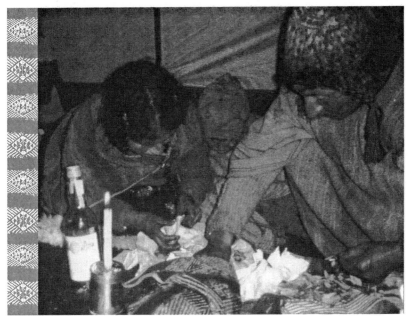

Doña Augustina, Gabriel and Don Mariano make a despacho

a brave and determined Priestess in her own right. Don Mariano at first appeared to be in charge. But then it seemed the one who was really running the show was, surprisingly, little Gabriel.

Gabriel was one of the most calm, quiet, and focused children I had ever seen. He was neither afraid of us, nor too interested in us. He sat staring intently at the *despacho* materials that lay spread before him, contemplating each item, before he confidently picked one out and handed it to his mother or father. They, in turn, invariably accepted, unwrapped, and used the substance contained within the tiny square folds of old newspaper. It was as if five-year old Gabriel was just one more priest officiating the ceremony.

I watched, spellbound. This young child never got impatient or distracted, but was as completely absorbed in, and a part of the hours-long ceremony, from beginning to end, as were his mother and father. His parents, on the other hand, never shushed him, shooed him aside, nor excluded him in any way from what they were doing. They worked together as a unified fourth-level priest-family. I was deeply touched, seeing them interact so tenderly, so respectfully.

The only thing little Gabriel didn't participate in were the ritual sips of *pisco*—Peruvian white lightning. These were splashed into the air, offered to the *Apus* on priestly fingertips, and then shared by Don Mariano and Doña Augustina. However, the priestess didn't look at all pleased by the little sips of *pisco* that she downed obligatorily, each time with a little shudder and a grimace. Don Mariano, on the other hand, appeared delighted with the brand new bottle of *pisco*, given to him by Juan for the *despacho* ceremony, and took an extra sip here and there whenever he could get one in.

Despacho ceremonies can last up to several hours, and certainly part of creating the sacred situation is the elongation of time. Time slowed down as the priestly family offered more *k'intus*, made prayers to mother earth, to water mother, to father sun, to the spirits of the mountains, the wind, and all the elements of earthly life represented in the *despacho*. As they did so, the separation between the worlds of matter and spirit evaporated. The sacredness in the air became thickly tangible, a deep sensation of harmony filled the space, and I felt my spirit relax and settle more deeply within my physical body.

One after another we let out long audible sighs; as if our spirits were saying, "Yes. OK. I can live here, in this body, in this place, in this material realm where sacredness is also being recognized." It was so soothing, so calming to spend time honoring, invoking, praising, recognizing, and being in the presence of the sacred. And *so* simple. Here, I learned everyday that "spiritual" was natural, not complicated, difficult, incomprehensible, painful, or hard to follow. Spiritual was simple, graceful, happy. Spiritual felt good, and relieved stress. And I now knew, best of all, spiritual was family!

The inner harmony I now experienced made me realize how disharmonious and conflicted my life had felt before Peru. Peru signified for me not only a return of the spiritual aspect of life, but a profound recovery of the feminine. Rich, warm, flowing, sensuous, earthy, and smitten; these were the essence of my femaleness now, having come to Peru. Instead of my previous embarrassment over, even denial of, my own sensuality and sexuality, I now felt pride in the power of my femaleness. Prior to my initiation, I had been a colder, more masculine, intellectually focused, and aloof woman. Now a soft feminine smile graced my lips on a permanent basis. I had come to understand, to know, take joy and revel in the fact that I carried the secret of life, the secret of creation within my own body. My inalienable connection to *Pachamama* made me feel and wear and respect my female power in a whole new way. I *was Pachamama*. Incredibly, when I first came back from Peru, I began to attract men—men I actually liked.

This was highly unusual for me, a woman certain almost since birth that she would never marry, knowing there was far too much to do. And who could be bothered to drag along a man on the kind of spiritual adventuring I knew instinctively I was headed for? And what man would go? I had known early on there were things in this life I had come to achieve, though exactly what, why and how I couldn't say. But that I would do them was unquestionable. I had some mission to accomplish, and men generally just got in the way.

My mother, a warm, extraverted, highly social, and also psychically sensitive being, was unhappily mismatched to my father, an aloof, ultra-introverted genius who often stated that he wished dinner came in pills so it wouldn't interfere with his work. I could see why my soul was attracted to their combination of genes, but the home atmosphere formed by their union, in which we children grew up, was a cold tundra of unspoken pain. As a result, relationships had always been difficult for me. Now I was amazed that I had been living happily with a man for three years. And I knew beyond any doubt that the recovery of my feminine nature in Peru had made this possible.

My dream that first night in Hatun Q'eros, of falling in love with John Lennon, had deep significance regarding the healing union of the feminine and masculine components of my psyche. Now, knowing about the concept of a *hapu*, and witnessing this *yanantin*, this sacred couple, performing the *despacho* ceremony in a harmonious and loving union, felt as powerful and auspicious as any dream. I was seeing for the first time in my life how a husband and wife could work together as a spiritual team! These two embodied my deepest criteria for a sacred marriage, and offered a living example, a guiding reference point, for my own marital aspirations.

I had read in Oscar Nuñez del Prado's account, written during the first expedition to Q'ero in 1955, that the Q'ero's attitudes toward sexuality were quite liberal. Adolescents of a sexually ripe age were allowed to romp in the fields with whomsoever they pleased and have multiple partners. However, once a young boy and young girl had chosen each other as mates, the couple had only the priest of the village to answer to. Parents or relatives had no right to interfere in mate selection. The priest alone—reading the coca leaves to determine whether or not the partnership was consecrated in the *Kausay Pacha*, or energy world—had the final say. In Q'eros, sexual was also spiritual.

The *despacho* ceremony was complete. Don Mariano blessed each of us by touching the tops of our heads with the *despacho* wrapped in his *mesa*. Then this *yanantin*-family, their work finished, each having contributed their essential presence and gifts to this potent ceremony, packed up and left. All they had done had seemed as natural to them as breathing. I sat in wonderment at what I had just witnessed. Even their child was an integral part of their spiritual work!

As the cooks prepared our dinner, the group sat around outside the cook tent on folding chairs in the schoolyard pasture sipping hot tea and staring down at the vibrant emerald green of the Amazon Jungle below. We all agreed that Gabriel was the most patient, attentive, and respectful five-year old that we had ever seen; and how honored we felt to have witnessed this high priest and priestess working together.

Inevitably a conversation followed about the problems of gender relations in our "modern" culture. It seemed odd to be discussing the "war between the sexes" in our unusual circumstance—perched above the Amazon in a sixteenth-century ceremonial village in the High Andes. It felt as if we were discussing an ancient feud afflicting a strange and primitive culture on some lonely planet in a distant galaxy.

After dinner we faced our last, and perhaps our most pleasant task—distributing the clothing, shoes, and school supplies we had brought as gifts to the Q'ero. We were amazed to learn that no one lived permanently in Hatun Q'eros. Yet each Q'ero family owned a house there that was ONLY used during their sacred festival times. The whole village of Hatun Q'eros was considered to be the *qosqo* or spiritual stomach of the community and was used for ritual cleansing of community *hoocha*! Just like the Qorikancha in Cuzco, Hatun Q'eros was truly dedicated to ceremonial use, and to the school, which was the only school in Q'eros. Its thirty-three children, the oldest of whom was thirteen, lived here alone. But they all took care of each other. Their teacher, the only adult, lived here part time.

These children—thirty boys and only three girls—were either too young to work in the fields, or else their parents considered an education important enough to excuse them from this traditional labor. The three girls must have had exceedingly modern parents, since an education was a privilege reserved primarily for boys. I never learned if this was an Inka prejudice, or the sexist influence of the conquering Spanish culture.

We had only to step out the door of the cook tent, to greet the school teacher who gathered all the kids together on the village green—the very same pasture where we had first frolicked together upon our arrival at Hatun Q'eros. This pasture had become our base camp, a haven not only to our cook tent, but to our two-person sleeping tents as well. Although this was a happy event, it also marked a sorrowful moment, for it would be our last night in the sacred center of Hatun Q'eros. Tomorrow we would begin a two-day march over eighteen-thousand foot mountain passes that would finally drop us down into the valley and onto the glacier where the famous Qollorit'i Festival has been held for centuries. I was sad to think about leaving this village which I had grown so fond of in such a short time. This magical place held many important experiences for me. But more than that, I felt so good here, so at peace. I felt home.

Thirty-three Inka children came out with big smiles on their faces, having been told they were to be given gifts. They formed a very polite and orderly line outside the tent and one by one each kid entered to receive his or, in three cases, her, gift. The kids were thrilled by the multicolored pencils, clean white sheets of paper, pens, erasers, and the small plastic animal toys we had brought with the bundle of school items.

The clothing, and especially the shoes, were a huge hit with the children who, like all the local Inkas, wore open toed sandals made from old tires, even in the freezing mountain weather. Each child was able to come through the line at least three times, and when all the gifts were distributed, they thanked us profusely and gave us all warm, dirty, affectionate hugs.

But the children wanted more than things from us ... they wanted to play. Another game of tackle-tag was clearly in order. We began chasing them, and they fled, trying to keep hold of their new belongings as they ran. The game ended again with us all falling in a glorious people-heap on the ground amidst a serious amount of laughter.

I asked the cook if we had enough food to invite all the children to eat with us. Miraculously, he said yes. So we all retired hungrily to the cook tent as soon as word of dinner got out. This had been a profoundly satisfying day on every level.

We took off from Hatun Q'eros early the next morning on the two-day horse-back ride that would take us through the 'back door' to Qollorit'i. We were literally following the hallowed pilgrimage route of the Q'ero to this ancient ceremonial site! In fact, Don Manuel was supposed to be catching up with us at any moment from his home town of Choa Choa. Before meeting Don Manuel I couldn't fathom how any eighty year-old man was going to hike two days through the High Andes over eighteen-thousand foot passes. Since my encounter with the spirit housed in that eighty year-old body, I wouldn't be fool enough to put anything past him now! In fact, I wasn't going to be surprised if we arrived to find him sitting comfortably chewing coca leaves, waiting to greet us with a "what took you so long," twinkle in his eyes.

The Festival of Qollorit'i is an event of supreme significance for any Andean *paqo*. I had heard about the "Ice Festival" since my first visit to Peru, more than six years before. A tourist had described it to me as a "really fun party." But once I had begun to study the Andean path, I understood the pilgrimage to Qollorit'i a to be the culmination of every initiates spiritual career. It was the superlative test, to see if one would be accepted by Sinak'ara—the great glacial *Apu* presiding over the festival. The truth was, I had always been afraid to go to Qollorit'i, feeling I was still unprepared for such a big step along the path. I had successfully avoided attending the festival until 1994, when Juan firmly suggested that it was indeed time for me to go.

One year prior to that, in 1993, Juan had left a *despacho* in the glacier asking permission to bring his first group of initiates to Qollorit'i. Juan himself had been sent there for nine years in a row by his master Don Benito; before he was satisfied that Juan really understood what the Festival was all about.

No doubt as a result of his *despacho*, in May of 1994, Juan and I took a group through the *Hatun Karpay* Initiation, and then on to the Qollorit'i Festival. Nearly everything that occurred on that trip had impressed upon me the power of a people united in their commitment to a greater purpose, moving toward, working for, and inspired by a shared vision. Now, as we wove our way through the magnificent mountain passes, returning again to the site of this legendary festival, I thought back to that first trip, almost a year ago to the day, and shuddered at the ordeal that still lay before us.

◆ ◆ ◆

That morning, we had loaded up our old yellow bus with food and camping gear. It was noon by the time we finally got on our way. We had found ourselves traveling on roads that would be considered dangerously impassible in the U.S.A., and probably would have been closed down. The seats on our rickety old bus were nothing more than wooden planks fastened between two upright metal poles. And clouds of dust poured in through quarter-sized holes in the floor of the bus and cracks in the windows. All our belongings and our clothes were soon covered in a fine gray powder, even our hair—we all seemed to have gone prematurely gray.

Our guides and the cook sat in the back of the bus. One was sick and coughed continually. We gave him all our cough drops. The dust on the road was so thick that at one point, when the driver had stopped to pee at the side of the road, I stepped down from the bus to get some fresh air and watched, horrified, as my foot disappeared above the ankle in dust. Juan, freshly up from his nap, was peering out the dust-covered window at me, and as I climbed back onto the bus he said, "Do you know how many people are going to travel this same road over the next few days?"

"No," I replied, not particularly caring to know.

"More than seventy-thousand!" The sheer number of vehicles it would take to transport that number of people boggled my mind. "Can you imagine how much dust all those vehicles will make?" he asked. "Up to here," he said, putting a hand up to his neck to indicate the height at which I would then be covered in dust. Then, at the look of horror on my face, he doubled over, lost in his own uproarious laughter. Although I was rather peeved at Juan, it was actually just the relief from tension the group needed. And everyone, including me, broke down in an absolute fit of hilarity, laughing until our tears washed clean tracks down our dusty faces. These extreme conditions begged for an extreme response.

I wondered how—considering the sheer numbers of pilgrims—we could have come this far without running into a traffic jam. Soon, my question was answered—in spades. By ten o'clock that evening we had begun to see many other vehicles on the road, and our rapid progress had slowed considerably. This was in itself a kind of relief for those of us who had been jounced nearly out of our seats every time the bus hit a pothole, which happened at least once or twice every few minutes. By eleven, we could only inch our way forward in a long line of battle-ship sized trucks and buses, along with numerous other rattle-bang vehicles of all colors shapes and sizes. We were just about to arrive at the town of Ocongate, "the half-way point" our driver told us, where we would be making a stop.

The women in the group nearly screamed with hysterical joy, hallucinating that "town" meant they would find a public bathroom facility available. I quickly set them straight. "You'll have to get over it ladies and take your pants down behind the bus, or," I half teased them, "down some dark alley." They were dismayed but undaunted. When we reached Ocongate, thumbing their noses at me, they made the driver stop at the local police station where they were offered a hole with a foot rest on either side behind a door that almost closed. Duly warned, they had come armed with their own toilet paper.

I chose the "dark alley" option myself and took my trousers down against a wall; several townspeople wandered by, some stared, some did not. I no longer cared. We were at an altitude of more than thirteen-thousand feet and the sun had set hours ago. It was immensely cold. As we clambered back onto the bus someone got out a stowed bottle of *pisco,* a Peruvian version of white lightning made from the seeds and skins of grapes, and we all chug-a-lugged.

Even I, who drank a thimbleful of wine on an average of once a year, found myself chugging down a hearty draught of the burning liquid. "Mmmm. Good," I said, handing it on to the next person. Funny how my purist notions about spiritual initiation had been completely routed out of their idealistic fantasy world. It had never crossed my mind that I would be consuming pure alcohol, decked out in polartec rather than a white toga, as I neared the culminating moment of my initiatory experience—Qollorit'i!

At the same time there was something absolutely satisfying about being in such extreme physical conditions. All layers of veneer and protection cushioning us from the real world had been removed—no space heaters, electric garage door openers, shopping malls, TV's, Jacuzzis, or electric blankets here—nothing to shield us from the raw experience of life and death in the Third World. So far on this trip we had seen not just dead animals in the road, but even, god-forbid, a human body. It was a shock to contend with a reality typically and quickly whisked away by the authorities in our country.

As the bus lurched forward on its way again we began to sing old Beatles songs at the top of our lungs. One bottle of *pisco* wasn't enough to get fourteen of us drunk, but it certainly had warmed our spirits and brought forth the more extroverted "Peruvian," side of us.

Juan had then told us we were within an hour's drive of the base camp of Mawayani. Not long after that, the bus had come to a dead stop. Juan went off to find out what was going on. From our windows we saw a long line of lights ahead of us; below and to our left, lighting up the circuitous route of switchbacks down the mountain. They were headlights of vehicles carrying the "seventy-thousand" pilgrims Juan had told us about.

I thanked God that we hadn't been able to see the frightening twists and turns we'd been making at the edge of these thousand-foot precipices in the pitch-darkness over the past several hours. I was amazed to have come this far, with all these thousands of people on the road, without incident.

But after about fifteen minutes, Juan came back to report that one of the huge trucks loaded with pilgrims had fallen into a hole in the road and tipped over. Miraculously, no one was hurt, but the truck was completely blocking the passage of any other vehicle. There was no way around it. This was the only road. The line of thousands of vehicles snaking through these towering passes and winding down the mountain had come to a grinding halt.

"Everything is alright," Juan told the group. "It will only be an hour or so. Just make yourselves comfortable." Juan was calm—I, on the other hand felt on the edge of a nervous break down, certain that by now the whole group was blaming me for all this trouble, and wishing they'd never come on this hellish journey in the first place.

"Elizabeth," Juan said, gesturing at me, "come with me." I had no desire to go out into the freezing night air, but Juan insisted. "Come, and you will see something amazing." Numbly, I followed him out into the darkness, our breath coming out in large misty puffs.

He led me past the long row of buses, all idling their motors in an attempt to keep their passengers warm. We skidded down an embankment holding onto trees and shrubs, and I realized we were making our way to the next switchback down. When we came back out onto the road again we were standing right in front of a huge red-and-white truck lying on its side one front wheel lost in what looked like a giant pothole. It seemed the truck had turned trying to avoid the pothole, fallen in and tipped over. The poor truck appeared for all the world like a huge helpless, wheeled bug. Miraculously again, no one had been hurt. The situation, however, appeared absolutely insoluble. I couldn't see how they were going to get a truck that size out of a hole that deep. And it was evident that the attempts they had already made to dig the truck out had had only dug it in deeper.

A large group of about forty men stood beside the truck, loudly discussing in Quechua what I could only assume was the "truck problem." Juan had translated for me. "They are saying they need to fill the hole with stones." Moments later I heard a sharp whistle at the switchback above from where we had come. A strong flashlight beam aimed in the direction of the sound revealed a man standing on top of a pile of large stones. Within minutes a line had formed and the stones were being passed hand-to-hand down the line and placed into the hole in front of the truck. After about fifteen minutes of hard work the hole was nearly filled. Then a loud shout was heard, also from above.

One of the smaller trucks at the upper switchback had broken free of the line, and with no regard for the fact that no road existed, came plunging straight toward us down the hillside, bucking and jostling violently over the steep uneven ground. My mouth literally dropped open in amazement. It was a stunt worthy of Evel Knievel, let alone a humble Inkan pilgrim on his way to Qollorit'i!

Yet the truck survived its harrowing descent, and came to a shuddering halt at the bottom by the side of the road. "Now watch what they are going to do next," Juan looked at me, eyes glistening. I watched as the men manipulated two huge wooden planks, setting the ends against the side of the overturned truck, and the other ends against the front bumper of the smaller truck, now idling just behind it. Then the smaller truck strained forward, pushing the two-by-fours into the larger truck. It took five or six attempts to push the fallen truck back up onto its wheels, where it was able to get enough traction on the stones to climb out of the hole. A great cheer went up from the crowd now gathered around the trucks. Juan turned to me and stated fiercely, "Now that is the power of collective work!"

The group had quickly filled in the rest of the hole with more stones. And the line of traffic had begun to move before we reached our bus. As Juan predicted, the entire operation had taken less than an hour. My desperate thoughts of wanting to go home, and my fears of being sued, or at least severely berated by the group, had been replaced with a sense of exhilaration at this "miracle of the trucks and stones," or more accurately, at this miracle of pilgrims united in body, mind and spirit, like one large *ayllu*—one spiritual family—overcoming all obstacles on the road to Qollorit'i.

CHAPTER SEVEN

Inka Prophecy

$\mathcal{S}$houts from our guides ahead brought me back from my reverie on last year's Qollorit'i trek. They had caught site of Qochamoqo, the last Q'ero village we would pass through before reaching Qollorit'i. Glancing around at the landscape we now traveled, gorgeous yet completely uninhabited, I shook my head in wonder at the difference between this year and last year's entrance into the Festival. How lovely it was to travel to Qollorit'i on this much more rugged and exotic, yet far less populated (and less dusty) path!

Qochamoqo, which means Mountain Lake, was the highest village in the Q'ero Nation, perched at well over fifteen thousand feet. After an all-day ascent in the burning high-altitude sun, we were grateful for the rest stop and lunch that would now take place at Qochamoqo. As our cooks unpacked their kitchen, we stretched our legs, chatted amongst ourselves, and gnawed on some appetizers of fresh fruits while trying to ease our saddle-sore behinds.

Two young Q'ero men approached us and tried to talk to us in a mix of Spanish and Quechua. I was surprised they knew any Spanish at all. We gave them our oranges, which they received like rare treasure. We tried to tell them that we were so out of breath because we lived at sea level. But our attempts to explain "sea level" elicited only a series of confused expressions. I thought the problem was our inadequate Spanish.

Finally Juan Murillo, Juan's brother-in-law and the sweetest Peruvian thing on two feet, explained why these Q'eros couldn't understand the

Alpacas at Qochamoqo

concept of "sea-level." They had never seen the sea! And in fact, didn't know that such a thing as "the sea" existed. The ocean simply wasn't in their frame of reference!

As we were in Qochamoqo (Mountain Lake) village, we tried asking them to imagine a lake so big that you couldn't see across it. But even the sea defied our attempts at explanation, and we gave up, ending the conversation with large, goofy, well-intentioned smiles that said, "we don't understand each other, but we like each other anyway." Soon, we would have the pleasure of seeing for ourselves how Qochamoqo, or Mountain Lake, had gotten its lovely name.

After lunch, we hurried back to our horses, hoping to get a jump on the afternoon sun. We had to arrive in Qollorit'i before sunset to avoid erecting our tents in the bitter cold of a seventeen-thousand foot high nightfall. Our horses labored on, climbing continuously, until we turned a sharp rocky corner that put us smack in the center of another world. Abruptly, all green ended, and we were back in the dull gray tones of Choa Choa, amidst an enormous boulderscape of weird wind-carved shapes. Below us and to our left, a mass of fluffy grey clouds covered what appeared to be a valley of indeterminate size.

This was it! We were at the top of the world. I pulled my horse Jack

Qochamoqo (Mountain Lake)

to a hard stop, and got my heavy-duty windbreaker and gloves out of my pack. The others went on, eager to see what lay beyond this, our highest pass. A few gusts of wind later, I was shouting to the group to get their buns back to my spot or miss the view of a lifetime.

The clouds over the "valley" parted to reveal it's hidden treasure—a pristine, cerulean-blue glacial lake resting at the bottom of a massive cleft in the mountains—Qochamoqo! The sides of the mountain surrounding the lake were so steep and sharp that it seemed only a mountain goat could possibly arrive at the shores of that entreating blue water, now glinting and dancing magnificently in the afternoon sun.

My cries brought instant results. The group gallumphed back to me in a wild disarray of horses and riders. Cameras were whipped out of backpacks, and dozens of photographs were snapped in quick succession to avoid the numbing of fingers in the biting cold wind. Moments later the guides were goading us forward again toward our goal: Qollorit'i.

◆ ◆ ◆

I felt it first as an impact of pure emotion; a subtle, exquisite sensation of sweet and holy pressure against my entire body. My horse and I had passed through an energetic membrane and into…? Another place…? Another feeling? It was impossible to describe, yet the visceral impact caused tears to spring to my eyes unbeckoned and course down my face.

Two-thousand feet above Q'ollorit'i Festival

It was several moments before my mind could assemble the facts. I was gazing down into a valley, more than two thousand feet below us—there a throng of tens of thousands of pilgrims were gathered at the foot of a giant glacier. I turned to Josh, who had pulled up his pregnant white filly alongside me—he too had tears streaming down his face. We were both overcome with inexplicable emotion and awe.

Juan, just ahead of us at the front of our single file line, turned his horse around and stopped cold, staring back at us, his face a study in intensity. Josh and I were abruptly forced to a stop. The others quickly caught up and gathered behind us in a tight little bundle. Turning around, I saw almost every face in the group streaming with tears. I didn't know what to make of it. We all looked at Juan, waiting for the Master to speak.

"Know that you are all very very lucky," Juan told us, his sparkling eyes gazing deep into ours. "Because you have received the *karpay* of don Manuel and we have come to Qollorit'i in this way—you have been sensitized enough to literally feel the impact of the sacred bubble of Qollorit'i."

So this was what had triggered the poignant emotional response in our group! So potent was the sacred energy of Q'ollori'ti that we had felt the visceral impact of its' ritual bubble—the living energy-field of the Festival itself—from two thousand feet above! No one spoke. Juan gave further explanation.

"I know that some of you realize the importance of this place to an Andean *Paqo.* But I don't know how many of you understand its significance in terms of the Prophecy," Juan's voice was somber and momentous. At the mention of the word "prophecy," some in the group nodded their heads in awe, while others simply looked blank. Between us, we possessed a wide range of knowledge and experience with the Andean path. But only those few who had passed through the complete ten-day initiation of *Hatun Karpay* grasped the full import of Juan's statement. He continued his explanation.

"The Andean Masters predicted a time of tremendous change known as a *Pachacuti.* This literally means "world turned upside down" in Quechua. Signs in the mountains and hillsides, the clouds and stars, and in the very bubble of living energy surrounding the city of Cuzco, deciphered by only the most advanced Masters, would tell when this next *Pachacuti* would begin. It was in fact don Manuel Q'espi himself, who came to my house very early one morning in January of 1990, to tell me the priests had seen the signs. The *Pachacuti* would begin at the Inka New Year, August 1, 1990.

"You see the Inkas didn't reckon time in the way of Western civilization—as a progressive, linear march forward. They considered time to pass in cycles, with one cycle being followed by a *Pachacuti*—a transition time—before the new cycle could begin. The *Pachacuti* is a time of cosmic re-ordering, a time in which the previous order is radically interrupted, perhaps even demolished and cleared away, so that a new birth may take place. The *Pachacuti* lasts for three years. And this time it is the harbinger of a new era, an era the Inkas call the *Taripaypacha.*

"*Taripaypacha* literally means 'the age of meeting ourselves again,' or the gathering together of the four corners of the *Tawantinsuyu,* the ancient Inka Empire, in preparation for the return of The *Sapa Inka* and *Qoya;* new spiritually evolved political leaders who will rebuild the Inka Empire. You see the indigenous people of Peru hold a sincere belief in the Inka's return, much in the same way Christians are awaiting the return of their messiah, Jesus Christ.

"You have all just been initiated into the fourth-level by virtue of having received the *karpay* of don Manuel Q'espi, a highly qualified fourth-level priest. According to the Prophecy, during the time of the *Taripaypacha*—a nineteen-year period lasting from August 1, 1993 to 2012—a great gateway of potential is open to the human race. We have the possibility not only to collectively achieve the fourth-level of psycho spiritual development, but some are predicted to arrive at the fifth-level—the level of the *Inka Mallku's.*"

"And just what does that mean?" asked Jeff, our ever cynical computer scientist. Yet even as he asked his question, his expression revealed that he was both deeply moved by the power emanating from Qollorit'i below, and completely enthralled by Juan's tale.

"There is only one test by which an *Inka Mallku's* fifth-level abilities can be fully established." Even though I had heard it many times before, still, I held my breath waiting for Juan to continue. "A true priest of the fifth-level must be able to heal **every** illness **every** time, with only a **single** touch. And to boggle your minds a bit further, the *Inka Mallku* is only the fifth level. The prophecy states that the emergence of twelve fifth-level healers priests is required to prepare the way for a pair of sixth-level priests—the *Sapa Inka* and his sacred partner, the *Qoya*! According to the prophecy, the Qollorit'i Festival, which we are now fast approaching, is the site at which the very first *Inka Mallku* will emerge."

Awed silence followed Juan's recounting of this prophetic Inkan lore. Still reeling under the energetic impact of Qollorit'i, and hearing Juan's detailed description of the Prophecy while perched on horse-back seventeen thousand feet above sea level, and two-thousand feet above the now visible sacred site at the heart of the prophecy itself, had the impact of a spiritual one-two punch. It gave us all something enormous to ponder as, wrapped in silence, we began the long and tortuous descent into the Festival of the Inka Prophecy.

◆ ◆ ◆

About an hour later we entered the valley floor and rode our horses into the midst of the massive hubbub. In the final fifteen minutes of our descent, the gray sky had darkened to black and begun spewing peach-pit-sized hailstones down on us. We now raced for the familiar haven of our cook tent, already set-up, and ducked inside. After a few moments respite, we were handed our two-person tents and notified that we would have to hurry and set them up before the ground became soaked. At this altitude and in this weather, all hands were desperately needed. In tent-mate pairs we raced out again into the hailstorm and set up our lodgings as quickly as we could.

Fifteen minutes later a bedraggled group of hail-pummeled, rain-soaked pilgrims crawled back into the cook tent in a futile attempt to get warm. Fortunately for us, hot water was on the boil. Either Juan found this an opportune moment for a history lesson, or he felt that we needed a distraction from the physical misery of the moment, for he began yet another fascinating tale.

"First let me reiterate that this sanctuary, Qollorit'i, is probably the most important place in terms of the Inka Prophecy. There is a myth, with many versions, about the origins of the Qollorit'i Festival. I'll tell you the version that I know best, to give you some idea about the entry of the Christian aspects into the festival." Juan paused just long enough for Lucas to pass around the cups of hot water. And as people stirred heaps of powdered chocolate or coffee into their cups, he continued his tale.

"The story goes that in the year 1780, a young llamaherd who lived in this valley was sent out with his brother to tend the family llamas. The elder brother was lazy and unkind, and left his little brother to do all the work. The young boy tried his best on his own, but it was just too much work. After several exhausting days, another young boy appeared to the llamaherd, offering to help him tend his llamas. Within a short time, and with the help of this new mysterious friend, the herd miraculously flour-ished. The boy's father wanted to reward his young son for such good work. The son insisted that his friend also be rewarded. When his father asked what the friend wanted, the son gave his father a piece of his friend's tattered tunic, saying, "All he wants is some more of this cloth to make himself a new tunic." So, the father walked all the way to Cuzco to purchase more of the cloth.

"In Cuzco he discovered that the cloth was actually made of a fine canonical material used only to make the robes of priests. The story came to the attention of the Archbishop of Cuzco, who sent his curate from Ocongate—the village nearest to the sanctuary—to investigate what appeared to be a heinous act of sacrilege. The investigating authorities went seeking the son and his friend and found them standing near a large rock. The mysterious boy ran away and seemed to disappear into the rock itself in a blinding flash of light. It is said that the image of Christ appeared at that moment, etched into the stone. According to the myth, the young Indian llamaherd died of shock and was buried beneath the rock. We know that this has been an important pilgrimage site since at least 1780, though we suspect that it was a sacred site long before that," Juan paused for impact.

"Recently another interesting theory has emerged amongst scholars of Inka history. The year 1780 also coincides with the powerful uprising of another Andean priest and political leader, Thupac Amaru. His leadership mobilized the entire Andean area and the movement nearly ousted the Spanish. Some would argue that the vision of Christ in the rock, although first seen by a humble Indian boy, was really a ploy on the part of the Catholic Church to help squelch the Indian rebellion.

"Who knows…that may be true. However, one thing the history books will not tell you is that every Indian uprising—from the *Taki Ongoy* movement of the sixteenth-century, to Thupac Amaru and the National Inka Movement of the eighteenth-century, on up to the Campesino rebellions of the twentieth-century—has had at its core the messianic expectation of the Return of the Inka. The leaders of all these movements have, of course, been sacred couples, or *yanantin's* of very charismatic *paqos*. In fact the leaders of the *Taki Ongoy* movement of 1590 were from this area. They were a couple of Andean priests named Juan Ch'oqñe and Maria Cleofe, whose "guiding star" was the Pleiades."

"The Pleiades!" I started. I had had a childhood obsession with the Pleiades. "Juan, I have always heard people call Qollorit'i the 'star-snow festival' and someone once told me this was because it had something to do with the Pleiades."

Juan shook head, clucking his tongue in disagreement, and then explained. "This occurred because of a mistranslation of the ancient word *qollo*, which means pure white, as *qoyllur*, which means star. It just so happens that the constellation that watches over the festival is the Pleiades, but this is because of the esoteric and energetic significance of the constellation. The Pleiades serve as *taqe* for the festival, meaning that the constellation emanates a powerful cosmic influence. This influence, of joining diverse living energies together into a collective whole, truly embraces the energetic and spiritual meaning behind the Qollorit'i Festival.

"For the Andean masters, the seven stars of the Pleiades represent the seven levels of psycho spiritual development. But the seventh level, beyond the emergence of the sixth-level Sap*a Inka* and *Qoya*, is as yet unrevealed. Little is known about the capacities or duties of seventh-level priests beyond the fact they will be able to resurrect their physical bodies, as Christ did.

"For the Indians of today, Christ is a very important figure, perhaps as important as the *Sapa Inkas* of old. For them, the image of Christ in the rock is a significant sign. The sanctuary building was only recently constructed around the stone to enshrine the miraculous image, and the electricity was only put in within the last few years. Twenty years ago only five or maybe ten-thousand pilgrims came here, but over the last eight to ten years the quantity of pilgrims has increased dramatically. I think the Prophecy is what explains this best. More people are drawn to this spot; they may not know why, but they come because they are called," Juan said, pointing to his chest to indicate the origin of the call.

"Certainly that's why all of us are here," Jeanette said, as other heads around the tent bobbed up and down in agreement.

Outside, the hailstorm had subsided and Juan opened the tent flap to reveal a view of the lighted sanctuary building that he had just been describing. A large rectangular building painted blue, with the now familiar corrugated tin roof, stood surrounded by pilgrims, even at this late hour. They were waiting their turn in an enormous line, and through all manner of weather, to enter this sacred shrine where the stone with the image of Christ etched in its surface could still be seen.

From my experience of the previous year, I knew that many who were standing now outside the sanctuary had walked for days through the mountains all the way from Cuzco with little more than the clothes on their backs. I watched them, full of awe-inspired respect, to see just how patiently and without complaint they were waiting to honor their lord of Qollorit'i.

 Qollorit'i Festival

*A*s we sat around the breakfast tent the next morning, even long sips from our hot beverages was not enough to warm us. The cloudy, cold, and gray weather outside seemed to have generated a mirror reflection inside us all. And when raindrops began pattering against our tent roof, that only sealed the deal. No one wanted to go anywhere.

"Elizabeth," Juan looked up at me with sudden inspiration. "I have a special *paqo* test for you."

"Oh?" I asked, groaning inwardly. My head ached from the altitude. Our base camp was now close to sixteen thousand feet and I had not slept much last night.

"Yes," replied Juan firmly. "Please describe to the group in detail how you entered the festival last year." I looked at him confused, through sleep-clouded eyes. "You do remember, don't you ... how you gathered your group *mesas?*"

"Yes, I remember," I replied groggily, trying to clear my sleepy head. I slowly sipped my tea, trying to gather my thoughts, searching desperately for a way to stall. "But Juan, don't you think you should explain to them what a *mesa* IS first?" I felt relieved to see Juan looking momentarily befuddled, a bit like an absent-minded professor.

"Yes, of course. Excuse me," he apologized to the group.

I had the good fortune and the cheeky impertinence to qualify as Juan's "*qollana*," the student who questions the teacher, pointing out any errors, oversights, omissions, or inconsistencies in the teachings. Juan had been Don Benito's *qollana*, and now, I was his. And it seemed I wasn't above using my informal position to get myself off the hook.

Though somewhat dismayed by this "test," I knew it was a good exercise, and far easier than others he could have given me. Because the Inka had no written language, their oral tradition, and memory was of paramount importance. Traditionally, the Inka had a class of priests called "the rememberers," living record-keepers dedicated to retaining, in exact detail, all of the Inka's oral history.

As an exercise in memory, Don Benito had once made Juan condense all his anthropology course notes for a year into twelve images, each image representing and virtually embodying all the course information for one month. Juan told me he had worked excruciatingly long hours, devising complex images that corresponded thoroughly and completely to the information, "containing" it like a computer chip. After finishing the drawings, Juan enthusiastically showed them to Don Benito. I can only imagine Juan's distress when his Master looked at them, and said only "very nice, very nice," then threw them into the fire!

This story helped save my sanity when, a few years later, I took my computer into the local computer nerd to have an updated machine made for me. I had asked him in advance if I needed to back up everything on my hard drive. "No, no. don't waste your time," he told me. "I'll transfer all the old data onto your new system."

When I returned to pick up my new machine, this renowned technical expert, for reasons unknown to himself or me, had formatted my old hard drive without transferring the data, effectively erasing everything on it. No information whatsoever was recoverable. I kept repeating to myself, "everything I really need is inside of me. *I* am the master computer!" I could almost feel Don Benito smiling and winking at me!

"I can best explain the *mesa* by showing you mine," Juan now told the group. And for the first time in our presence, Juan opened his sacred pouch. He normally carried this small bundle in his backpack, protected in a white canvas drawstring bag. We had all seen the small eight by eight inch fat little bundle, whose inner objects were wrapped in a brilliant black, pink, and white alpaca cloth. This small folded bundle of traditional Q'ero cloth was woven with the square hourglass-shaped design that was called *ch'uncho*, and represented the jungle dancer.

We had all felt the touch of Juan's *mesa* at our various ceremonies, and wondered about its mysterious contents. Yet none of us had ever dared to ask him what it contained. The others gathered closely around Juan, burning with curiosity to see what was inside, while I took the opportunity to go over in my mind the events of last year's Qollorit'i festival.

The group sat mesmerized as Juan carefully unwrapped the colorful, expertly folded bundle. It held its shapely folds as if by magic, like a large cloth Andean origami. Once it was fully opened, we saw that this small almost square ceremonial cloth, called an *lliklla*, was about twenty-five by thirty inches. A thin panel of pink and white snowflake designs ran along each of its outer edges. Inside each of these ran two large black panels, followed by a third pink and black and orange panel with *ch'unchos* running down the center. Folded inside this first *lliklla* was another plain gray alpaca cloth fastened with a long silver pin.

Juan withdrew the silver pin and opened the second bundle to reveal its curious contents: one two-inch long Christian cross made of dark *chontah*, a very hard wood from the Amazon jungle; several sea shells of the type used in *despachos*; four tiny crosses made of gold and silver; two tiny paper images of saints I didn't recognize with plastic coverings and black felt backs; and a number of small, oddly shaped stones, some black and round as a marble, some flat and white like quartz, and some that looked like ordinary gray stones you might find on any city street. I recognized one as the round gray stone that had carried Don Benito's voice to me during our coronation ritual at Wiraqocha Temple on the last day of the *Hatun Karpay* Initiation.

"These are all my *khuyas*, gifts from my masters. *Khuya* comes from the Quechua verb *khuyay*, which means to love passionately. A *khuya* represents the love between a Master and a student, or the passionate love of a couple. This *khuya* represents both kinds of love," he said holding up one of the gold crosses. This is a gift from one of my greatest masters—my wife."

Though Juan laughed as he said this, we could see that he clearly meant it. Our group had not met his wife, Lida, but we knew that he regarded her as a very spiritually powerful person. Andean priests had always worked in sacred alchemical couples, called *yanantin*—we had recently met one such couple in Q'eros. Only now did it dawn on me that Juan and Lida were also a *yanantin*. Juan had once told us that Lida had unlocked the secret of Qollorit'i for him, but he had never fully explained this comment. I now took the opportunity to ask him about it.

"Ah yes," Juan replied, recalling the story. "Most of you know that I began working with Don Benito because of an extraordinary mystical experience I had at our first meeting. I was interviewing him for my academic research on the spiritual beliefs of the Quechua Indians, when he began to speak with me in a strange language that transmitted images and complete comprehension of what he was saying directly into my mind. Somehow, during those two hours, I too was capable of speaking this same strange language. At the time, it seemed completely natural. Only afterwards did I realize what had happened, and my mind, my whole rationalist framework, was totally blown. I couldn't explain what had happened to me with this little Indian man," he told us, placing his hand a little over four feet high to indicate Don Benito diminutive stature.

I was an extreme rationalist when I first began working with Don Benito, only observing facts, data, like a typical anthropologist. My master was trying to teach me about direct perception of the world of living energies. I think he must have become very frustrated with me many times. Anyway, during my training, Don Benito sent me to Qollorit'i eight years in row. Each time I returned I would tell him, 'Master I saw this and that, and blah blah blah.' And Don Benito would only shake his head patiently, amused at my apparent lack of perception. With all my training and intelligence, I was missing the most important part of the festival—what you experienced as we arrived here—the living energy! So, he would just smile and send me back the next year to observe again.

"On the ninth year I brought Lida with me. Lida was not a trained priest, but she is of course a woman, with the female perceptive powers. She participated in everything and observed the rituals carefully. On the last day of the ceremony she remarked to me casually, "Oh Juan, look how in the final procession they are making a huge collective bubble!" I nearly ran back to Don Benito with this insight. He smiled and nodded to me, saying, "Finally you are beginning to understand." Juan laughed until small tears appeared in the corners of his eyes.

Everyone had enjoyed his story and I could feel he was getting ready to hand me the floor. "Elizabeth, I believe it is now your turn."

I was ready.

"It was a year ago to the day," I began. "We had survived a veritable bus ride from hell—all the way from Cuzco—and arrived at a base camp just below Qollorit'i but on the opposite end of the sanctuary from where we came in yesterday," I paused for dramatic impact, noting that I had the group's full attention. "Of course last year, I had no idea that there was a "back door" to the Festival that passed through Q'eros first, because had I known, I certainly would have taken it the first time," I pronounced giving Juan a sharp glance of pretend reproach. Juan played along, raising his eyebrows in mock offence. "But *at least* Juan did tell us we would be participating in a ritual at Mawayani base camp church," I continued to chide him. "And now I know that Mawayani is indeed Qollorit'i's front door entrance!" As I warmed to my subject, images and vivid details of last year's Festival, my first unforgettable pilgrimage to this sacred site, flooded back into my mind in living color just as if I had gone back in time …

◆ ◆ ◆

"Today is a very important day," Juan told the group while we were sitting around our campsite just below Mawayani, finishing breakfast. "First, you are going to have a chance to create your own *mesas*; and second, we are going to fulfill a prayer that I made last year." Juan regarded us for a moment, his dark eyes kind yet somber. "I have always come to Qollorit'i either by myself or with only one or two students. This is the first time I will bring a group of *paqos* to Qollorit'i. Last year I left a *despacho* in the glacier of *Apu* Sinak'ara, the *Apu* who presides over Qollorit'i. I made the *despacho* to ask for the permission and help of the *Apus* to bring a group with me the following year. And, here you are!"

Juan smiled at us with obvious pleasure. And we buzzed happily in our excitement over the opportunity to have our own *mesas,* and in our joy to learn that we were, in part, the fulfillment of Juan's dream. "In a few minutes we will walk up this hill and enter the base camp of Mawayani. There we will attend a mass at the church and receive the blessing of the priest of Mawayani. Then we will hike the six-kilometer trail, the route by which pilgrims enter the sanctuary area. The walk itself is a ritual … as you will see," Juan explained.

We gulped down the last of our breakfast and crammed our small daypacks with sun-glasses, sunscreen, water bottles, cameras, extra sweaters, moleskin, power bars, and lots of toilet paper. While we carried these essentials on our backs, our porters would carry the rest of our camping gear, and enough food for the three days of the festival. Yet with all their extra weight, they would still arrive hours before us and set up our camp.

The physical hardiness and human warmth of our porters and guides never ceased to amaze me. At three a.m., the night before, we were drinking hot chocolate around a campfire as our guides industriously set up our tents and even went as far as unrolling our sleeping bags for us. These men had just lived through the same hellish twelve-hour bus ride we had to arrive at the base camp. Then they had to set up our camp and had even gone the extra mile to make us hot chocolate! Later that night, when Maryann was puking her guts out from altitude sickness outside her tent, one of the guides had actually gotten up and gone to rub her back and bring her fresh water. The tremendous loving care and humanity of these people who had so little material wealth was a lesson to us all. I think that due to their good example, in a very short time period, the group had become more open, kind, and caring toward one another.

The next morning, I discovered that our main guide, Lucas, the man who had daily hoisted our baggage, seen to our lunches, and was now in charge of all our camping gear, was himself a *paqo.* He knew what we were doing and therefore felt an even stronger duty to take care of us.

We had been doubly blessed!

We headed up a hill and came out into a huge flat valley filled with all kinds of vehicles. It was like a giant parking lot with a large market area, where hundreds of make-shift stalls were made of bits of plastic tarp nailed to strips of wood. Vendors were selling everything from soda crackers and cigarettes, to crosses and tiny images of the Lord of Qollorit'i. These were mostly gold framed photographs of the image of Christ in the stone, blown up to an enormous size and superimposed above the glacier itself, making Christ appear bigger than the glacier, and a tiny sanctuary building in the foreground, for perspective.

We arrived at the door of the church, a small simple wooden building with perhaps ten rows of pews and a simple altar, covered in burning candles, beneath a large wooden icon of Christ on the cross. Other framed photographs and statues of the Lord of Qollorit'i and the Virgin Mary were also prominently displayed on the Church walls. Aside from our group there were about twenty other pilgrims present, but we stood out as the ONLY *gringos*. Juan, with occasional whispers, apprised us of the unusual and eclectic ritual that followed. A full-blood Indian priest presided over a Mass that demonstrated the syncretization of the Andean and Catholic traditions. After performing a small part of the formal Catholic ceremony, he sang some traditional Quechua *huancas*, or sacred songs, and then ended by calling on *Apu* Sinak'ara and *Pachamama*. The entire ceremony took perhaps fifteen minutes.

Juan then instructed us to silently pray for permission from the *Santa Tierra*, or sacred Earth Spirit of the church, to enter the holy pilgrimage route that led up to the sanctuary. Next, the priest of *Mawayani* dipped a bouquet of red carnations into a white plastic bucket of holy water and shook the flowers at us, blessing us all with a good dousing of holy droplets.

As we exited the church, Maryann looked at me, astonished. "Wow! My stomach ache is gone!" she exclaimed. "My gut was hurting so bad I thought I was never gonna make it to the church, let alone up that trail. When we got inside I just started praying, and poof!" She snapped her fingers. "This stuff really works!"

"Let's hope our luck holds," I said. "People look like they're in pretty rough shape. " I was becoming a little concerned for the physical well-being of the group. The faces of about half of the initiates had gone a very light shade of green with the rising altitude. We would be ascending to nearly sixteen thousand feet.

Juan now handed us each a little hand-woven bag. "Before we leave this area, each of you must gather twelve stones from the grounds of the church and place them into your pouches. Keep this *mesa* separate from your personal *mesa*, which I gave you on the first day of the *Hatun Karpay*. This *mesa* has a different purpose. Your personal *mesa* contains your river *khuyas*, and should be used for your own prayers, practices, and when you do healing work. This *mesa* is uniquely for group work, for the gathering of your *ayllu*." The *ayllu*, Juan had told us, was our spiritual family, the group with whom we should practice the Andean techniques, similar to the idea of the Buddhist *sangha*. "I suggest that you choose very small rocks, for you will have to carry them with you over the next six kilometers."

The few group members unaffected by the altitude scampered around the church grounds like kids looking for marbles. The rest of us moved more slowly. After we had gathered our stones, we returned to the circle to await further instructions.

"Now we, as *paqos*, have an extra duty to enter the Qollorit'i sanctuary in a sacred way." Juan looked into each initiate's eyes with his dark intensity. "There are twelve crosses stationed along the pilgrimage route up to the sanctuary. At the foot of each cross you will see a pile of stones called an *apachita*. At each one of these stone piles we will perform the same purification ritual. You will each take one stone from your pouch, infuse it with all the *hoocha* from your bubble, and then place it as an offering on the *apachita*. Then you will charge your bubble with refined energy, pick a new stone from the *apachita* that represents this refined energy, and place it in your pouch. In this way, you will have completed this cleansing ritual twelve times by the time you come to the final cross on the door of the sanctuary itself. And you will have also replaced your *hoocha* stones with stones imbued with *sami*."

I had seen many such piles of stones at the top of many mountain passes during my two years of living in Cuzco. According to my readings of Garcilaso de la Vega, a half-Inka, half-Spanish chronicler of the sixteenth century, *apachita* was the mistranslation of *apacheqta*, an expression of gratitude pronounced by the Indians to their God, *Wiraqocha*, when they reached the top of a mountain. It meant something like "surely Lord you have carried me here." After uttering this prayer they would add a stone to a pile to mark their passing, and show to their respect. The Spanish, according to Garcilaso, ignorant of the religious significance of the word, mistakenly assumed that it referred directly to the pile of stones. In time it had come to mean exactly that, as it now does in modern Quechua. I mentioned this to Juan.

"I think many of these types of mistakes must have occurred," Juan responded. "This is a warning to all of us anthropologists. I have come to the conclusion that one cannot understand another language without understanding the values and spiritual philosophy of the people who speak it. Clearly, the Spanish saw the Indians as "heathens," a people without religion who worshipped rocks. As you so well know, nothing could be further from the truth. One could argue that perhaps the Inkas possessed such a refined spiritual nature that the Spanish, and especially the conquistadors, were incapable of understanding them. There are scholars today who are beginning to find evidence for this point of view."

We trailed behind Juan like delinquent children, staring after the few dancers and other colorfully costumed people lingering in *Mawayani*. Every minute, more people arrived in the "parking lot." Disembarking from their vehicles, they too would make their way, up the trail to the top of the mountain sanctuary.

The first cross, apparently made of iron, was planted halfway up the steep hill towards which the majority of pilgrims now swarmed. It indicated the beginning of the pilgrimage route. A blue and white satin cloth tied to its horizontal arms waved in the mountain breeze, making it appear more like a festive flag than a Christian symbol. After a steep, grueling, twenty-minute climb, several of us reached the first cross and its *apachita*. We sat down, panting to catch our breath, and waited for the others who were not far behind. When everyone had arrived we performed our ceremony together.

I chose a roundish gray stone as my gift to the first *apachita*. I held it in my hand focusing on all the heavy thoughts and feelings in my mind and heart, as well as all the aches and pains in my body. Then I simply thought of all this as nothing more than heavy energy. I concentrated on releasing all my heavy energy to the little stone, feeling it flow out of my body, down my arm and hand, and into the stone. It was good … I felt myself become lighter for the climb, in both body and spirit, and I knew that I was on the right track.

I placed my *hoocha* stone on the *apachita,* offering it to *Pachamama*. I waited a moment, drawing in the delicious refined and always refreshing energy from *hanaq pacha,* the upper world, until a bright white stone, different than all the other stones in the pile, caught my eye. I picked it up and prayed to *Wiraqocha* to charge the stone with refined energy, and to give me the strength to go on to the next cross. I had been feeling dizzy and out of breath, not only from the altitude, but also from sleep deprivation and the exhausting bus ride of the day before. Now, after this short and simple ritual, I was renewed, refreshed, and ready to go on.

"You may all feel free to go at your own paces. Don't worry. There is only one trail, and it will lead us all to the same place." With this comment, Juan liberated us from our group mindset and from any feeling of dilemma. We now splintered naturally into pairs or threesomes along lines of hiking abilities, friendships and affinities that had developed along the way.

The longer I followed the Andean path, the more deeply I experienced the truth of its' teachings. There was no rigid dogma, no cult rules to follow; only simple principles of sharing, and ritual interactive communion with the divine power of the universe itself. Juan was never domineering; he never forced anyone to do what was uncomfortable for them. But he gracefully encouraged us to move beyond our limitations, inviting us to partake of what he was offering.

I paused in my long tale to take another sip from my teacup, and noticing I still had the group's full attention, I continued my recital of last year's entrance into Qollorit'i and the gathering of our "group *mesas*."

"We left the first cross and stepped onto a well-worn dirt path that wound ahead of us through a barren, yet beautifully austere valley. A line of bobbing human figures, devoted pilgrims, marched ahead of us into the distance as far as we could see. Having embarked on the main route, the path became progressively more crowded. During the three days of the festival more than seventy thousand people would walk over this same road.

"We continued up the road at our own paces, performing our cleansing ritual at the base of each cross we came to. At the fifth or sixth cross I began to feel my second wind. The other pilgrims came, placed their religious icons on the *apachita* for a short while, and then took them on to the next one, apparently performing a version of the same ritual as our group.

"All at once, I heard behind me what sounded like an old Salvation Army Band. I turned and saw a ten-piece marching band approaching the *apachita*. They stopped reverently before the *apachita*, played a mournful dirge, and immediately followed that with a happy, upbeat number. Juan was standing a few feet away, having just completed his ritual. Teaching by example, Juan always performed each ritual that he asked us to do, never wasting an opportunity to renew his own initiation. Our eyes met and, as usual, he answered my unvoiced question.

"Yes. They are doing with music what we are doing with our ritual at the *apachita*. They are offering their sorrow—their heavy energy—in the form of a sad song to the *apachita*; then they play a happy song to bring in a feeling of joy and lightness. It is only a different method for accomplishing the same purpose." I was impressed with the depth of Juan's understanding, garnered in his nine years of attending this festival.

By the eleventh cross, the stream of people going and coming from the sanctuary was unbroken. After about three and half hours of hiking, with long breaks to catch our breath, we turned the final bend, came over a little hill, and received our first stunning view of the sanctuary site—Qollorit'i!

A circle of huge snow peaks formed a bowl around a brown, black and green valley roughly the size of ten soccer-fields literally covered in a carpet of wildly colorful pilgrims and their creative temporary dwellings. Throngs of sequined dancers flashed brilliant colors, turning and spinning in the Sun to the lively beat of Qollorit'i music. Pilgrims in garish costumes greeted us, wearing elaborate feather or sequined headdresses and masks of demons, animals or red-cheeked white human faces with foot-long noses that mocked the Spanish conquistadores. The valley was awash in celebratory music as a constant drumming and trumpeting of numerous bands all played what we would come to call the "Qollorit'i theme song." It was an annual Andean Woodstock with a venerable history going back centuries.

As far as we could see in any direction, every available inch of this valley was taken up by people—dancing, cooking, making music, setting up camps—whose poncho tents of every color of the rainbow, propped up on sticks, would form their only shelter against the rain and freezing cold. Many *campesinos* lay together in great human piles on plastic tarps or on the bare ground, just to keep warm. Every area, except for the market place and the sanctuary building, served as both campground and congregation. The wild uproar was clearly part of the great fun that Lucas had been talking about. There was nothing dull about this party.

A woman passing in front of me wearing a brilliantly colored *lliklla* on her back brought me up short. I realized how completely this charismatic crowd had captured me. I felt an urge to leap head-long into the foray. Before me, I saw Juan waiting in a rather long line with the rest of the group, standing before what appeared to be Inkan stonework. It looked like some kind of fountain or waterway. I ran up to them.

"Elizabeth," Juan looked at me quizzically, then nodded. "Ahh," he observed in his uncanny way my powerful energetic state. "I see you've had a touch with the bubble of Qollorit'i."

"Yes ... I ... it's quite powerful," I mumbled, still overcome.

Juan continued to speak and the group, also deeply affected by the power emanating from this snowcapped bowl and its crowded festival, drank in his words.

"This is the last place of purification before we enter the sanctuary area. We will now go and have a touch with this *ñust'a*, the female nature energy inhabiting this creek. Cleanse yourself with her holy water that comes from the glacier, the *Apu* Sinak'ara himself. When you finish, we will complete our ritual with the last of the twelve crosses. This last cross is known as the 'doorway to the sacred sanctuary of the earth,' and it is one of the four *huacas* or sacred shrines of the sanctuary area."

Our brief period of rest and the power of Qollorit'i seemed to have invigorated the group. These previously green-faced individuals now looked as if they had more or less adapted to the altitude. We waited in a line with a few dozen other pilgrims to fill our plastic bottles with holy water from the *Apu*. We gradually approached the last *ñust'a* we would see on this trip. With the press of people behind us, we had time for little more than washing our faces. But I touched the water again to the "eye" of each of my energy belts: forehead, throat, heart, *qosqo*, and the base of my spine, and prayed to the *ñust'a* to be spared another case of parasites—why not, it couldn't hurt!

We followed Juan through the enormous throng of pilgrims, literally squeezing through the crowd—somehow there was always just enough room. We finally reached the base of an enormous cement cross about twelve feet high. Rising into the sky against the backdrop of the glacier, it was covered in blue satin with rich gold embroidery. A priest stood there, whom Juan apparently knew.

"*Hermano!*" (Brother!) They shouted and hugged each other in a joyous greeting; this was only the first of many such encounters Juan would have over the next three days. The priest shooed the dallying crowd away, allowing us to approach the cross. Not bothering to introduce us, Juan immediately began the ritual, bowing his head in silent prayer. We followed suit as we performed the final cleansing of our energy bubbles, and exchanged our last *hoocha* stone. Here, there was no *apachita* and we had to scramble in the earth around the base of the cross to find our *sami* stones. I found a beautiful green stone with two humps that looked like the shape of a real human heart—albeit a little lop-sided—and carefully placed it into my *mesa* bag.

"Now, place your completed *mesa* at the base of this cross and let it absorb the power of this *huaca*," Juan guided us.

We all jostled for a place to put our *mesas* around the little cement ledge at the base of the cross, and prayed for them to absorb the cross' power. Other pilgrims had left lighted candles there, sticking them to the base with melted wax. After a few moments Juan nodded and we retrieved our *mesa* bags, feeling a sense of deep surrender and completion.

Just then a group of stunningly costumed dancers, heads bowed, approached the cross. They wore black shoes, with white leggings and their knee pants and short bolero-like jackets were embroidered in a literal explosion of rainbow sequins that glinted brilliantly in the sun. The Priest shooed us out of the way, as if saying with his gesture, "Alright, your time is up!" We all stared, stupefied, at this group of shimmering human beings, who simply knelt in deep and humble reverence before this shrine. The cross, I noticed, was placed directly across the field from the foot of the great glacial *Apu* Sinak'ara.

As I watched their lips moving in silent prayer, suddenly I realized that the dancers were praying equally, at one and the same time, to the Christian symbol of the cross, and to the *Apu*, the mountain spirit Sinak'ara! This image of sacredly adorned human beings bowing before God and Nature with the same deep reverence, etched itself forever in my mind as the ultimate symbol of Qollorit'i.

Prayer Candles at Q'ollorit'i

◆ ◆ ◆

"And that is how we entered Qollorit'i last year, and how we created our 'collective *mesas*,'" I completed my recital to the group. While I had been talking, the rain outside had gradually died down. Now I waited, impatient for Juan's approval of my narrative.

"Not bad...not bad" Juan smiled and chided me, regarding me out of the corner of his eyes. Then he rose abruptly and said, "but you have forgotten to mention one or two highly important factors. Let's go and see them now." He exited the tent and we all followed him out onto the soggy sacred ground.

CHAPTER NINE

Keepers of the
Spirit of the Inka

*W*e had to fall into a half trot to keep up with Juan's enormous strides as he headed toward the first *huaca*—the large cement cross, draped in blue satin, at the "front" entrance to the Qollorit'i Festival. This was the final cross where, the year before, we had performed our *hoocha* ceremony and gathered the final stone for our group *mesa*.

We moved in an exotic and fascinating world, walking at a mad pace through a sea of people dressed in wild sequined costumes and bizarre, multi-colored outfits, some with real stuffed baby alpacas hanging from their backs. Many of them were dancing, or playing the three-bar Qollorit'i theme song on a variety of Inka instruments. Some were jovial, others more serious in their concentration, still others—probably ones who had been dancing or playing music for more than twenty-four continuous hours—looked as though they were in a deep trance state.

We could only point, oggle, and guess at the meaning and significance of their varied attire, ritual music and dances. Every act here had a meaning, and everyone a purpose. Even the vendors, who were selling everything from soda crackers, Coca Cola and cigarettes, to crosses, plastic virgins, and various sized images of the Lord of Qollorit'i in bright gold frames, were part of the sacred celebration.

Ukukus, Q'ollorit'i Festival

We were nearly halfway across the sanctuary when Juan stopped before a small group of pilgrims. They wore dark gray, brown and black-fringed costumes emblazoned front and back with large red or white crosses. They seemed to have stepped straight off the set of an old movie of King Richard the Lionheart and the Knights of the Crusades. I recognized them from last year as the *ukukus*—the bear men.

This group of three men had a tiny *ukuku*-in-training with them, and they were all laughing and chatting together. When I asked to take their picture, they began typical *ukuku* antics, speaking in shrill voices and mock fighting one another. I asked about the little one and was told he was the nephew of one of the three bear men. He was only two and a half years old!

"These are the *ukukus*, the 'bear men'" Juan told the group instructively, with a pointed glance at me. And I realized, I had forgotten to mention the *ukukus* in my recounting of last year's festival. We both knew it was a significant omission. "They have many functions here at the festival," Juan continued, "but really they are part of another, entirely different spiritual path … separate from that of the *paqo*, yet related. They are spiritual warriors in training. They are also part of the prophecy."

"How?" Josh asked, panting. We were all breathing hard.

"Every year they serve as the keepers of order at the festival. And you must watch what you do, or you may feel the bite of an *ukuku* leather whip," Juan warned us.

"Will they hurt us?" Jeanette asked Juan, rather frightened.

"No, no. They will simply let you know when you are disrespecting the rules in the sanctuary area. You will see that, at times, the crowds can be quite intimidating. The *ukukus* are here to keep order. You will find them very friendly, and funny too. The *ukukus* are not only warriors, they are also our sacred clowns, a curious contradiction. They are the keepers of order, yet they are also sanctioned to break the social rules by acting a little crazy. They speak in very silly, high-pitched voices and are constantly playing gags on each other.

"Very interesting," remarked Nina, "so the Qollorit'i police are also the local clowns. I like it." Juan chuckled and then continued on a more serious note.

"But it is the *ukukus* that go up on the glacier and stay there all night, to prove that they have the power to keep company with the mightiest forces of nature. If they survive the night, they gain the right to cut and carry down a piece of the glacier with them, often a huge chunk of ice cut in the shape of a cross. By passing this test, they have shown that they can incorporate the power of the *Apu* into their bubble. They then melt the chunk of ice and bring it back to serve as holy water for the people of their village. In fact, they are carrying the power of the *Apu* back to their people. They undergo a great ordeal of training and preparation in order to form the spiritual army of the *Sapa Inka*. For you see, they, too, are awaiting the Inka's return. In this way, they play their role in the fulfillment of the prophecy as well.

"On a more practical level, the *ukukus* remain at the festival after everyone has gone, to clean the area, returning it to its original pristine condition. In this way they are the guardians of the sanctuary, and servants of both the *Apu* and *Pachamama*."

To me these *ukukus* looked more like teenagers in strange Halloween costumes than spiritual warriors. In fact they seemed downright playful. Then again, I had never felt the sting of their whips. Yet one thing I was learning was that here in the Andes, spirituality and play went hand and hand; and the most religious event for the Andean people was not a somber and grave affair, but rather celebratory, carried out with great joy. I asked our guide, Lucas the *paqo*, about this. He was a small, square, handsome man with jet-black hair, and a classic Inka nose. He even sported a small ponytail.

"Oh, the *Apus* would not have it any other way," Lucas told me. "They would not enjoy something solemn. We are here to honor them and what they love best is a good party. You see each *Apu* has a different kind of personality. Some are raw power, like *Apu* Salkantay, some authoritative, like *Apu* Ausangate, and others are wild partiers, like *La Mamita* Veronica."

I knew that the ice-capped Veronica was, like the green and luscious *Mamita* Putukusi, one of the rare female mountains, visible on the road to Machu Pikchu.

"If you need more authority in your personality," confided Lucas, "or if you need to learn how to have more fun, you can go on a pilgrimage to the *Apu* that possesses those characteristics you wish to incorporate in yourself. But at the festivals, all the *Apus* want to see us enjoying ourselves. What father does not want to see his children happy?"

Lucas turned the questioning back to me. He had a point. I liked the idea that the Andean gods wanted their people to be happy. It seemed like a very healthy spiritual system. I believed that God wanted us all to be happy.

Juan charged forward again through the throngs of dancers and musicians still playing the endless three-bar Qollorit'i theme song. I knew from last year it would be played ceaselessly, twenty-four hours a day, for the next three days and nights. The repetition, if it didn't drive you crazy, moved you into a kind of trance. We arrived at the base of the cement cross and Juan motioned us to gather together.

One dance troupe had finished their turn at the cross, and another had gathered, waiting for the signal from the officiating priest. It was the same man I had seen here last year. Now he spied Juan.

"*Hermano!*" he cried. "*Hermano!*" replied Juan. They exchanged a brief, yet enormous embrace, and the priest went right back to his job, signaling the next group of dancers to approach the cross.

Something in the reverence and grace with which these dancers approached the cross immediately captured our attention. They wore gorgeous rainbow-color headdresses and sequined outfits, with ornate square plaques sewn on their backs depicting stories, village scenes, or sacred names. As we watched, entranced, they began to turn, dancing slowly in the sun before the giant cross, wearing the most devout expressions I had ever seen.

They were singing as they danced. And as they sang, shining tears began streaming down their faces. The holiness of the moment was overpowering—tears began streaming down all our faces as well.

Juan turned to me and translated the words of their song from Quechua to Spanish. Through my own tears, I translated them into English for the others as best I could. And as I did so, I began to understand.

"Oh great and glorious God, Oh Lord Jesus Christ, O *Pachamama*, Oh powerful *Apu*! We are here to dance for you, to honor you for your power and your beauty, and to thank you for the gift of living this past year. And if you desire to give us your blessing, if you grant us this gift, the power to live for yet another year, we promise to come back and honor you again."

Many of the dancers had by now stopped turning and were on their knees, weeping in prayer before the shrine. Juan and I exchanged tearful glances. There was nothing to say. The dancers, through their movements and in their song, had spoken it all. These people knew life came from the Gods, and that only with the Gods' blessings did we continue to live each year. Here, in the high Andes, where life teetered on a precarious thread and was clearly precious, these people had not forgotten how to give thanks.

Now our turn had come. With the permission of the priest, we placed our *mesas* or sacred objects at the base of the

Qʾllʾriti Dancers Pray to Apu Sinak'ara

giant cross to absorb the power and beauty of this place, of this moment. Then Juan was off in a mad dash again, leading us to another shrine directly up the mountain from the cross. This was an enormous *apachita,* the size of a house. Juan told us it was for the Virgin of Qollorit'i—the feminine deity connected with the festival. Placing our *mesas* against the base of this shrine, we prayed for her to empower us, and our *mesas.*

I knew that any good Andean priest gathered his or her *mesa* by collecting *khuyas,* usually rocks, energized by the power of the sacred place. The more powerful *khuyas*—and *mesas*—you had, the more powerful your healing abilities, and the more potent your bubble. A potent energy bubble meant long, healthy life, prosperity, and therefore a greater ability to serve the *Apus* and *Pachamama.* Q'ollorit'i was clearly one of the most powerful sanctuaries, and certainly not easy to get to. We all instinctively knew to gather as much of this sacred energy as possible into our *mesas*!

A sudden shout caught our attention. Looking up, I saw Jeanette, perhaps a hundred feet above the virgin's shrine, being dragged away by a Quechua woman. She was waving frantically, but smiling too. "Let's go!" Juan shouted, and turned to race up the hill after Jeanette. How she had gotten up there so fast, I never did find out. But when we reached her she was standing inside a little enclosure made of rocks, her arm securely clamped inside the arm of the young Quechua woman who had a determined, yet distinctly mischievous gleam in her eye. It was clear that she was not about to release her captive. Juan was trying hard to contain his laughter.

"Juan, what's going on?" Jeanette asked, laughing but looking a bit discombobulated. "What does she want?"

Juan, his smile spreading all the way to the creased corners of his eyes, explained, "You have entered the 'gaming area' Jeanette. Now you must play!" She looked at him aghast.

"I've entered the what? What are you talking about? I just came up here to look around...and she grabbed me and she won't let go!"

I cursed under my breath, cognizant of another significant omission in my supposedly exhaustive description of the Festival. Juan was now beside himself with laughter, both at Jeanette's expression and perhaps,

I guessed, at the collision of Western woman with Inka ritual. Once he calmed down, he spoke in Quechua to the native woman. She spoke back to him smiling broadly.

"Let me explain," Juan now said. "This particular area above this shrine is part of a large and very ancient collective ritual—part of a system of 'magical economy' if you will." The others looked at Juan expectantly, not quite comprehending. "This is a place where you play out your dreams and true desires. You can buy a toy representation of whatever you want to manifest or accomplish in your life, and ritually act it out. But be careful because once you enter this area, you are free game to be chosen as part of the ritual acting out of anyone else's true dream as well." Jeanette's expression changed from a puzzled frown to a look of interested astonishment. "This woman wants to open a store in Cuzco—a small exclusive market selling meat and beer."

"Well that's just perfect!" Jeanette burst out laughing, "seeing as I'm a vegetarian who doesn't drink a drop."

"It doesn't matter." Juan continued, "She chose you, Jeanette, because you are American, and you Americans have an impeccable business reputation around here. For her, your bubble is filled with the power of material success. She wants you to play the Godmother of her new store. She wants you to give your power of good business, your living energy, to bless her store."

"Well alright! Bring on the ritual!" Jeanette roared, enjoying her predicament immensely now that she understood its purpose. The Quechua woman was beside herself with delight. For she now had eight North Americans in her "shop," a small square enclosure she had marked out with stones. She gaily passed out long thin stones that, Juan explained, represented Peruvian bottles of beer. We all raised our stones, clicked them together, toasting her bountiful success in her new enterprise, and took make-believe sips from the "bottles." Jeanette gasped aloud. "I swear I can actually taste the beer!"

Juan gave further explanation, "Once you play the ritual, it is said that if the dreamer has a vision of the lord of Qollorit'i—at any time during the festival—his or her enacted dream will come true!"

"Juan, I like this game," Jeanette said. "I have a piece of land I've been trying to sell for years."

"Well let's go over here and buy the deed, then you can mock sell it to whomever you wish!" Juan replied. Jeanette was off in a flash to the man selling the gaming accoutrements. At another pile of rocks sat a man selling toy taxis, houses, hotels, and fake documents of every kind, for about ten U.S. cents. In a matter of minutes, with Juan's help, Jeanette had bought a play deed to her land and sold her property to a Peruvian man, who then asked Jeanette to act as an American immigration officer and stamp his pretend Visa for the United States!

In no time everyone was in on the game. Before the end of the afternoon, Juan and I bought a Hotel in Cuzco and opened a school of Andean Mysticism; Nina had Juan play her groom in a mock wedding to her soul mate; and Josh funded and produced his next Emmy award-winning documentary. Of course, we all hoped for a vision of the Qollorit'i Lord to turn our fantasies into reality.

As it turned out, years before, Juan had actually received a grant to write a thesis on this tradition of "magical economy," underwritten by the Ford Foundation. "I guess you saw the Qollorit'i Lord that year!" I chided him.

As the gaming frenzy died down Juan resumed his anthropology professor personae to continue our *paqo's* education on the festival. "There are four principal *huacas* in this sanctuary: the cross where we have just been, this *apachita*, the sanctuary building itself with the rock housed within, and that black stone over there." Juan pointed to an enormous jet-black boulder jutting up on the side of the mountain directly opposite the sanctuary building. "Two are feminine and two are masculine…can you guess which ones are which?" He had to yell a little to be heard above the din of the musicians and the milling crowds.

I looked over at the boulder and noticed there seemed to be a lot of pink and black ponchos nearby. It was the "stone of Q'eros!" I had seen it last time. It was the special place of honor for the Q'eros who presided over this festival as "Keepers of the Spirit of the Inka." We noticed that no one else besides the Q'ero, out of the tens of thousands of pilgrims at the festival, approached the stone. Juan waved us over, and gingerly, we drew nearer the massive boulder.

There were about fifty Q'ero men, women, and children, sitting or standing around the stone. And there was Don Manuel himself, smiling at our approach. I almost didn't recognize him, dressed as he was in a pinstriped blue wool three-piece suite, complete with silk tie!

I asked Juan about it and he said, "Don Manuel is offering the highest honor to the *Apu*, so he must wear his very best clothes. Don Manuel is a curious kind of paqo; he never does what anyone expects. For him, his very best clothes are the ones he is wearing—his very "exotic," and for him very expensive, pin-striped suit, vest, and tie!"

I was surprised and glad that all the Q'ero didn't feel the same as Don Manuel. Of course it made sense that Western clothing would seem unique and exotic to him!

Don Manuel smiled and offered to sell one of his beautiful multi-colored Q'ero ponchos to any buyer in our group. A great debate ensued as to who should be allowed to buy it. I didn't notice how the matter was resolved, nor if an actual purchase took place. I was too pre-occupied with other questions.

"Juan, what exactly is the position of the Q'ero here at this ceremony?" I asked, deeply curious.

"The Q'ero lead a curious sort of double-life because of the way they are treated in the community. In Cuzco, no upper-class Peruvian would want even to be seen with a Q'ero. They disparage and tease the Q'ero for being backward and "primitive." Yet if a family member is ill, or if they need a *despacho* ceremony, or a coca leaf divination, that very same upper class Peruvian would be the first one stealing out the back door, under cover of night, to meet a Q'ero if he heard one was in town. The Q'ero's powers as priests are renowned throughout Peru. Yet modern Peruvians are afraid of seeming backward or low class if they use the services of a Q'ero priest."

"What a strange life for them!" I said to Juan, turning his words over in my mind.

"Yet here," Juan pronounced triumphantly, "they are amongst mostly indigenous people; and in this community, and at this festival, they are honored for their direct lineage back to the Inkas, and for their loyalty to the ancient ways. Here, they are known as the 'Keepers of the Spirit of the Inka.'"

Juan was suddenly called away by Don Manuel, and I was left to ponder the strange predicament of the Q'ero, these priests of the supernatural. Even here at the festival the strange aura around them was tangible. I sensed how the other indigenous people seemed to treat these Q'ero with a combination of respect and fear.

They were a paradoxical group; so rich in wisdom and spiritual gifts, yet so materially poor they often lived at the edge of starvation; proud of their Inka heritage whose ancient body of knowledge they kept alive, yet humble as only simple peasants can be; and revered, feared, disparaged and sought after by various sectors of the populace whom they served as needed. What an interesting fate it must be to be born a Q'ero!

A Westerner whose psyche had been profoundly reconfigured by contact with this Andean priestly caste, I often found myself contemplating the Q'eros with a kind of longing that was almost nostalgia; examining their unique and ancient culture alongside my own. They possessed spiritual treasures that we Westerners longed for, and a peace bestowed only through deep and direct contact with the powers of nature and the universe. We, on the other hand, possessed all the astonishing comforts and wealth of the modern world, which they desperately needed for survival. It seemed that a powerful cultural *AYNI* was in order. The Inka Prophecy declared that this was the time to share. But how to accomplish this necessary sharing of diverse yet essential gifts between our two cultures?

My musings were brought up short by Juan, who called us over to the spot where he had been conversing with Don Manuel. "Our master has offered a most generous gift. He says we are allowed to have a *karpay* with their stone." We looked at each other, bewildered. "You may make an energy exchange with the 'Stone of Q'eros'," Juan tried to explain. "OK," he said finally, a little exasperated by our seeming obtuseness, "go and offer your living energy to the stone, and receive the living energy from the stone back into your bubble!"

I guessed the confusion sprang from the fact that, while we could understand exchanging living energy with another human, and thus our *karpay* with Don Manuel, our Western minds still thought of stones as "things" rather than living beings possessed of their own kind of living energy. So at first, the group didn't catch his drift. Besides, our inner circuitry was hard-pressed to assimilate the abundant energy to which we had already been subjected.

Finally, heads nodded around the group and we all went off to find a private bit of boulder to lean against and perform our *karpay*. I thought of how much energy this massive stone must have received over the centuries from untold thousands, perhaps even millions of pilgrims like myself who had had *karpay* with this immense black, solid, mysteriously sacred piece of the universe.

I pressed my back against the stone; it felt amazingly cold to the touch. As before every Andean ritual, I adjusted my mental perspective and began to focus my mind on the living energy flowing through and all around my body. I began to think of myself no longer as solid matter, muscle, blood and bone, but instead, as a contained field of living energy made up of various frequencies, some finer and some denser. I humbly offered my living energies to the rock.

Now something came over me … the world began wavering slightly before my eyes. As I became a field of living energy, so did the rock. Suddenly, a tremendous flood of warmth and power exuded from the glacial stone. It poured into my back, a sort of throbbing, sensuous life force I had come to associate with the Q'ero and nature energies. I tried to take it into my bubble, then I stopped, frightened by its pulsing intensity.

This energy felt similar to that of the infamous "Black *Ñust'a*" that we had met in the underworld cave during our *Hatun Karpay* Initiation in Machu Pikchu! Juan had told me that this force, brought under control by an Andean Priest, gave them the power over life and death! The black stone of the Q'ero was another black *Ñust'a*! I knew I had solved another one of Juan's *paqo* tests. Yet while I could recognize this power I was intimidated by it, and I certainly had absolutely no clue as to how to handle it! However, my experience with this mystical path had already revealed that I could develop in ways I had before never thought possible. Now, I could only hope that one day I would learn to use the sacred and dangerous power of the Black *Ñust'a* as well.

CHAPTER TEN

A Passport
for Don Manuel

*J*had been home almost seven months now—back
from the Festival of the Inkan prophecy. I, and the rest of our group, had
been integrating the inner riches of our Q'eros pilgrimage into our North
American lives… lives that had certainly undergone profound transformation in Peru! It seemed each of us had some mystery to ponder, task
to perform, or unaccountable blessing to savor.

On her return, roughly two weeks after her ritual real-estate sale in
the "gaming area" above the Virgin's shrine in Qollorit'i, Jeanette had sold
her Northern California property for a good price. Nina, one month after her return, had met an old high school sweetheart and was now deep
in the throes of a romantic involvement. Josh had called inviting me to
be on the board of directors for an organization he was forming to make
a series of documentaries on Indigenous Traditions. For myself, six
months after my return, in early February, 1996, I officially founded the
Wiraqocha Foundation for the Preservation of Indigenous Wisdom, an
organization designed to help accomplish the great *AYNI* I had begun to
feel was so vital. Basically, the Foundation's mission was to get material
aid to the Q'ero Indians of Peru, help to preserve all indigenous wisdom,
and to teach the philosophy of living in harmony with nature to the

world. And, perhaps this would be the first step to the esoteric school Juan and I had mock-founded in Qollorit'i.

Who knew where these beginnings would lead? Yet our Qollorit'i rituals certainly seemed to have born tangible fruits, moving us along toward our personal goals, and stimulating our individual growth processes. If Peru was the land of dreams and visions, the USA was the place of carrying them out—the land of "getting things Done."

As I sat in my living room, sipping tea and gazing out at the budding Spring foliage, the thought flashed through my mind that I was now truly "living my dreams." I thought of my best girl-friend, Cyntha Gonzalez, an exotic half Irish, half Mexican-American beauty. It was she who had first taught me this magical art of intentional manifestation. Cyntha was the reason I had gone to Peru in the first place. Not too surprisingly, the phone rang at that moment—it was Cyntha!

"Lizcita," Cyntha's normally melodic voice was a sea of trouble.

"Cyntha what's wrong?" I responded instantly.

"My situation here is getting really serious," I heard deep alarm in her voice through the crackling of the long distance connection. "The *gendarmes* actually came looking for me at one of my old addresses!" It seemed her Visa had expired, and the French were clamping down on all non-French citizens working in France, especially Paris.

Cyntha and I first met while we were studying psychology in graduate school in 1986. We quickly became best friends, then "soul sisters" as we discovered we shared the same spiritual longings and high-spirited, passionate natures. While we were both fascinated by articles we read on traditional indigenous healers, Cyntha was the first to bravely plunge in—she went to Peru and studied for a year with Shamans on the Northern Coast, in order to get information "straight from the horses mouth."

I went to Peru to visit her near the end of her stay, and right in the middle of my PhD. program felt a powerful call to move, lock, stock and barrel, to the high Andean city of Cuzco. Oddly, at the same time, Cyntha felt called to Europe. And being Cyntha, she went. Over the last seven years, while I had been going back and forth to Peru, Cyntha had built up a highly successful healing practice in Paris. She taught spontaneous painting, while introducing unorthodox practices like auric healing, tarot, and esoteric shamanic healing methods to the Medical community of Europe. Her career had really taken off. She was hired as a consultant for a well-established company that offered alternative educational programs to European health professionals. She soon became their queen bee by inventing most of the alternative programs the company offered. So I was shocked now to hear that things were not well with her.

"Cyntha, why don't you come stay with me," I suggested. "You can help me with the Foundation for a couple of months, while you decide what your next move will be!" I was delighted at the possibility of spending some real time with her.

"Done!" She said ... I could almost hear her packing her bags.

Cyntha was a woman of action, and the "queen of manifestation." She, more than anyone I knew, was living her dreams. For Cyntha to have an idea was to make its fulfillment inevitable. She was the one who had first taught me how to manifest my dreams. Her formula was simple, and powerful. "You just visualize or write down all that you really want in life," she often told me, "and then you *make* it happen!" This was no hollow formula. Cyntha actually lived like this! Traveling with her in Peru had been a wild adventure. And intentional manifestation had been our pivotal practice. Whenever we were going to a new town, Cyntha would say, "Ok, let's do a meditation on exactly what we want to happen when we get there!" We would do this together, creating a future script as it were, and visualizing it in deep meditation with great intention. Then we would watch as, miraculously, our visioning unfolded before us in reality. It was pure and simple magic.

On my very first trip to Peru, I went to see Cyntha in the coastal town of Trujillo. Before leaving Trujillo to travel together to Cuzco and Machu Pikchu, we sat on top of the ancient pyramid of the Sun and visualized our ideal itinerary, beginning with easy, accident-free transportation to Cuzco. We saw ourselves getting a hotel whose owner had an esoteric bent, and doing tarot readings for a little extra cash. Our visualization manifested almost unerringly, although we ended up at a Cuzco

Hotel across the street from the one with the esoterically oriented owner. Upon my return from my three-week 'vacation' to Peru, I knew I had to move there. Curiously, in the same month that I first decided to move to Peru, Cyntha realized her time there was up, and accepted her "call" to Europe. We planned to synchronize our transitions, and to travel around South America together before moving into our new lives and locations. Spontaneously, two dear friends—fellow transpersonal psychology Graduate students Dave and Jeannie—decided to join us. So the four of us wandered together through Peru and Ecuador, using the "Cyntha travel method" of visualization=manifestation. Our month together was full of wild adventures. We journeyed through mountains and rain-forests, met with shamans in dark hotels, attended exotic healing rituals, danced in jungle discos, and even managed to get robbed!

In one of my most memorable experiences, I was approaching a bus that would take us to an Ecuadorian jungle, when I stepped into a pot-hole and heard my ankle snap. In agony, I hobbled onto the bus, afraid to look. In seconds Cyntha was holding my ankle in her lap intoning some archaic Japanese chant. Dave saw a bolt of green light extend from Cyntha's hand to envelope my ankle. I didn't see the green light; but I do know that twenty-four hours later, I was walking around nearly normally on an ankle that had been swollen to the size of a baseball the evening before! This was testimony to Cyntha's healing powers, as I had had no other medical intervention aside from her "green lightning bolt" treatment. Luckily, during the rest of our journey, I didn't need any more.

Our travels together were studded with Cyntha's miraculous displays of witchy power; Jeannie's unstoppable belief, proven time and again, that you *can* have whatever you *really* want; my constant psychic impressions and deja vus of ancient cultural phenomena and events; and Dave's impossible jocular wit.

Dave was a gay man traveling with three rather wild female creatures in a Latin country. Invariably, and amusingly, Latin men would approach him to either ask his permission to date one of us, or beseech him to explain how he had landed three women! Dave played these moments to the hilt, with a delicious sense of irony, almost rubbing his hands with glee. He would begin his little charade by telling them that we were all VERY sexually experienced, and that they would have to be *muy potentes*, or real sexual athletes, to be with any of us. And his grande finale, if they hadn't run off by then, was to explain in fatherly tones to our potential suitor that he could chose whichever of us he liked, as long as DAVE got to try him first! At this point, most of these young Latin men would run off with a shriek, or , Dave had a date! He found either result highly satisfying. On several occasions Dave disappeared, and returned to tell us of bidding wars he'd held between three or four men who wanted to buy us—his *tres chicas!* Fortunately for us, the bidding never went high enough for Dave to consent to our sale.

At one point on our trip, it occurred to us to apply this same visualization process we were using to travel, to our lives as a whole. We did a group meditation/visualization and discovered some interesting things. First, we all wanted true love in our lives, although none of us had really ever had it! Jeannie wanted more than anything to find and marry her soul mate, and live a dedicated spiritual life with him. She felt intuitively she had already met the man nearly a year before. At the time, he wasn't available, but she had been dreaming constantly about him during our trip. Dave wanted love and meaningful, spiritual work that he was well paid for, minus the bureaucratic entanglements of a psychotherapy license. On a more mystical note, Dave wanted to find a witch doctor he had seen in a vision one evening, as the wind howled with spirits in a dark Hotel in Northern Peru where we awaited an appointment with a Shaman. Cyntha wanted to find her soul mate and to be a well-paid witch, an unorthodox wish that fit her like a glove. And along with love, I wanted more than anything to find my true spiritual purpose, achieve it, and fully unleash my creativity along the way. This shared ritual would cast its long shadow forward in our lives, and bear significant fruits in each of us.

Now, seven years later, we were all magnificently well along the paths we had first visualized in South America. Dave had found his true love, and achieved a fantastic reputation as coordinator of several school based health centers, as well as developing incisive tarot reading powers. After traipsing through a few South American jungles in search of his witch doctor, Dave came to understand this character as a symbol of his own shadow and his spiritual power. Jeannie had found and married her soul mate, a lovely man named Jeff who was dedicated to creating sustainable forestry projects in the Amazon. She had used her own kind of magic to pull him in. As soon as Jeannie returned from Peru, she examined all her fears masking her true desires for love. That night she dreamt about him, and the next morning—after a year with no contact—he simply appeared on her doorstep! Now, seven years later, they had just had their first child, Julia, and lived a deeply dedicated, spiritually directed life together. I had discovered and trained in the Andean Mystical tradition, later secured a book contract with a major publisher, then written and published an account of my spiritual experiences! I had also fallen in love and was now living with Jacques, a psychology professor from Montreal. As for Cyntha, she had indeed become a well-paid and highly respected "witch" in France. In the process, she had set Freudian psychoanalytic Europeans on their ears with her rational-mind-defying concepts, practices and healing techniques that gave new meaning to the term "wish fulfillment" by healing doctors, nurses, *and* patients!

Although Cyntha had had no lack of relationships, she was the only one of us, or so it seemed at the time, who had not yet found her mate. So when she arrived at my home the first week in March of 1996, I was not surprised by her answer when I asked her, "So, my queen of manifestation, what do you want next in your life?"

"You know Lizcita," she told me, a look of great vulnerability in her large blue orbs, "I just want my husband, and to live in a nice house in the country, and start a family." It seemed almost difficult for her to admit. My once career-driven, globe-trotting, world-shaking, aura-zapping, tarot-wielding, witch-friend wanted what most people want—a simple, peaceful, happy life. I wondered briefly if, now in our mid-thirties, we were just getting old.

"Alright darling, let's see what we can do about that!" I told her with a wink. "But first I want you to meet Jacques!" I proudly introduced my tall and handsome lover who was just coming down the stairs wearing his fencing uniform. His long black hair and goatee, not to mention the fencing foil in his hand, made him look just like one of the Three Musketeers.

"Great to meet you at last!" Cyntha said, giving him a big hug.

"You too!" Jacques replied. "It's like meeting a legend!" We laughed. Then, turning to more mundane matters, he asked me, "Darling have you seen my fencing gloves? I have practice in ten minutes and I can't find them anywhere!" At the request for help, Cyntha came on like a light bulb.

"Missing fencing gloves? No problem," she chimed. "OK. Psychic search!" She pronounced, closing her eyes in concentration. "Located!" She exclaimed a few seconds later, pointing her finger in the air to some invisible target. "Yes. They're upstairs in the closet on the left, behind some stuff!" This was the first time Cyntha had been to our house. And she had never been upstairs.

Jacques, eyes opened wide, turned without a word, and disappeared upstairs as if commanded by some unseen force. He reappeared moments later, staring at Cyntha, something between fear and total awe on his face. His fencing gloves hung loosely from his left hand.

"Where did you find them sweetheart?" I asked.

"In the closet…on the left…behind some stuff…" he spoke like someone in a trance, and seemed to be trying to collect his jaw from the floor. "Uh…Do you mind if I ask you how you did that?" he asked Cyntha, his black eyes shining with curiosity. Jacques was French Canadian, and his grandmother had been a powerful healer. He was interested in his own spiritual potential, but still somewhat spooked by the prospect as well.

"Sure. It's easy!" Cyntha replied cheerfully. "You just close your eyes, visualize the house, ask 'where are the fencing gloves,' and wait to see what area lights up!" She spoke as simply as if she were giving out a cookie recipe to a third-grader.

"Ah, just like the good old days," I sighed, giving Cyntha another welcome squeeze. One thing was certain; we were all in for a good time!

Meanwhile, there was endless practical work for us just to begin to accomplish the mission of my new Foundation. First, we found a spiritually-oriented MBA intern to help us write up a business plan. Then we spent hours brainstorming, ordering priorities, deciding short and long term goals, and drawing "mind maps" of how to put it all together. A few months earlier I had submitted a proposal to the International Transpersonal Association that was having its annual conference in Manaus, Brazil, suggesting they bring Don Manuel Q'espi down out of his mountain home to speak and participate in the conference. The theme of the conference was Technologies of the Sacred ... a perfect fit! By the end of March we received a letter from Stan Grof, director of the ITA, saying they had accepted our proposal and would love to sponsor Don Manuel's participation! The timing was perfect and we were ready. In fact, this would be the first project of the Wiraqocha Foundation!

Now came the hard part. I had informed Juan of this possibility, and he was on alert in case the invitation came through. Of course Juan would be needed to escort Don Manuel from Peru, and to serve as his interpreter. In the material world, Don Manuel Q'espi had never been further than Lima, Peru, where he had gone once by airplane in his early forties. And here a very earthly problem arose. Don Manuel, a mystical priest whose consciousness communed with nature and the spirit world and traveled at will into other realms, did not have a passport!

Juan had a scant two months to get Don Manuel's papers in order. And as events unfolded, we discovered that neither did Don Manuel possess a birth certificate, nor did any of his official documents of identity, such as his *libreta militaire* and his voting card, bear any resemblance to one another. On paper his identity was contradictory, if not schizophrenic. Even more problematic, his military card showed he had not served his required military time. Now the Peruvian government began insisting that Don Manuel do his time or pay a big fine, despite the fact that he was in his eighties!

A comic opera ensued in which Juan ended up filing three lawsuits against three different municipalities, two in Cuzco and one in Lima, who had incorrectly filled out Don Manuel's official papers, and were now filing lawsuits against him! I had to wire Juan over two thousand dollars just to cover his legal bills to get Don Manuel off the hook. And I had to send endless pages of documentation proving that Don Manuel was actually invited to the conference, and that we would be financially responsible for him while he was there. The last absurdity in this fiasco was getting permission from the Ministry of Culture for this humble, honest village priest, Don Manuel, to bring his ritual coca leaves with him. Although chemically speaking, bringing coca leaves into the States was no more similar to transporting cocaine, than carrying a bottle of poppy seeds was transporting opium—and everyone knew it! Still, the officials raised an official stink. With a few rational arguments, Juan finally overcame this obstacle.

In fact, it seemed Juan had solved most of the major problems. Now, we could only wait, on pins and needles, to see if Don Manuel's passport and Brazilian Visa would actually come through in time!

Finally, five days before the conference, Juan called me, elated and triumphant after his two grueling months of non-stop effort. "We got it Elizabeth! I'll receive Don Manuel's passport tomorrow. We're coming!" I congratulated Juan, heaved an enormous sigh of relief, and hung up the phone.

In the meantime, another crisis was brewing on the home front. Cyntha, who had been working faithfully with me for two months, and had made many of the arrangements for our trip, suddenly decided she didn't want to go.

"But Cyntha...Brazil....c'mon, it's BRAZIL Cyntha!" I was shocked; first of all, that go-anywhere-at-the-drop-of-a-hat Cyntha Gonzalez, the world's most mossless human, was resisting so tempting a trip. But we both knew there were larger forces of destiny at work here. Cyntha had had many hints from the universe, including her own dreams and visions, telling her that she would one day marry a Brazilian doctor, or a doctor that had something to do with Brazil. Even a teacher at our graduate school had spontaneously stopped Cyntha in the school parking lot one day, to tell her he had had a vision of her marrying a Brazilian doctor.

Cyntha had actually traveled to Brazil several years earlier, to try and find this illusive doctor, but to no avail. Perhaps this is why she was hesitant now. She couldn't bear to be disappointed again. I didn't blame her for wanting her spiritual mate—her *yanantin*, as I had now learned from Juan and from the Q'ero—was the Inka term for this kind of partnering.

Yanantin, in Quechua, literally meant 'harmonious relationship between different things.'" This was a key to Inka spiritual philosophy and one of the real psychological steps to achieving the fourth-level. Applied to our modern day culture I could see how this concept was central to achieving real diversity in society. You had to be able to allow differences, yet maintain a harmonious relationship. In other words, you had to lose fear. Wasn't this really the key to ANY successful relationship—be it individual, or societal—and especially between two such diverse creatures as Man and Woman? This seemed so different from our Western fantasies of the "soul mate" which always seemed to imply some nearly symbiotic kind of relationship, based in immediate, perfect mutual understanding. The Inka concept of *yanantin*, that acknowledged differences and implied work to achieve harmony, seemed much more practical, realistic, and down-to-earth.

"Ok, now is the time to tell you, Cyntha," I said. "Two nights ago I had a dream. We were on our trip and you met him."

"Who?" she said, looking at me with a mixture of dread and delight.

"HIM!" I told her emphatically, "Your Doctor…your *yanantin*," It was true. I'd been saving this piece of psychic news as leverage; sure it would work in a pinch. But she didn't budge. It was time to apply emotional leverage.

"Look, Cyntha, I am going to need a ton of help while I'm there. Please come, if not for your own sake, for the Foundation. I need you! We have over seventy people signed up for our workshop! Please!" I pleaded. Finally, she gave in.

Sure, it was emotional blackmail; but it was all true. Once word got out that the spiritual leader of the descendants of the Inka's was going to be at the conference, everyone and their mother had signed up for our workshop. The "real thing" was coming. People could smell it. And they wanted it!

Cyntha took charge of our travel arrangements. Curiously, the mistress of manifestation had all kinds of trouble booking our flights to coincide with our Hotels. The travel agency kept screwing up our reservations. When Cyntha called to double check, she found they had booked our flights on the wrong date! They had us traveling a day early, leaving us with no accommodations on our first night there. Cyntha raised hell with the manager, and made them give us an extra night's lodging free in restitution for their host of mistakes. Finally, everything was ready. Nothing could stop us now ... or so I thought.

The night before we left, the phone rang. It was Juan. "Elizabeth, I think it will be a miracle if we attend this conference!"

"Why Juan? What's wrong? I thought everything was in order!"

"The morning after I last spoke with you, I was to go and pick up Don Manuel's passport. But the passport office called me and said they wanted to make sure I was bringing Don Manuel with me. I felt something was wrong so I went alone, and sure enough the Police were there waiting to arrest Don Manuel!"

"What?" I shrieked in outrage.

"It seems he has the same name as a dangerous member of the *Sendero Luminoso* that they are looking for!" Juan told me.

"What? The Shining Path—the Terrorist group? But Juan they can't be serious! Isn't it obvious that he can't possibly be the one they're looking for?" I felt both despair, and fear for Don Manuel.

"You would think that would be the case, seeing as the Don Manuel Quispe that they are after is twenty-five years old! But it seems that in the case of terrorists you are guilty until proven innocent." Juan replied.

"But Juan, what are you going to do? What are WE going to do?" I felt helpless at the other end of the phone line, so far from the battlefront.

"Don't worry Elizabeth. I have a plan, and I think it will work," Juan spoke confidently. "Just go ahead to the conference and we'll see you there. My guiding star is with me, telling me what to do. That's how I knew not to bring Don Manuel to the passport office. I believe everything will work out. The *kausay pacha* is in our favor!"

His confidence and clarity were like an infusion. Somehow, in spite of this disturbing news, I too felt strangely at ease. I just knew Don Manuel was meant to be at this conference, and that Juan and I would get him there, come hell or high water!

"Alright Juan," I told him, trying to match his confident tone. "I'll see you two in Manaus, the day after tomorrow!" Although some part of me knew everything served a hidden purpose, and that this was going to work out just fine, I still felt that what was happening to Don Manuel was an outrage. And it was clearly happening because he was an Indian. Had he been a white, upper class Peruvian, this scenario would NEVER have occurred!

The next morning Cyntha and I performed our "manifestation meditation," visualizing everything working out fine for Juan and Don Manuel. Then Jacques took us to the airport and we boarded the plane with a great sense of anticipation. It was eighteen hours from San Francisco to Sao Paolo, where we would have to change planes for Manaus. I was exhausted and tried my best to sleep on the flight. However, sometime in the middle of the night I was awakened by Cyntha, weeping miserably in the seat next to mine.

"Cynthanita, what's wrong?" I said tenderly, addressing her in the Spanish diminutive.

"Oh … all these visions about my husband … I just can't take it anymore. It's driving me crazy. I have to know once and for all, will it really happen? Will I ever really meet this doctor? Or is it just all a bunch of bullshit? Every time I meet a man I wonder 'is it him?' I hate this! It's such a weight on me…so much pressure!" She broke down and sobbed pitifully, while I handed her tissues and patted her consolingly.

"You know what I think?" I said.

"No. What?" She asked, her lower lip protruding like a child's.

"Forget the visions! Forget all this spiritual stuff! Just go get laid!" I had meant to create a little comic relief. But my joke had the opposite effect … she only cried harder.

"I can't!" She wailed. "I tried … but I just can't!"

Cyntha hadn't been seeing anyone since breaking up with her last boyfriend, about a year and a half ago. It had been really hard on her, witnessing all her best friends in loving relationships. Now living with Jacques and I, who were so affectionate and harmonious together, had brought it all to a head. It made her feel her loneliness more acutely than ever. We had tried to set her up on dates, just for fun. But she wouldn't even touch a guy if she didn't feel the "right" spiritual vibe. I gave up and just let her cry. There was nothing more to be Done. We could only wait and see.

When we arrived in Sao Paolo, I was beat. I hadn't gotten one wink of sleep on the plane. All I wanted to do was get our bags, check in, and find a place to lie down during our four-hour wait for our connecting flight to Manaus. But Cyntha, to my chagrin, was suddenly all chat and enthusiasm, her mood the polar opposite of mine.

"Ohh another country! How exciting!" She bubbled. It seemed last night's catharsis, which had drained me completely, had left her refreshed, even exuberant. All I could think was, 'Oh God, I am NOT excited. I don't care where we are, I just want to lie down!' Cyntha kept up her enthusiastic chatter, while I mumbled half responses and held onto our baggage cart for dear life. She didn't seem to mind.

We entered the line to check our bags onto the next flight. Cyntha struck up a conversation with the man ahead of us in line. "Better him than me," I thought, leaning drowsily on the cart, my eyes fluttering slowly shut.

"Oh you're going to the conference too?" I heard him say to Cyntha. I looked at his shoes … they were all I could see of him with my eyes at half-mast. Terrible shoes… all beat up. Then the horrible thought crossed my mind that he had seen our names in the program and would want to hear all about Don Manuel. Above all, I did not want the conference to start early, here in the airport. I resolved to do my best to avoid him. But he seemed glued to Cyntha. After all, he was going to the same place. We couldn't really get away from him. I pushed the cart forward and we all checked our bags onto the Manaus flight. He followed us up to the waiting area, he and Cyntha chatting blithely together. I growled my answers whenever he addressed me, and he quickly caught on.

They went and sat together on the black vinyl airport chairs, while I found a bench a few yards away, stretched out with a huge cat-like yawn, and closed my eyes. I was just dropping off, when a prickly sensation went up my spine. All at once, I felt as if the bionic woman had just loaned me her left ear. Their conversation, which had been a mere background murmur, grew suddenly distinct.

"So Yahia, what do you do?" Cyntha asked. His name was Yahia. He was an Egyptian who had lived in London for the last twenty years.

"Oh, I'm a Doctor," he replied.

For one brief second, time stopped, and the hairs on the back of my neck stood straight up. Then I shook off the feeling. In the momentary pause that followed, I wondered what Cyntha's expression looked like. "No," I thought, "it can't be him. It CAN'T be! Not with those shoes." Having reassured myself, I dropped off to sleep.

When I awoke a few hours later, he was gone. Relieved, I got up and went to sit beside Cyntha. I didn't know if it was just natural sisterly protectiveness, my state of exhaustion, or some other instinct that made me cautious of this man.

"What happened to that guy?" I asked, somewhat warily.

"Oh, he went to change his flight." She replied, not quite looking at me directly. There was a strange buzzing sensation all around her. I was still exhausted.

"I'm going for a cup of coffee." I told her. I knew she wouldn't come. Cyntha hated coffee.

"OK," she replied, looking past me excitedly. He was coming back. I took my cue and strode off to the café. Shortly after I came back, they announced our flight and we walked together to get onto the airplane. Now that I was more awake, I noticed that Yahia was actually a relatively handsome older man, with dark black hair, a light olive complexion, and glasses that gave him a benign, trustworthy, intelligent look. He was almost exactly the same height as Cyntha. He took his seat in the middle of the plane, and we took ours in a nice exit row on the side.

"So, what's up with this guy?" I had to ask her.

"Oh he's really nice. He's a Leo, but he just told me he's fifty! That's almost as old as my MOTHER!" Cyntha exclaimed. "Whew," I thought to myself, "can't be him then." Again, I couldn't exactly explain my initial distrust of this seemingly friendly person. Perhaps over the years, I had formed my own image of who Cyntha's husband and spiritual partner would be, and like all realities, he just didn't fit my image. But more than anything I knew how vulnerable Cyntha was and I wanted to protect her from being hurt.

Once we were in the air, and exactly five seconds after they turned off the seat belt sign, Cyntha was up. "I just have to ask him something!" She told me, and scurried over to the empty seat next to him. She was still there when we landed in Manaus. After we had gotten our bags Cyntha dragged her heals, chatting with Yahia whose bags had not shown up yet. Our bus to the Hotel was waiting for us.

"C'mon Cyntha. Let's go," I was somewhat confused as to what she was waiting for. She looked at him, looked at me, and looked back at him.

"C'mon let's go. You'll see him at the Hotel!" I was surprised at her. I'd never seen her behave this way around a man before.

"OK, let's go" she told me, waving goodbye to Yahia.

Manaus was in the heart of the jungle, and there were no paved roads into the town. Our bus drove through an incredible landscape of lush jungle vegetation and huge flowers. We couldn't help oohing and ahhing over nature's magnificence. I later learned that in fact, the only way into this city was by boat or plane.

We got to the Hotel and checked in at the front desk. On the way to our room we saw a beautiful pool, complete with a fake waterfall and swim-up bar. But as soon as the door of our room closed, Cyntha began squeaking wildly, "It's him. It's him. Oh Lizcita, I think it's HIM!"

"Whoa Whoa Whoa, Cyntha. Slow down. Wait a minute here. You mean *THE him*?" I struggled to take in the significance. "Wait. On second thought, don't answer that. Let's go to the bar. I need a drink." Amazingly, Cyntha didn't argue. The only thing she hated more than coffee, was alcohol.

We both put on our swimsuits and headed out the back door to the tropical pool bar. It was about ninety degrees. Both Cyntha and I, who almost never drank, proceeded to down four pina coladas each, one after another. We were so high, from the excitement, that the alcohol merely started to make us feel slightly grounded.

"Cyntha, are you sure?" I asked her for the fourteenth time.

"Lizcita, he told me all about his esoteric dreams on the plane! That was one of the signs by which I was told I would recognize him. I really think it's him. I really do."

"Still, even if it is, don't you think we should do an FBI check on him or something?" I felt all my protectiveness coming out. But I also knew that Cyntha never reacted this way to anyone.

"Yes," she said, "I guess you're right. No you're not. Oh, I don't know. I don't know anything. I just know that I feel wonderful!" she replied giddily.

An hour later we went back to our room and I lay down on the bed, wiped out. The pina coladas were catching up with me. Cyntha, all afire, wrapped a sexy scarf around her hips, making a little skirt over her bathing suit.

"I think I'll go to the front desk and see if I can't get us one of those rooms up there with a balcony," she told me, pointing out the window at the upper floors. As she waltzed out the door of our room, I knew beyond a shadow of a doubt that she wouldn't be coming back anytime soon.

CHAPTER ELEVEN

An Inka Returns

*T*he front desk rang my room around ten the next morning—Juan and Don Manuel were waiting for me in the Lobby. I rushed from the room nearly galloping through the long circuitous hallways of the six-hundred-plus room Mega-five-star "Hotel Tropical" of Manaus, anxious to see my two most cherished Andean teachers.

I burst into the lobby and saw Juan sitting in a gorgeous white and burgundy silk-upholstered mahogany chair, wearing his standard blue jeans and wrinkled white cotton button-down professor shirt. Don Manuel was almost unrecognizable in a pair of brown polyester trousers, white button-down shirt, *à la* Juan, and matching brown Chicago Bulls cap! I knew Juan had dressed Don Manuel intentionally in Western clothes, to get him inconspicuously in and out of Lima and La Paz, Bolivia, where their plane had had a four-hour layover. Still, the effect was shocking. Out of his traditional garb, Don Manuel looked like a little old brown man. Then he glanced up at me, and there were those laser eyes, still beaming a brightness that no costume could ever dim or disguise.

"Juan! Don Manuel!" I shrieked with delight, planting a hearty traditional Peruvian *beso* on each one of their cheeks.

"*Hola* Elizabeth," Juan said, eyes shining.

"You made it!" I exclaimed. Juan and I exchanged a hearty congratulatory handshake and knowing glance, remembering the monumental effort it took to get Don Manuel here.

"Does Don Manuel remember me?" I asked Juan.

"Papa," Juan spoke to Don Manuel who was staring around, eyes wide with wonder at his exotic surroundings. Juan asked him something in Quechua and Don Manuel responded. "He says yes. You came to his house in Choa Choa." Juan translated. I almost blushed I was so flattered.

"What does Don Manuel think about this Hotel?" I asked, noticing his all-consuming gaze taking in every detail. He had entered another world, and was giving his full attention to it. Juan translated my questions, and then Don Manuel's answer.

"He says it is a very BIG village," Juan told me, and we chuckled at the response.

"Well tell him I'm VERY happy he's here. Would you like to say hello to the Rio Negro? She's right outside!" I felt certain Don Manuel would be interested in greeting the local nature deities.

"Yes, we'd love to," Juan replied without hesitation. Turning to Don Manuel he said, "*Haku* Papa, *haku.*" Which I soon discovered was a very useful phrase, meaning basically, "C'mon, let's go!" in Quechua.

We walked out the doors opposite the ones from which they had entered, and descended the elaborate staircase toward the dock. An airplane passed by overhead and Don Manuel stopped and looked up for a long moment. There was something primal in this gesture ... like a man gazing in wonder at a magnificent bird. This was one of many times that I found myself gazing at him in the same way, hopelessly trying to fathom what was going through his timeless mind. What did he see, this man newly shorn from the womb of nature, and thrust into the chaos and modern magic of the "civilized" world?

We strode out onto the little dock spanning this small section of the mighty Rio Negro. The river, true to its name, was a deep, dark, madly careening force of black liquid power. The leaves falling from the thickly surrounding jungle foliage disintegrated in the water, causing not only the dark color, but also an extremely low acidic condition that created a unique ecosystem along the river. Only certain species of fish could survive in such low acidity.

We approached the water not like scientists, but like priests. Don Manuel immediately took from a small Q'ero woven alpaca pouch a few coca leaves and began blowing on them, preparing to offer them to the river spirit. At that moment a loud, fancy white motorboat whizzed by, completely capturing Don Manuel's attention. He watched, fascinated, until it disappeared around a bend in the river. Then, without missing a beat, he took right up where he had left off, holding up his coca leaves, and saying prayers to the spirits of this mighty river. Staring intently into the river with a look of deep concentration, Don Manuel edged ever nearer the dock's end. He appeared to be in a light trance state.

"Pay attention to his bubble," Juan spoke to me in a whisper, not wishing to disturb Don Manuel's priestly concentration. Juan's words brought my attention directly into the feeling of the living energy surrounding Don Manuel. Indeed, once I directed my attention, I could sense that his field of living energy was hugely expanded. As I tuned into his energy bubble, a delightful, cool sensation washed over me; like being in water without being wet. Next, I felt immersed in an enormous, flowing, living liquid mass. It was as if I had, through Don Manuel, somehow merged with the consciousness of the River herself!

Suddenly, Don Manuel gasped and a huge smile split his face, show-

Don Manuel offers coca leaves to the spirit of Rio Negro

ing his broken, and mostly missing teeth. The delight on his features was irresistible and I smiled back. He approached me, and hugged me. I had long ago learned this was one way that Andean priests transferred their living energy to you, like a *karpay*, but less formal. I received his hug and felt a doubly strong blast of the cool water sensation. Don Manuel hugged Juan also, in the same trancelike way, and began to speak to Juan in Quechua. I waited patiently until he was done, intently observing the look of wonder and awe that spread across Juan's face as he listened to his Master.

"He says there are hundreds of them—*Ñust'as*—the female water spirits of this river. He says they appear like gorgeous young, nubile, women. He thinks that we must be very close to the borders of *Miskayani* for there to be so many!" Here once again was a reference to this esoteric city of highly advanced female spiritual beings. I felt some essential reality lay behind this idea, this myth of the esoteric city of *Miskayani*. Like a haunting memory, or an elusive dream, it had gotten under my skin … it was an itch I could not scratch.

Shortly, it was time for lunch, which entailed quite an expedition. Just

Don Juan and Don Manuel meet Rio Negro Ñusta's

getting to the lunch buffet required traversing endless corridors, reading maps and other directional signs along the way. To Don Manuel, accustomed to the landmarks of epic nature spread out beneath a glittering map of constellations, finding his way through this enclosed man-made maze must have seemed a hopeless task. He followed us obediently as we trotted along, oblivious, talking of this and that in a typical, Western "get things Done" kind of way. Don Manuel however, took his time, absorbed in this utterly artificial landscape, fascinated by everything.

At one point he stopped cold in front of a large tank of tropical fish. He stood staring, eyes wide, and his open mouth curved slowly into a smile of pure, childlike delight. As Don Manuel gazed at the fish, Juan nudged me and said, "look…rather…feel his bubble now."

Juan and I had been in the middle of an intense discussion about how to conduct the workshop we would be teaching in two days time. Now I had to stop a moment, catch up with myself, and tether my awareness in the present. My mind had traveled far and away into the future. Don Manuel, on the other hand, was all present moment. As I tuned into him again, I sensed his total absorption in his regard for the fish. And I felt in him a potent yet remarkable simplicity that seemed the very essence of living power.

"This is the power of an Andean Priest," Juan told me, shaking his head in wonder at his Master. "They have an enormous capacity to contemplate nature."

That was it! That was the word: Contemplation. The Andean Path wasn't about nature meditations, nature exercises, or even rituals or prayers to nature. It was about cultivating a state of contemplation that made absorption into the very power of nature, and a subsequent life transforming exchange of living energies between nature and human beings, possible. The essence of this path was at once so simple, natural and ordinary, and yet so utterly mystical. And this contemplation was like a kind of spiritual breathing that easily conducted these miraculous energy exchanges.

We stood before the fish tank for nearly forty-five minutes, absorbed in Don Manuel's "contemplation." Finally he gave a contented little sigh and looked up at us, as if to say, "well, shouldn't we be going?" I had barely noticed the passage of time. But my stomach had … by now it had begun to growl. We slid into the lunch buffet just minutes before closing time!

Lunch itself seemed to pose a unique set of challenges for Don Manuel. He had NEVER seen so much food in his life, nor in such variety. In his small village he had lived for more than eighty years on little more than potatoes, yucca, and jungle corn. He probably didn't recognize most of the foods he now saw laid out before him in great, heaping, artful displays. He sat motionless, his slow gaze sweeping over the fecund table, as if he were absorbing and digesting it all with his eyes. When Juan asked him what he wanted, he cast down his eyes and replied simply, "I will take whatever you give me."

It took days before Don Manuel grew bold enough to go and choose his food for himself. Juan later divulged to me that he had only the week before, in a restaurant in Cuzco, shown Don Manuel how to eat with silverware. Apparently that first steak had sailed across the restaurant under Don Manuel's initial attempt with knife and fork.

During lunch, after much goading from me, Juan finally explained what had transpired on their last days in Cuzco, and what obstacles and tests he and Don Manuel had passed through to come to Manaus.

"It was unbelievable Elizabeth," Juan said, his mouth half full. Don Manuel regarded Juan with what seemed a look of polite disdain, and Juan chewed and swallowed before continuing. "Excuse me," he said, wiping his beard with his napkin. Although Don Manuel had only recently acquired them, his table manners already seemed better than ours.

"Tell me all!" I prodded Juan, chuckling at this amusing interchange between he and his Master. It was obvious that much had happened between these two on the road from Cuzco to Manaus. "OK," Juan, recovering his composure, began again. "As I told you on the phone, when the passport office called to make sure Don Manuel was coming personally to pick up his passport, I had a strange feeling. So I went alone and found they were laying a trap for him. They didn't care when I told them Don Manuel was an old man, the priest of his village. They were actually prepared to put him in jail! They told me Don Manuel would have to go to trial." At Juan's recital I could only think of how Don Manuel must have felt.

"Don Manuel was fed up by this time … he didn't even want to come anymore. He almost went back to Q'eros. Our legal system is a terrifying thing for any Q'ero to face," Juan continued nodding toward Don Manuel. "He really wanted to run away. I almost thought he was right—after all he had been through! How could I keep telling him it would be worth all the aggravation and suffering?" Juan's face was clouded with emotion.

"Then, I came up with a plan. It was my guiding star Elizabeth!" As Juan spoke, the cloud lifted and his eyes became huge and bright. "And I had to tell Don Manuel that the plan came directly from my guiding star in order to convince him, and to get him to go along with it."

"What Juan? What was the plan?" I'd been waiting days to hear this.

With a little smile of incredulity at himself, Juan continued. "I learned which judge would be hearing Don Manuel's case and went to speak with him. And I convinced him to meet Don Manuel and I outside of Cuzco in a little village. I still honestly don't know why he agreed!" I glanced back and forth between Juan and Don Manuel.

"By luck or fate, this judge understood Quechua. So Don Manuel was able, in his own words, to tell the judge who he was—just a simple man, a humble village priest who tended his sheep, read the coca leaves, and performed healings for his people. He told the judge he didn't know why the police would want someone as unimportant as him, and that he was very frightened.

"His simplicity, the innocence with which he spoke, his … " Juan searched for the right words, "his *ingenuousness* … I can't say exactly how it happened, but by the end of the conversation, the judge was in tears! More importantly, he was completely convinced that Don Manuel was not their man and dismissed the case!"

"*Unbelievable!*" I gasped. And it was, for I well knew the odds against a poor Q'ero in the grip of the Peruvian justice system. Don Manuel was lucky not to be languishing in jail at this moment, awaiting trial.

"No. It was a miracle," Juan said, gazing fondly at his master. "*Un milagro, no es cierto Papa?"* Juan asked Don Manuel to confirm his story. Don Manuel looked very serious for a moment. Then he nodded, a huge smile spreading across his face, and in Spanish with a Quechua accent he concurred, *"Milakaro!"*

We now determined that, in this ninety-four degree heat, the best activity after lunch and a rest was lounging by the enormous pool with its artificial waterfall. Neither of them had brought a swimming suit, which wasn't common accouterment in Cuzco. So while they went to rest, I went to purchase suits for both of them in the Hotel gift shop. An hour later we met at the pool. Needless to say, Don Manuel's trunks looked enormous on him. But it didn't stop him from enjoying the water in which he swam and played like a child.

As we lay on the lounge chairs basking in the sun, who walked up but Cyntha and her new love, Yahia! "Well fancy meeting you here!" I chided her, reaching out with a smile to shake hands with Yahia. Both their faces were flushed and they had the shy, tender look of two people newly and totally in love.

At seven that morning Cyntha had breezed into the room, grabbed a change of clothes, and breathlessly commented on the absolutely un-believable planning on the part of the "Love Angels." Because if she and Yahia hadn't met at the Sao Paolo airport yesterday, they would HAVE to have met this morning, being the ONLY TWO out of eight hundred people at the conference who had signed up for the day long jungle tour! It seemed the "Love Angels" had had a back-up plan. They were just now, at five p.m., returning from their 'private' safari. Their guide had even asked if they were on their "honey-moon!"

I quickly introduced them to Juan and Don Manuel. Yahia seemed quite impressed that his new love had such a direct "in" with some of the main presenters at the conference, and especially with the guest of honor, Don Manuel!

"So how was your jungle tour?" I asked, curious as to what they had seen.

"Oh it was quite amazing," Cynthia enthused. "Nature here is fantastic. *La Pachamama de aqui es muy bonita!"* She spoke to Don Manuel in Spanish and he nodded politely, no doubt understanding this simple phrase. "But Lizcita, it's terrible, the deforestation and the destruction of species. We are killing the earth! *La Pachamama esta llorando!*" She told Don Manuel, meaning, "The *Pachamama* is weeping because we are killing her." Then she asked Juan to translate this to Don Manuel.

Juan hesitated, saying "But they don't see it like we do ... they ..."

"Please tell him what I said," Cyntha insisted. Juan shook his head, knowing what was coming, and dutifully translated. As he finished, Don Manuel—to our utter surprise—burst out laughing. Certainly, it was the exact opposite of what we had all expected. In fact, he guffawed himself into an absolute fit of hilarity. He laughed and laughed until he was crying. Finally he had to lie down, holding his stomach. I couldn't help but be amused. His laughter was contagious. Cyntha looked utterly perplexed. Juan, wiping the tears from his eyes, tried to explain.

"You see for the Inka, the *Pachamama* is the biggest and most powerful creative force that exists. For us to think that we could kill her ... well ... to them it's ... ridiculous. Absurd. It's like saying we're going to kill God. From his point of view, we are only alive because of the generosity of *Pachamama*. She has only to move her shoulder like this," he said, implying an earthquake, "and we are ALL dead! In reality, he is right. Because even if we destroy all the forests and species with pollution, *Pachamama* will not die. She will go on, cleaning herself again, and making more forests and species. The truth is," Juan said thoughtfully, "we are only killing ourselves."

Complete silence reigned in our little group. My perspective had just been spun around one hundred and eighty degrees. That we were killing, or even could kill Mother Earth, or that we could save her, was an idea that I, and most ecologically minded groups, easily espoused. Yet Don Manuel's response, and Juan's explanation, revealed behind that assumption a kind of blind, egocentric delusion of omnipotence. The shift I experienced in seeing this from an Inka perspective was clarifying and refreshing! Human beings holding the power over the life or death of Mother Earth? Rather, it was SHE who had that power over us! Don Manuel's reaction was indeed absolutely appropriate.

We parted company quietly, chewing over the deep, and brutally honest perspective that Don Manuel's laughter had brought to us. Indeed, that was exactly why he was here. We walked back to our rooms to prepare for the opening ceremony, where Don Manuel would be performing a *despacho* before a conference of eight hundred people ... more people than the inhabitants of his entire Q'ero Nation.

A few hours later, Juan and Don Manuel stepped into the Great Hall. I was already there saving our seats in the front row. Don Manuel and his *despacho* ceremony were the opening act! I was nervous. But Don Manuel looked completely unconcerned, now dressed fabulously in his *unkhu*, a traditional black alpaca ceremonial shirt, his multi-colored woven *chullo*, with beaded ear flaps, a beaded sleeved undershirt, short black alpaca pants, sandals, and a glorious multi-colored Q'ero poncho over the top! The technical help was trying to figure out exactly where to attach his lapel mike. I wondered whether anyone had had the presence of mind to explain to Don Manuel what a lapel mike was. Just then the illustrious psychologist Stanislav Graf, veteran explorer of altered states of consciousness, took the podium.

"Good evening ladies and gentleman ..." he began in his deeply melodic richly accented voice. His charismatic presence immediately captured everyone's attention. After a brief and eloquent introduction to the conference, Stan graciously introduced Juan and Don Manuel, giving the ritual the floor.

At Juan's signal Don Manuel moved to the stairs and ascended the stage where he would make his *despacho*, the traditional Andean offering that preceded any sacred or important work. Don Manuel had had chronic lung problems for years, and ascending the stairs caused him to draw deep breaths that could be heard room-wide over his lapel mike. At this noise, he looked around bewildered. I cringed. Then, realizing the sound had come from him, he began to chuckle. When that too was heard room-wide, he let out a hearty laugh that spread contagiously through the now-thoroughly-charmed audience. Don Manuel had clearly discovered what a lapel mike was for.

Without missing a beat, as if he had performed *despachos* on stages before large audiences all his life, Don Manuel went about his business.

Juan translated his simple, humble prayers to the spirits of the Mighty Rio Negro; to the *Santa Tierra's*, the Earth Spirits on which the Hotel was built; to *Inti Tayta*—father sun; to *Pachamama*—mother Earth; and finally to *Wiraqocha*, God of all creation. He invoked the many natural and supernatural beings, asking their permission for, and help with, the conference, and petitioning them to bless, heal and keep safe all of the people attending the conference. As his prayers were translated, Don Manuel blew on his coca leaves and built the offering, element by element. With each coca leaf, bit of yarn, flower, and piece of candy he humbly, lovingly offered to *Pachamama*, he touched and opened eight hundred hearts. The entire process lasted about twenty minutes. Throughout, the audience witnessed in awed silence this Andean Master, leader of the descendants of the Inkas, going about his work. His mastery of living energy made apparent by the huge love bubble he had just single-handedly created.

When he was through, he simply got up and walked off the stage with Juan trailing after. The audience exploded in applause and Don Manuel smiled and nodded his acceptance.

For the next hour or two there were the usual speeches, acknowledgements given to those who had worked so hard to make the conference possible, plus an overview of the conference schedule. The high point was Stan Graf's compelling presentation urging that psychology be held and practiced within a spiritual framework. "Without that," he told us quite bluntly, "our psychological theories, and our therapeutic interventions are absolutely meaningless." Finally, the end of the presentation was announced and people got up to leave. Both Juan and I stood up, completely unprepared for what happened next.

First one, then two, then five people came up and knelt down on the floor, heads bowed, at Don Manuel's feet. Within minutes a kind of spiritual contagion swept over the entire room, and there were nearly three hundred people kneeling on the floor before Don Manuel, awaiting his blessing. They were also effectively blocking any possibility of our leaving the room. I looked helplessly at Juan. "What should we do?" I whispered to him over Don Manuel's head. "Should we pick him up and carry him out of here?" Juan looked at me, contemplating the moment, and then did an immensely practical thing. He simply asked Don Manuel what *he* wanted to do.

"Yes of course, I am going to give them all my blessing. What do you think I'm here for?" came Don Manuel's immediate reply. Juan translated his words to me, laughing. For the next nearly two hours, we stood on either side of Don Manuel, like body guards—but also lending our living energy to him—while he placed his hands over each head that appeared before him, and invoked the spirits and the Gods on that person's behalf. Finally, when only about twenty people remained, Don Manuel nodded to us. He was spent. And with that, we took him away, exhausted, but thoroughly happy!

During one of the last days of the conference, something happened that taught me more about Andean healing techniques and philosophy than any other single event before or since. Juan and I were sitting having lunch with Don Manuel, who had just gone to the Men's room. Just then, Christina Grof, Stan's wife, came over to our table. Christina is a very warm and beautiful woman, and at the same time an imposing figure, standing nearly six feet tall. She sat down with us and briefly told us that she had injured her back in fall from a boat down at the docks. She was in pain and was wondering if Don Manuel could help her.

Juan replied with an immediate "yes." At that moment, as if on cue, Don Manuel reappeared. Before anyone could say a word to him, he grabbed Christina's wrist and looked as if he were listening intently to something. He spoke quickly to Juan. "She has had a shock. I can help her." Christina smiled as Juan translated his words and instinctively moved to stand up.

Now it was Don Manuel's turn for a shock, as he looked up at the woman whose wrist he was still holding, towering above him. In his customary way of handling surprise, Don Manuel began to laugh. Then he and Christina disappeared. When they returned ten minutes later, Christina reported that pain in her back was gone. (It was still gone the next day, and that night she slept comfortably and had beautiful dreams!)

This scene caused a commotion, and soon a crowd had gathered in the dining room around Don Manuel and Christina. I begged Juan that we take Don Manuel and slip away somewhere—I was dying to know exactly what he had done and how he had done it. Apparently, Juan had the same thing in mind. And he knew exactly how to lure Don Manuel away. He told Don Manuel that we wanted to take him out for a beer. Don Manuel LOVED beer! In fact, we'd have to watch him carefully lest he drink himself sick on the stuff. Of course, he immediately accepted our invitation, and we were off, searching out one of the dozens of little bars scattered throughout the colossal Hotel complex.

We found the perfect little out-of-the-way bar, far from the conference area, and ordered three large beers. Don Manuel, grinning like a kid in a candy store as his beer arrived, had to put both hands around the enormous glass, eyes huge, as he tipped it slowly into his mouth, savoring every drop. As for me, I could not contain my bursting curiosity any longer.

"Juan, can you please ask him to explain how he knew something was wrong with Christina?" I asked. "And exactly what he did to 'fix' her?"

I had been unable to tell just from looking at Christina that anything was amiss. And I wondered what Don Manuel had "seen." Juan spoke to Don Manuel for quite a while, asking many questions, laughing, and asking more questions. I sat fiddling impatiently with my beer glass, taking frequent sips. Finally Juan looked at me, light dawning across his face.

"Yes, I see now," he said. "I understand things much better."

"That's nice Juan," I said, feeling both teased, and like teasing back. "Now could you PLEASE let ME in on it?"

Juan knew of my serious interest in healing, and answered directly.

"First," he said, "you must remember that everything in the Andean world has both a physical aspect, and a spiritual or energetic aspect."

"Yes, yes, I know. And…?"

"When the physical body receives a shock, a little piece of the energy body is lost…it falls out at that spot…the place where the shock occurred. We call that *susto* in Spanish. You call it 'trauma' I believe."

"Yes. I follow you. Keep going." I goaded Juan.

"Don Manuel, being a *kamasqa*, someone who is able to perceive energy directly—what you would call a 'clairvoyant' I think? Well, he noticed immediately that Christina was missing some of her living energy. He only needed to hear the story of her accident to know where it was."

"On the dock?" I ventured.

"Right," Juan confirmed. "Then all he had to do was use his *mesa* to call that part of her spirit back. First he lured it into his *mesa*, and then he blew it back into her body, where it belongs. It's a simple procedure, especially if the shock is quite recent. Then he noticed that one of her vertebrae had been knocked out of alignment in the fall, and he used gentle pressure to move it back into place."

"So when you put the physical and the spiritual aspects of the person back where they belong...*voila*...you have healing!" I exclaimed, fascinated as always by the simple elegance of the Andean explanation.

"Precisely!" Juan confirmed. "And speaking of putting things back where they belong, do you realize what we have done in this trip?"

"No Juan, but I'm hoping you'll tell me," I chided him.

"Recently an archaeologist discovered some of the Inka Royal Pottery here in Manaus. Then I saw Don Manuel's reaction to the Rio Negro, and his declaration that we are close to *Miskayani*. To me this is not only further confirmation of the ancient Inka myths, but it also extends the previously accepted border of the Inka Empire, all the way here to Brazil. So in bringing Don Manuel here, we have returned the Inka from Cuzco, the center of the empire, to his ancient border!"

An Inka Returns: Don Manuel in Manaus, Brazil

CHAPTER TWELVE

Pachamama
New York City

*M*ission accomplished! Don Manuel, through his simple presence and his wise words, had made a spectacular impact at the Manaus conference, teaching and influencing many people. He'd given numerous interviews on video and in newspapers and magazines. For this humble village priest, the hardest thing had been talking repeatedly about himself. He had never, in his eighty some years (no one knew exactly how old Don Manuel really was), had to tell people about himself. Everyone in his village both knew him, and knew all about him.

For Don Manuel, telling strangers who and what he was, where he came from, and what he had Done in his life, while they aimed cameras or recorders at him, or scribbled his words down, soon went from VERY strange to downright unbearable. As a result, almost purely in self-defense, he began falling asleep during the interviews. This was especially funny on videotape, where I was often caught gently nudging Don Manuel awake.

One story the journalists couldn't get enough of was Don Manuel's initiation story. Although I had heard several times that Don Manuel was a very unusual kind of Andean priest, called *kamasqa*—meaning he had received the fourth-level initiation not from other fourth-level Masters, but directly from God—I didn't understand exactly what this meant until I heard Don Manuel tell the story of his initiation in its entirety.

We were sitting in a fancy suite of rooms with its own private balcony that our interviewer—a Canadian journalist—had commandeered from the Hotel for the videotaped interview. Although she knew very little about the Andean path, her keen questions stimulated fascinating answers. She wanted to know how Don Manuel had become a priest.

"I first entered onto the Path when I was about twenty-one or so, only because I was very sick, and very desperate. There was blood coming from my male member. And I was close to death. I sought help from other Andean priests, but no one could heal me. My father finally told me to go and ask for a miracle in two of the sacred sanctuaries near Cuzco—the sanctuaries of Ocururo and Wanka. The sanctuary of the Señor de Wanka, renowned for its healing powers, proved especially important. There I received a vision of Jesus Christ as a *mestizo* (white man) wearing spectacles, very elegant clothing, and shining brightly. Jesus told me, `You will be completely healed, but you must go to Qollorit'i sanctuary.'

"Obedient to my vision, I went to Qollorit'i sanctuary. There, Jesus came to me in a vision again and told me, `You must go to the snow peak and perform the initiation ritual.' I didn't know how to do that ritual. But I was with my father who, though he was not an Andean priest, still knew how to perform the ritual. After performing the initiation ritual at the snow peak, I had a third vision of Jesus. He told me to take a ritual bath in the glacial lakes of Qollorit'i, and then make and offer several *despachos*. Faithfully, I did all those things. Then, Jesus came to me in a final vision and told me, 'You must become an Andean Priest. You must come back to Qollorit'i three times and you will receive your *mesa.*' After that, I returned to my village, and I was totally healed."

The journalist was very impressed with Don Manuel's story, but also confused. "It seems quite odd," she told Juan, "an Indian person having a vision of Jesus as a white man. Can you ask him why he thinks he had a vision of Jesus and not an Inka?" But Don Manual began speaking again before Juan could ask, and in his own way, addressed her question.

"The answer goes in another direction, but it is very interesting," Juan informed us when Don Manuel had finished speaking. "Don Manuel said, `When I had the vision of Jesus I also received the flame of the Holy Spirit in my head and in my body, and I was healed. This is why I can speak of these things. If I hadn't received the flame of the Holy Spirit in my head and in my body, I could not talk about these things. I could not do the things I can do.'"

"Does he mean healing others? Or transmitting that energy to others?" The journalist had unwittingly asked a very key question. Suddenly light bulbs went off in my head. During the *karpay* ceremony Don Manuel had performed for us in his house in Choa Choa, I had received a blinding "cross of light" in the top of my head. Could this be the flame of the Holy Spirit he was just talking about?

"Jesus and the Holy Spirit—these are very Catholic or at least Christian terms," the journalist kept at the subject. "Isn't it odd for an Indian to use such Christian terms?"

"There are two factors here." Juan said, giving his learned explanation. "The first one is psychological. When a white man has a sacred dream or vision these days, the messenger will often take the form of an Indian. The psyche delivers the sacred message via the person of someone exotic or different. So why shouldn't Don Manuel see the sacred coming in the exotic form of a white man, wearing glasses?" What Juan said made good psychological sense.

"There is something else you must understand," Juan told her, now putting on his anthropologist hat. "First, the Andean spiritual system has always been very inclusive. In Inka times, there was a great diversity of religions being practiced all together. In fact, there were over fifty-two different religions that all kept their idols in the Qorikancha, the central sun temple of the Inkas in Cuzco. As a new group became part of the Inka Empire, they were not forced to practice a homogenous religion. They were allowed to keep their religious freedom and identity. Their idols were simply added to the others in the Qorikancha."

"So, when the Spanish arrived with their Christian religion, it was easily integrated by the Indians, for they understood it deserved a place among all living faiths under the sun. Over time Jesus simply occupied the ancient place of *Wiraqocha*. Yet, even today you will see that the basic structure of the religious practices, ceremonies, even the processions of Catholic Saints, is still Inka. For the Inka system is based on one of the fundamental underlying principles of the universe—living energy—and is therefore like a super-ordinate system that can hold all other religious systems inside it; including Catholicism."

This journalist's mind was blown! Not only by Don Manuel, but by the idea that an ancient system like that of the Inkas could be so advanced a model of religious tolerance and diversity, and so resilient and deep-rooted that it could subsume the Catholic Church into itself as one of its many parts. Indeed, this was the beauty and power of the Andean system, and part of the reason it had survived so to this day.

By now, Don Manuel was tired. He told us, in fact, that so much talking was bad for the spirit, that we were pulling words out of him now, and he had talked too much. "My heart is crying blood," he said, giving the classic Inka metaphor for having done something 'til it hurts." Still, the conference had been a wonderful success, and all including Don Manuel had had the time of their life!

On a more earthy plane, Cyntha and Yahia, within three days of meeting each other, had gotten engaged. She had decided to move to England with him, and they were plotting the purchase of a house in the English countryside. It had all happened so fast. Especially when Cyntha announced that Yahia and she had picked out her engagement ring in one of the Hotel shops! It was a beautiful two-karat Tanzanite, a gorgeous purple-blue stone, surrounded by two small diamonds. As it turned out, the shop didn't accept Yahia's British credit card for some unknown reason, and I ended up purchasing their engagement ring on my Visa card. I felt like the fairy-god-mother of their meeting!

On our way home, back through the Sao Paolo airport, Cyntha and I made a video taped re-enactment of their entire meeting. We filmed each place in the airport where some significant part of their encounter had taken place, and Cyntha narrated the story. After all, it was now an historic event she had been anticipating for years! Still, for some reason

I couldn't fully explain, even to myself, why I wasn't entirely convinced. Visions are visions, but they have to be played out in real life, down here on the earth plane.

I loved the Christian Mystics test of a "real" vision as opposed to a delusion or hallucination. First, the vision had to mark a powerful tangible change in the person's life with a turning toward the spiritual. Second, it had to set forth and give real instruction on how to accomplish a spiritual task. And third, the task had to be carried out in the real world, and be of service to the larger community. Certainly I was happy for my dearest friend, but I decided to reserve judgment and see how it all worked out over time. I knew from experience that spiritual meetings needed to go through the earthly test of time to see if they could be successfully grounded in everyday reality.

Shortly after we returned to California, Cyntha was off to her new life in the U.K. A few months later, she was pregnant and they were living in that house in the English countryside they had visualized together. Within six months Cyntha created everything she had told me she wanted upon coming to California. She was indeed still the Queen of manifestation. The circle was complete!

◆ ◆ ◆

A few weeks after my return from Brazil, I received a concerned telephone call from my literary agent. Having heard no word from my USA publishers regarding my completed manuscript, which they had received five months before, she had telephoned my editor in New York to make sure the book was still on schedule. She had received vague assurances that it would soon be published, they just weren't exactly sure when. It sounded like trouble.

We decided the best thing was for me to go to New York and meet with my editor personally … let her see that I was a real live person. It might be the stimulus needed to get my publishing ball rolling. I knew I could stay with Linda, my international agent, who had so successfully sold my book abroad. Fourteen countries had now purchased publication rights, each in their own language. And they weren't happy about the delay of the American publishers.

I arrived one afternoon the following week at Linda's 54th street New York office. In the past, big cities like New York, the city of my birth, had intimidated me. This time, however, I felt deliciously at home. The streets, the people, the buildings, Central Park, all felt exciting, fascinating, and surprisingly welcoming! Previously, a city's chaotic stimuli had seemed overwhelming to my sensitive nature. But my work on the Andean path—the strengthening of my personal energy bubble, and my increased ability to handle and integrate different kinds of living energies—gave me a new sense of clarity and stability. Rather than overwhelmed, I felt empowered!

Linda and I had a lovely dinner together, discussing my Peruvian adventures and the unusual experiences that had led me to write my book. Linda, a very sensitive, intelligent person with her own spiritual interests, was also a shrewd businesswoman. She had been a psychotherapist for years prior to becoming a literary agent, and was a very good listener. We discussed my plans for the next few days, and she suggested I take in a museum or two while I was there. Her West End Avenue apartment was within walking distance of the museums in Central Park.

My meeting with my editor wasn't until the afternoon of the next day, so I decided to spend my morning museum-browsing. When I awoke, Linda was already gone. I took a shower, made a cup of tea, and perused Linda's scribbled directions to the nearby Metropolitan Art Museum—they sounded simple enough.

Before heading out the front door, I gathered everything I needed for the day, as I would be going directly from the museum to my publishers. I walked two and a half blocks with the nagging feeling that I was going in the wrong direction. Yet I was clearly on course for the museum ... I could see the park up ahead. Then suddenly I had the distinct sensation of someone trying to get my attention. "What is going on?" I asked myself, stopping on the spot to listen within.

Instantly, an image began forming in my mind. An inner voice, with a most forceful personality, echoed through me, "And just where do you think you're going, my girl, without first honoring me?" The image coalesced into the flowing form of a powerful river...the Hudson River. She was speaking to me!

"Where are you? I can't see you?" I was so surprised, I spoke aloud— then self-consciously clapped my hand over my mouth.

"I am here, behind you," came the river's reply. "Just two blocks from your friends front door. Do you really think you can do anything here, in New York City, without first honoring me?" Her tone, friendly yet chiding, had an awesome force behind it.

"No...I'm sorry...I didn't see you...I wasn't aware you were here," I stumbled over my words, absolutely flabbergasted, and a bit embarrassed. After all, I *was* an initiated priestess of nature with an affinity for water, yet I hadn't thought enough to make an offering to the city's sacred river. Meanwhile my small, personal ego was agitated about having my museum trip interrupted. This was all out of control.

I turned and looked behind me. There was no sign of any river. For a moment I wondered ... was this communication real, or an audio-hallucination, some bizarre effect of a guilty conscience? Now, my rational mind kicked in, looking for logical explanations, demanding facts. I saw a kiosk up ahead at the corner of the block. "I'll get a map of Manhattan and we'll see," I told myself. "I'll clear all this up."

Striding confidently up to the kiosk I casually purchased a city map, certain I would soon be, once again, on my way to the museum. I moved out of the way of the sidewalk traffic, opened the map, and quickly located West End Avenue. "Uh oh!" Again, the words escaped my lips aloud, as my eyes landed on the Hudson River, five blocks behind me, precisely two blocks from Linda's front door! The river called indeed ... and the museum would have to wait. A crazy combination of emotions churned within me as I, stupefied, humbled, and secretly delighted that this magic communication was real, folded the map, turned around and walked, head bowed, back toward the river.

After all I had learned and experienced, I still arrogantly doubted my own direct experience when it came! What a fool! I didn't doubt for a moment the reality of the ubiquitous advertising billboards, with their questionable messages, towering above West End Avenue. Yet part of me was still reluctant or afraid to believe in that information-laden reality perceived through my subtle senses. Conversely, I did trust that reality in Peru. So why not here in New York City? Why should the Big Apple not have as much mystical power and as many nature spirits as an Inka ruin in Machu Pikchu?

As I walked, I contemplated. This wasn't the first time I had encountered the power of a New York City Nature Spirit! But the collective mentality of New Yorkers did not accept the reality of Nature Spirits, whereas the Peruvian collective mind DID! Perhaps that was why it was so much easier to feel 'the spirits' in Peru, where you had the collective energy field backing you up. I thought back to my experience with the Santa Tierra of the Avenue of the Americas, nearly a year before. After recalling that incident, plus my experience with Rivers, and the example of Don Manuel in Manaus, I knew what I had to do. I came to a beautiful grove of shady trees and gathered some greenish-golden leaves for the k'intu offering I would make to the River. It was hard to imagine a river so close by, hidden by a screen of trees and busy, traffic-engorged city streets.

A few minutes later I arrived. There she was—the magnificent Hudson River—streaming and sparkling brilliantly in the sun! I spoke my prayers into the leaves, holding them out in front of me, and with great reverence and respect, offered her my living energy. I blew three times on the leaves, giving the power of my body, the power of my heart, and the power of my mind, into her service. At a certain point, I threw the leaves out over the little embankment, where they were immediately caught up into the current and swept away.

"There ... that's better," came the River's rich melodic-voiced reply. I too felt a kind of relief sweep over me, as my energy bubble slowly, naturally, began to expand. "Come closer my daughter, and let me show you something," she commanded. I was already as physically close as I could get without going over the embankment. I realized she meant something else. I consciously expanded my bubble further, visualizing it reaching out to merge with hers, as Don Manuel had shown me, by example, how to do at the Rio Negro in Brazil.

My first thought was of the tragic pollution that poured daily into this beautiful river. When I thought this, I saw only the garbage floating on the surface. Then immediately a cool, refreshing liquid sensation filled my senses, and the power and force of that flowing water, the living energy of the river herself, enveloped me, carrying my consciousness away. Suddenly I saw that pollution and all human influence was only a shallow skin over the immense life force of the river, and a tiny spot upon the Infinite Power that was Nature herself. At once, as from a bird's eye view, I saw and felt the River as a singular being stretched upon the continent. I saw her beginning and her end as I merged with her, and flowed together with her toward the great ocean, *Mama Qocha*. A tiny silverish scab lay upon the land beside a fraction of the immensity of her length. That tiny little scab...was New York City!

I continued to flow with the River, and as we merged into the great living awareness of Mother Ocean, our power increased to such a degree that the dry land of the earth took up only a small portion of our awareness. Human beings and their affairs occupied only a relatively tiny aspect of our vast consciousness. I exulted in the immense life force of the planetary awareness before ever so slowly, gently returning to my own minnow-small body, and my ego-self.

Suddenly joggers, skateboarders, dogs, babies, traffic, and two rollerbladers whizzing past me in colorful sports attire jostled my consciousness more fully back into my body. There I sat on a riverside cement park bench, trying to catch my breath, still intoxicated by the vision the Hudson River had just granted me. I laughed, recalling my initial distress at missing the museum.

Returned to my miniscule individual human perspective, I realized I had been given a tremendous gift. I had seen New York City from the perspective of the Hudson River. And for one brief moment, I had glimpsed humanity from the perspective of *Pachamama*! Whew!

"And that's not all my daughter," *Mamita* Hudson River spoke to me again, and I paid close attention. "We spirits of the Earth can access not only the larger cosmic perspectives, but we are also privy to certain human level problems. Let me tell you that you won't be meeting the Vice

President of your publishing house today, as you had hoped. But when you meet with your editor you must tell her...."

Remarkably, a clear and incredibly astute series of instructions followed on how to handle a completely human interaction, in order to achieve the best possible outcome for the book. And in fact, I followed these instructions to the letter, and the situation turned out exactly as predicted by the river spirit. I shouldn't have been surprised, considering that a waterfall spirit near my home in California had showered me with creative ideas and broken my writer's block a year before. I profusely thanked the Hudson River deity and, armed with peerless knowledge for my meeting, went to hail a cab. This had certainly been far more educational than any museum visit!

In the cab I marveled at how kind, generous, and helpful the spirit of the River had been to me, almost like a mentor or dear friend. It occurred to me that my book does inform people about nature beings. Perhaps she was only helping her kind to get some "good press" with humans? No. It was much more than that. I had sensed a warm affection flowing from the River, some kind of special and highly personal connection between she and I.

Then it hit me! Lake Waskar is the place near Cuzco where we go to connect to the living energy of *Waskar* Inka—last ruler of the Inka Empire—on the first day of the *Hatun Karpay* Initiation. We go there because the Lake is his *paqarina*—the nurturing Nature Spirit of his birthplace. I was conceived in my parents New York apartment just blocks from the Hudson River, and was born in Mount Sinai Hospital on Central Park, also mere blocks from the Hudson. The pieces of the puzzle clicked into place as, all at once, I realized that the Hudson River must indeed be **my** *paqarina*, the most special and intimate Nature Spirit of my birthplace. I knew that in the Andes, one's *paqarina*, so integral to a person's identity, was usually incorporated in some creative way into one's name at birth. As such, according to Andean tradition, my name should be Elizabeth Hudson River Jenkins.

With the help of the Hudson River Ñust'a, and after my meeting with my editor, we were now certain my book wasn't being cancelled.

Although we didn't know exactly when it would be published, we were assured it would be out within the coming year.

This trip to New York was further proof that my mystical experiences with Great Nature and Nature Spirits had clearly extended beyond the borders of Peru. Even here in New York city, one of the worlds most materialistic centers, equal but opposite to Peru's spiritual center of Machu Pikchu, I could still converse with Nature Spirits. I guess it goes to show; you just can't keep a good nature spirit down! But perhaps this also spoke to the deepening of my fourth-level initiation and our *karpay* with Don Manuel. In the Andes it was easy to remain for days in mystical trancelike states. But here in the USA, I felt that I had to constantly move back and forth between ordinary consciousness and mystical perception. Now the two states of mind began to flow more naturally together within me, no matter that the collective energy field of the United States did not support it. The power of mystical perception was in my bubble wherever my bubble happened to be.

I found I could be doing something completely ordinary, like working on my taxes, pause to commune in energetic ecstasy with the hummingbird outside my window, and return, in a heartbeat, to my taxes again. The integration of the mystical into ordinary consciousness, ordinary life, was for me one of the great gifts of this tradition. But the physical, energetic, and emotional gifts of this practice were also becoming more apparent to me.

Last January, Jacques and I had gone on vacation to the Hawaiian Islands. It was my first trip to Hawaii, and we had chosen the lovely and natural setting of Kauai, the famed "Garden Island." The first morning of our stay, we awoke and headed straight for the water, our little hotel being located directly on a stretch of white sandy beach.

Instinctively, I picked three leaves and a gorgeous enormous pink hibiscus, fashioning it into a little *despacho*. I slipped into the water and placed my offering, filled with prayers of love and gratitude to *Mama Qocha* (Mother Ocean), onto a huge out-going wave. The *despacho* instantly disappeared. But *Mama Qocha* responded equally swiftly and gracefully. For the next wave tossed a delightfully sculpted piece of white and purple coral directly into my left hand. And I felt the words, "Thank you my daughter, you are welcome here!"

She had given me a *khuya*, a female power object. I knew it was female because it had come to my left hand, and I also knew that it was to be placed into my *mesa*. This was a very powerful *khuya* from the *Mama Qocha* herself!

Later that morning, we drove North up the coast to Hanalei and decided to hike all the way into the famous three-hundred foot waterfall of Hanakapei. We had been warned that the path was muddy and difficult due to the rains, but we were determined to get there.

After nearly three hours of hiking on a trail that appeared and disappeared more times than I could count, we were caked in mud up to our knees, and convinced that we were lost. Several times already I had felt I was so exhausted that I was ready to turn back. But the hoped-for thrill of seeing the enormous waterfall had spurred me on. Now, as I looked up at the quickly blackening sky and realized we were in for more rain—I could feel my exhaustion—I had hit my limit. Suddenly, it dawned on me that we would have to hike all the way back, at least another three hours, and probably in the rain.

"I have to stop. Jacques we have to go back. I don't have anything left. I can't make it." Just as I finished my last sentence the wind must have changed. Suddenly the great gushing sound of the waterfall could be heard distinctly. We looked at each other and charged forward in the direction of the sound. Five minutes later we stood before one of the most glorious sights we'd ever seen—an immense three-hundred foot ribbon of silver water gushing out of the rock face of the cliff, spilling aquamarine into a sculpted rock pool at our feet.

Just then the sun came out, making rainbows dance in the abundant frothy spume above the pool. Before I knew it, Jacques stripped naked, clambered over the rocks, and dove headlong into the pool. He waved to me, splashing about in the water wearing nothing but a big grin. I had no choice but to follow suit, or rather, to follow suitless. And I did.

As I climbed into the icy water, whose cold impact froze my breath in my lungs, I heard the sound of the falling water suddenly change. It was now roaring with greater force. "This is for you ... I give you more energy," came a delightful voice. I immediately recognized it as belonging to the waterfall.

"Open your bubble," I told Jacques, "receive the living energy of the waterfall. She's giving us a gift!" Jacques, now used to and actually comfortable with my strange behavior, immediately stopped splashing and concentrated. I felt a wave of power, lightness, a bubbling, living energy come pouring into me. Instinctively, we both moved closer to the falling water, enveloping ourselves within its rainbow spume.

"AHHHHHHHHH!" sighed Jacques after about five minutes of silent concentration. We dove and splashed a few more minutes until our lips had turned blue with cold. Teeth chattering, we exited the water, shook ourselves dry like young dogs, and numbly put our clothes back on. From the depths of his pockets Jacques produced a few chunks of dried, sweet papaya and we munched happily, shivering on our stone ledge beneath the glory of the magnificent waterfall.

From out of the rainforest, a young couple appeared at the far side of the pool. We were surprised to see anyone else here, as we had encountered nary a soul on the trail. They must have been close behind us. They too, stripped off their clothes and entered the water. Once again, I heard the noticeably amplified roaring of the waterfall as she delivered the blessing of her living energy to this couple.

"I offer my living energy to everyone who comes here." The waterfall being confided in me, "but few are aware enough to receive it! My blessings to you!" We made an offering of leaves and tiny pink flowers from the surrounding bushes, in *ayni* for her gift. Then we started back down the path home.

This time we easily found the right path back and cut off nearly twenty minutes from the journey. I had noticed more than once how every time I put myself in harmony with the nature of a place, everything became easier. It was as if our feet were being guided in the right direction. Though feeling near-total exhaustion upon our arrival, we were now both so energized by the waterfall that we literally **ran** most of the way back!

Wherever I traveled, I marveled at gifts bestowed on me by my knowledge and practice of the Inka path. Beside the enormous physical benefits and ongoing feelings of well-being and happiness, it had revealed to me that the universe I inhabited was magically alive, full of new and interesting friends. Meaningful encounters could occur quite naturally with non-human entities or spirits.

Such experiences didn't require the use of drugs, extreme physical conditions of pain or self-denial, or the feeling of impending madness that supposedly accompanied so many "mystical" experiences I had heard and read about. I was now more stable, balanced, and happier than I had ever been. The more I learned, practiced and shared my knowledge with others, the more calm, grounded and at ease I felt in my life. Phrased another way, the more mystical I became, the more ordinary I felt. And the more real spiritual knowledge I gained and applied, the more I was able to accomplish in the physical world. My earthly life, I saw, was so deeply satisfying precisely because it was now based on and guided by my spiritual vision.

And the spiritual world continually dropped unexpected fruits into the material realm, first as possibilities. In Kauai, the spirit of Waimea Canyon had spoken to me as the Hudson River had in New York, giving me clear, step-by-step instructions on how to go about setting up the Wiraqocha Foundation. I had envisioned it before, but never so complete nor so clear until then. I had taken that offered possibility and planted and nourished it like a seed in the world through my dedicated actions. That vision had grown, ripe, and ready to be plucked from the vine of dreams and made into a living reality. I believe this spiritual intervention allowed me to so easily accomplish the founding of the Foundation, only one month after my return from Kauai.

Six months later, upon my return from New York City, I knew the time had come to take the next significant step in the manifestation of the dream, first set in motion in a high Andean mountain village, one year before. It was time to share the beauty and gifts of my Andean family with my North American brothers and sisters. It was time to bring Don Manuel and the Q'ero to California.

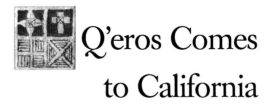 Q'eros Comes
to California

$\mathcal{J}$t was mid-July when I got back from New York
and I wasted no time. Immediately, I telephoned Jeanette. She and I had
exchanged a look of knowing that cold night in Choa Choa—the night
we first met Don Manuel—that we would one day bring Don Manuel
and other Q'ero priests to California. Jeanette was a dynamic organizer,
and once I explained the brief outline of my plan, she jumped at the
chance to be my organizational king-pin. I hired her that night.

We had exactly two months to put the whole program together
which included: obtaining all official documents (meaning passports and
US Visas for Peruvian Indians!), renting teaching space, writing and distributing all publicity for four different events in four cities, setting up a
fundraising dinner, and gathering all the participants. We had absolutely
NO idea how all this would turn out, or if we could even accomplish
these imposing tasks in the allotted time frame.

By utter magic and from out of the woodwork, people appeared with
concrete offers of help and support to make this dream program a reality. People offered suggestions and help we didn't even know we needed,
and a group of several dozen volunteers formed almost on its own. We
also received generous Donations from the Angeles Arrien Foundation,

Michael Harner's Foundation for Shamanic Studies, and my dear friend and colleague Carol Adrienne. A magnificent creation began to coalesce, all accomplished by a huge collective effort.

After a month of Jeanette and I putting in eighteen-hour days, the program was set as follows. In mid-September a team of three Q'ero priests, headed by Don Manuel, would arrive in Los Angeles. The younger priests—Don Augustin Pauqar Qapa, from the village of Q'eros Totorani, and Don Leoncio Juan Pauqar Espinoza, from Choa Choa (like Don Manuel)—each had a different specialty. Don Augustin was a *pampa misayok*, a ritual specialist in *despachos* and coca leaf readings. Don Juan Pauqar, a fourth-level mystical priest or *altomisayok*, had been initiated in the most traditional manner, chosen by Great Nature herself. He had been struck three times by lightning and survived. Thus he could speak directly with the beings of the *hanak pacha*, the superior world. Don Juan Nuñez, my teacher, thought the best combination was to have the young-est and brightest Q'ero talent together with the eldest and most venerable.

From Los Angeles, the team would head to Redlands University, also in Southern California, where they would give several lectures on campus, and perform an evening *despacho* ceremony outside under the full moon at the college fire pit. A wonderful professor from Redlands, California who had met us in Manaus arranged everything, including coverage in all the local papers. Another woman we had met in Manaus arranged a public lecture at the famous Agape Church in Los Angeles, and then offered her house in Malibu for the weekend workshop. She agreed to coordinate participants there.

Then, from Los Angeles we would fly to Phoenix, Arizona. There we would meet a special woman who had arranged a private encounter in Hopi Land between the Q'ero, and the secret clan leaders of the Hopi Elders. Before securing this invitation we had to swear an oath not to reveal the names of the Hopi leaders or publish them in any form. We were to go from a very public venue, to one of utmost secrecy. The pur-pose of the Hopi Land trip was to bring together two ancient brother cultures. The public was not invited. Everyone agreed. After a week in Hopi Land came a three-day grand finale, with a lecture, workshop and fundraising dinner on home turf, in Marin County, California.

By some strange magic, our Hopi Land contacts acquired the name and telephone number of an influential CNN intern who turned out to be very interested in our project. We sent information and several dozen slides to CNN and they agreed to cover the Marin evening lecture, barring any breaking news. After all it was, as far as anyone knew, the first time in history that the Q'ero, the descendants of the Inka, would be publicly invited to the United States to share their cultural and spiritual wisdom—certainly an event worthy of a news report on CNN!

But there was one real glitch in the works—the two younger priests had arrived at the appointed time in Cuzco, yet it seemed all was not well with Don Manuel. We didn't know exactly what had happened. Juan, after all his efforts to acquire Don Manuel's passport, had been a little reluctant to give it to him. Juan feared that other groups, who had only recently made contact with the Q'ero, would want to exploit Don Manuel. The childlike Q'ero were naïve and easily seduced. Who knew if we had done the right thing in bringing Don Manuel out of the country the first time in Manaus! We felt a painful fear that others might not feel the same protectiveness, familial care and concern toward Don Manuel and the other Q'ero that we did.

In the end Juan, being a lover of personal freedom, had to give Don Manuel his passport, and thus free will over his movements outside the country. After his Manaus debut, many people were now vying for the time and attention of the Q'ero, and especially from Don Manuel. A drama erupted even before his departure. First, official word came that he was sick and wouldn't be able to make the trip. Immediately, unofficial rumors followed that other groups who were vying for Don Manuel's exclusive attention were actually holding Don Manuel's passport, forcibly restricting his movements out of the country. It was all just a bunch of ridiculous hearsay, and there was no proof of any of it. I realized by this experience how rumors create *hoocha*. Spreading rumors, at times a great temptation, served no purpose but to create more heavy energy.

Juan, a solid fourth-level priest, refused to pay these rumors the least bit of attention. "Rumors are only rumors; they breed no good will," he said. "We shall not lend them our living energy. We'll continue our work with the two younger priests. After all, **they** are the future of the Q'ero Nation. Don Manuel may really be sick. And besides, whether or not he comes is his own decision." I respected Juan's "high road" position. Yet I felt in a bit of a quandry, having already announced in dozens of publications that Don Manuel would be appearing at all our events. All we could do at this point was to inform our participants that Don Manuel would not be in attendance, and let them decide if they still wanted to come or not! Whether I liked it or not, that was the situation. And after swallowing and digesting my disappointment, I came to accept the fact that Don Manuel would not be present.

Still, I was optimistic, enthused and proud of what Jeanette and I had accomplished in so little time. The itinerary was set, hundreds of participants had signed up for the workshops and lectures, and passports had been obtained. Now the only thing lacking was actual possession of the young priests' Visas to the U.S. It seemed we were in the clear with all green lights, which was fortunate for me, as I had a family celebration to attend in Montreal—Jacques parents' fiftieth wedding anniversary!

Badly needing a break, both Jacques and I left for the family festivities with happy hearts. That same day, Juan left with the two Q'ero priests for Lima, loaded down with a ridiculous overabundance of documentation that we hoped would ensure the easy acquisition of their U.S. Visas. I promised Juan I'd call him from Canada to see how he was getting on in Lima.

A few days later, now ensconced in Jacques's family home, I found a moment amidst a host of celebratory events to call Juan in Lima, only to receive some very discouraging news. In their first U.S. Embassy appointment they had presented all their documentation, and been flatly refused Visas. Juan seemed unperturbed. He knew from many accounts that the Peruvian U.S. Embassy almost never accepted local applications on the first round. Their next appointment was set for three days later. I wished him luck and said I'd call in three days to see how the interview had gone. In the meantime, Jacques and I decided to simply relax and enjoy the family, food, and fun on our mini-vacation.

Three days later, at the appointed time and hour, I called Juan. Once again I received bad news ... they had been turned down again. Now things were getting desperate. They were supposed to come to the States in less than a week! I called Jeannette in California and asked her to track down the U.S. immigration officer in charge of their case. I would speak to him or her personally!

I also had Jeanette gather official endorsement letters for our project from the Angeles Arrien Foundation, Michael Harner's Shamanic Studies Foundation, Redlands University, and the Agape Church in Los Angeles. I had Jeannette fax these letters to the US Embassy in Lima, to the attention of the officer in charge of their case, along with a detailed schedule of the priests' itinerary, their interviews with the press, and the numbers of people pre-registered to see them. There was no way I was going to allow this project to be stopped at this point in the works. I had to rent a cellular phone in order to call all the necessary people, or be available to Jeanette for questions or updates at a moment's notice.

Jeanette got the name and phone number of the officer in charge of our case and I called him directly. I explained the nature and scope of our project, and promised that we would be completely responsible for these two Q'ero Indians while they were in the States, and would ensure their safe return on schedule. He promised to review the case personally, and said he didn't think there would be a problem. Then I managed to reach Juan, who seemed relieved to hear the news. They had spent the past seven days in Lima on an errand they had expected to take only three.

The next day was one of miracles in reverse ... things unexpectedly went from good to horrible in no time at all. Juan and the two Q'ero, having to pay a several hundred-dollar fee for each U.S. Embassy visit, had by now shelled out a substantial sum of money. When they tried to get to their appointment the next day, their taxi got a flat tire in rush hour traffic. They arrived late to find a woman throwing a hysterical fit in the Embassy office. By the time they reached the Visa window, our "man in Lima" had gone home. Needless to say, his replacement refused their Visa for the third time!

I had to sit down to control my rage when I heard the news. This was an obvious case of racism, pure and simple. All their documents were in order—in fact they had issued Juan a Visa good for ten years. But they had taken one look at two poor Indians in the Embassy office, and automatically refused them! I had had enough. On the spot, I made a perfectly lucid decision ... I was going to sue the U.S. Embassy for Racism! I was ready at that moment to go out, hire a lawyer, and throw the book at them.

The next morning I called the immigration officer at the Lima American Embassy. Itching to go ballistic if they refused us a fourth time, I mentioned that with all their documentation in order, the only problem could be that they were Indians. The officer instantly assured me that if Juan came to see him, personally, there would be no problem. And, he added, it was a funny coincidence, that he was himself half Native American! There was only one hitch ... Juan and the two priests had to be at the Embassy in less than two hours.

I immediately got on the phone to call Juan. He was, of course, nowhere to be found. I called every Lima phone number I had. Then I made some up. No luck. In a last desperate barrage of repeat phone calls, I found him and told him the news. He grabbed the two priests and they raced across town, arriving at the embassy just as the officer was walking out the door. Each priest was given a three-week Visa, but only after Juan had sworn a solemn oath to personally escort the two Q'ero to the immigration office upon their return. Ridiculous! But it clinched the deal.

With our vacation almost over, and most of mine spent either on the phone or pacing up and down with phone in hand, I was finally able to relax. Poor Jacques showed remarkable tolerance and understanding of the urgency of the situation. I had dreamed of bringing Juan and the Inka knowledge to the USA for nearly a decade. Upon first arriving in Cuzco, I had had a vision of a white rainbow bridge stretching from Cuzco to California, and known I was to be part of a migration of spiritual information from ancient Peru into our modern Western culture even then. It was central to my destiny. Now it was finally happening!

I flew home a few days before Jacques to help Jeanette with last minute details. I timed my arrival in Los Angeles to coincide with that of Juan and the Inka priests from Lima, making sure I would be waiting to meet them when they came through customs. All came off without a hitch. It was easy to spot two Inka priests descending the Aero Peru jet-liner, despite their Western clothing. They still wore their beaded *chullo's*, covered by Peruvian leather hats with the traditional Q'ero beaded hat-bands. I raced up to them and Juan and gave them all lung-crushing bear hugs, beside myself with delight.

I could sense at a glance that these two young priests were going to be lots of fun, and that due to their youth and energy, would have an easier time adapting to this strange new world than their octogenarian Master, Don Manuel. I almost felt a flash of relief that Don Manuel would not have to contend with Hollywood!

Don Juan Pauqar, Don Augustin and Elizabeth

Juan Pauqar Espinoza, the elder of the two priests, was about forty years-old, with a medium-sized square build, jet-black hair, sparkling black eyes and a rather serious fatherly expression that could change at a moment's notice into a brilliant child-like smile. Don Augustin, on the other hand, was all rascality. A mere thirty-four years old, his handsome face often wore an impish grin, and the devil-may-care gleam in his eyes told me at once that we were in for appealing trouble with this one. He was constantly cracking jokes in Quechua that made Don Juan Pauqar's paternal composure dissolve completely into fits of laughter. Though I understood almost none of his wise cracks, they seemed to have mostly sexual or at least naughty overtones. Both of them spoke a fair bit of Spanish.

Our Los Angeles connection and hostess met us outside and swept us immediately off to Safeway to purchase lunch for a picnic on the beach. I captured these two young priests on videotape, taking in their first hungry glances of the Los Angeles landscape, picnicking on the beach, and performing a sincerely devotional *despacho* ceremony to the *Mama Qocha*, the mother ocean. The *despacho* ceremony both thanked her for their safe journey here, and asked her blessing for the successful completion of their USA teaching tour.

Juan told me later how, for most of the flight, both priests had stared in trepidation out the window of the plane, astonished by the never-ending water-body of the *Mama Qocha* stretching below them from horizon to horizon. They had asked Juan repeatedly if he was sure they were not going to fall in. Aside from the short one-hour flight from Cuzco to Lima, this had been their first real plane ride! And thus their offering of thanks to the *Mama Qocha* made worlds of sense.

◆ ◆ ◆

One of many memorable incident occurred on our preliminary tour of the Redlands University campus in Redlands, California. Arriving at the brand new library, the two priests stopped and stared, dumbfounded by an enormous globe about six feet in diameter adorning the entrance, an exquisite icon of *Pachamama*. Don Augustin circled the orb as if it were a sacred shrine, muttering his prayers in awe. We showed them Peru, Cuzco, and where Q'eros must have been, on the great continent of South America. They stared, aghast. Finally, Don Augustin said in Spanish, "*Con razon! Con razon, la Mama Qocha es tan poderosa. Mira su tamano!*"

"Of course, of course…now I understand why the Mother Ocean is so powerful. Look how big she is!" Being a fully trained Andean priest, his knowledge of the world came through his direct perception of its living energies. He had personally experienced the energetic force of the *Mama Qocha* and knew how powerful she *felt*. Now, for the first time, he was seeing a visual representation of her size and power.

It amazed me to think that he first knew the great Ocean as an enormous and conscious being of living energy, and only later learned the abstract factual data about her size. For us it was knowledge in reverse. In the West, such "facts" formed almost our sole conception of *Mama Qocha*, diminishing both our relationship to her, and our awareness of her mysterious, even cosmic nature. It was delightful to see the world through the eyes and perceptual fields of these two young mystical priests.

That evening at the University lecture hall, Juan Pauqar told the powerful story of his initiation into the Andean Priesthood. Before almost four hundred people, Juan Pauqar stood in front of the microphone after being introduced by Juan Nuñez. His initial nervousness had been overcome by a ritual of mutual empowerment performed by Juan Pauqar, Juan Nuñez, and Augustin. Prior to going on stage they had together performed *saminchaska*, filling each other's bubbles with *sami* by placing their *mesa* on each other's head and invoking the refined living energy of the superior world to enter their bubbles.

Now his determination to serve in his priestly job, made him plant his feet firmly on the stage, remove his hat (a ritual act amongst the Q'ero, signifying the following words as sacred) and speak, albeit gingerly at first, into the strange contraption called a 'microphone.'

"I want to tell you that I am an *altomisayoc* (a high priest) because I was chosen by lightning." Once the "oohs" and "ahhs" from the crowd assured Juan Pauqar of the audience's enthusiasm, he continued with a little more confidence. "After the lightning struck me I was sick for almost one month. I went to look for other Andean Priests who could help me—who could read the coca leaves and tell me why the lightning chose me, what I must do about it, and how I can be cured of my sickness. I finally found Don Andres Espinoza (a very famous and powerful Q'ero Priest) and he read the coca leaves for me. He said, 'You have been chosen to serve the *Apus*, the spirits of the Mountains. And if you follow the call, and enter into service to the Mountain Spirits, you will be healed.'

"Don Andres then told me we must do an initiation ceremony called a *karpay*, in the same place where I was struck by lightning. Because that place, for me, was the equivalent of the sacred sanctuary of Qollorit'i. Then, he told me, I would have to go to the Qollorit'i sanctuary to perform another ritual. So I went with Don Andres and performed the first of these two rituals." Juan paused here, briefly, looking somewhat embarrassed, and when Juan Nuñez and I nodded our encouragement to him, he continued again with an almost childlike, resolute thrusting forward of his chin.

"Now, I must tell you that my father had abandoned me, and my mother had a physical defect so that she could only walk with one leg. Understand that in my community I was a very poor young man. I couldn't satisfy the requirements that Don Andres asked of me for the second ritual, which was payment of two cows, a sheep, and a llama. Since I couldn't afford to pay this Master, I couldn't complete the last ritual with him. And because I couldn't complete the last ritual, I continued to be sick. One side of my face was terribly swollen, and the other side was contracted so that I couldn't eat and had to be fed with a small spoon.

"So with another, less expensive priest, a *pampa misayoc* named Martin Girillio, I went to Qollorit'i to complete the second ritual. This Martin Girillio, God bless him, took me up into the sanctuary of Qollorit'i and gave me the ritual bath of initiation in the glacial lakes. Then he made the initiation offering at the sacred stone of the *Mamacha Carmen* (a sacred female place in the sanctuary). After completing the *despacho* offering to the *Mamacha Carmen*, the Priest left me inside the door of the sanctuary Chapel, alone with my *despacho*, to discover my own destiny and to discover the will of the *Apus*, and the will of God. In the middle of the night, which I spent awake near the door, I heard a terrible noise inside the chapel, as if the roof were caving in. The priest, sleeping lower down the mountain, heard the noise as well. He thought something grave had happened to me, and even feared that I might have died.

The next morning when Martin Girillio saw that I was not dead, he read the coca leaves and found in them confirmation that I must follow the path of the *Altomisayoc* (high priest). The thunder within the chapel had been a sign. He said I must not distinguish between any of my brothers, but must serve everyone equally. I now serve any of my brothers who come to me, so that we may all have and share a good life. And I offer all that I have to anyone who wants to learn from me, and who desires to live a better life."

Don Juan Pauqar completed his story, and the audience, charmed by his ingenuous sincerity and sweetness, juxtaposed against the pain and power of his initiation story, responded with thunderous applause. According to Andean tradition, he was a mystical priest because he had been chosen by the lightning itself, a conscious supernatural being with a living spirit—as opposed to a "thing" or a mere scientifically explainable phenomenon of nature.

Now, Don Augustin's turn came to tell his story. For Juan Nuñez del Prado, Don Augustin was "the most gifted and powerful Ritual Priest, or *pampa misayoc*, in Q'eros."

Don Augustin, a natural clown, began his story humorously by seemingly accidentally banging his forehead against the microphone as he bowed his "good evening ladies and gentlemen" to the crowd. Speaking more rapidly than Don Juan, and with abundant hand gestures, his tone quickly changed from funny to serious as he told his story.

"I came to the path of a priest not for fun, nor even by my own choice. I came because my wife, whom I loved very much, died. In my grief I went to a high priest, an *altomisayoc* named Don Andres Espinoza, asking him to read in the coca leaves the meaning of her death, and tell me what I needed to do. So he read the coca leaves, and told me it was a sign of my spiritual calling.

"My grandfather was called to be an Andean Priest in his youth, but he had refused the path. My father too, was called to be an Andean priest, but he also refused the path. He died, I think, because of this. I had many dreams as a young boy, dreams that the village priests told my mother were calling me to the path. But I was poor and never answered the call. Then, with the death of my wife, I knew I had to answer this calling."

At this point a woman in the audience wanted us to tell Don Augustin that she was very sorry about the death of his wife, and to ask him when it happened.

"That was five years ago," he said. "But don't worry I have another wife now." Everyone laughed, and Don Augustin continued his story.

"I found another Andean Master who told me that I had three stars (spiritual guides). One of these guides was the bull. When this master performed my *karpay* ceremony, he told me the bull came to him and said that I could become a very powerful *altomisayoc*, but I would only have the power for a few years and then I would lose it. This master said that if I refused the bull, I could become a *pampa misayoc* and have this power for all my life. So, I thought about this for a long time. I chose to refuse the bull and become a *pampa misayoc* instead. It seemed less dangerous. And I thought it was better to have the power to help people for my whole life, instead of just a few years."

Don Augustin must have been in his mid-to late-twenties when this initiation occurred. This seemed like great wisdom, especially for a poor young man, to refuse abundant power—which always meant more money for an Andean priest—for a life of longer, yet lesser power. I wondered if any our twenty-eight year olds, faced with such a choice, would have shown the same wisdom.

I was struck by the initiation stories of these two priests, and how they had found the cultural support to go through their ordeals. It made me realize how so many of us in the West lacked initiation rituals of any sort. In fact we were spiritually isolated, cut off from those sources that might help us to endure and digest our own unorthodox, or visionary experiences, so that we might use them to guide our lives. Was this not after all their purpose? Being a North American psychotherapist, I knew how our culture labeled and stigmatized people who had visions and heard voices from the "Great Beyond," treating them as crazy and their visions as pathological symptoms, rather than acknowledging their untapped wisdom and spiritual potency.

I could not help feeling that we had it backwards. In Q'eros it was the priests, healers, or "doctors" who had visions and heard voices from the great beyond. It seemed their visions gave them the power to heal. Further, in many cases the onset of physical illness was the initiatory call, marking one as a healer or priest—this made them seek their own spiritual vision to guide their lives and to serve the community. For Q'ero priests, to be cut off from the world of visions would actually be the real pathology, and would eventually rebound on one's own physical health.

There was definitely a common theme running through the initiation stories I had heard (including Don Manuel's) ... that the call to the spiritual path often came through death, illness, or spiritual affliction, and that accepting that call led to life, health and wholeness. This theme, knowledge from an ancient cultural tradition, held important clues about the mysterious, intricate and vital connection between our spirits and our physical bodies. And it raised other equally important considerations.

Western medical science was only beginning to consider the crucial role of the mind in physical health (let alone the body's relationship to "spirit" which Western science could not yet even begin to acknowledge). And what of the incredibly sophisticated and delicate interrelationship between our bodies and Nature? Our relationship to Nature, which truly bordered on the mystical, was completely unaccounted for in our medicine. In Andean medicine, maintaining harmony with the natural world was part and parcel of human emotional, mental, spiritual *and* physical health.

I recalled one experience I had had watching an Andean healer treat a man with one leg swollen to double its size. "Have you offended any water spirits?" Was the first question the priest asked his patient. Sobbing, the man admitted to having pissed in a sacred stream during a ceremony. The priest, supplying the man with herbs to reduce swelling, told him the critical part of his cure would be to make amends with the spirit of the stream, and that the element of water was out of balance in his body due to his disrespect. His act had created a disharmony between himself and the natural world.

Again and again my exposure to this tradition had revealed to me as obvious the fact that on levels often too subtle to notice, human beings, plants, animals, nature and mother earth all constantly communicated, affected, and exchanged vital energy with one another. And that should these incalculable inter-species exchanges cease, life itself as we know it would also cease. Together, we formed an immense living system in which each part performed some necessary service essential to the survival of the whole. The more I learned, the more I glimpsed an exciting and intimidating vastness, a limitless order of inconceivable complexity, operating in perfect harmony, which would ever elude my miniscule grasping mind. Perhaps only the heart could fully understand.

Don Augustin completed his recital to another thunderous applause from the audience. The *despacho* ceremony that followed, performed outside beneath a full moon by the two Q'ero priests, was a beautiful and poetic event. The students were delighted to participate in a ceremony in which their local mountain spirits were invoked and honored.

The fire made for the burning of this *despacho* glowed brightly in the

Fireside Priests

night, and the offering was fully consumed by the flames, signifying the *Apus* accepted and appreciated this collective *despacho*, and returned their blessing upon everyone present. This simple ceremony and the enthusiastic delight of the crowd made me feel rich and warm inside. Not only was our purpose in bringing the Q'ero here to the States indeed being fulfilled, but also it gave me hope that perhaps it *was* possible to bring a modicum of spiritual connection back to the people of the United States. Perhaps the collective soul of our materially obsessed society wasn't actually dead yet. Perhaps if we *could* still respond to the magic of spiritual communion with Nature we could be saved!

CHAPTER FOURTEEN

Inka Meets Hopi

*B*ack in Los Angeles three days later, after the Q'eros' highly successful lecture before nearly four-hundred people at the Agape Center, and a well-received weekend workshop in Malibu, our now thoroughly bonded team boarded a plane for the next stop on our itinerary: Phoenix, Arizona.

From the Phoenix airport, we rented a van and drove to the home of our hostess in Flagstaff, the woman responsible for our appointment with the Hopi elders. Barbara was a very special person. A tall, thin ethnobotanist with long brown hair nearly reaching her buttocks, she had been collecting herbs and flowers from the Hopi lands for over thirty years.

Through the lens of modern ethnobotany, Barbara was both re-discovering and re-confirming the spiritual plant wisdom of the Hopi. She was also using these ancient remedies to treat the health problems of the modern Hopi people. And because of her intelligence, sensitivity, and proven dedication to their well-being, they had taken her, a white woman, into their confidence, and even adopted her as a kind of daughter. She seemed to know everyone and everything that went on in Hopi Land.

That night at her home, she made us a wonderful and nutritious dinner, and told us stories about her life and her work with the Hopi. Early

Making Despachos

the next day we went to make a *despacho* offering at the sacred Kachina Mountain called, curiously enough, the San Francisco Peaks. Here we asked that all go well in our meeting with the Hopi Elders.

As the priests were finishing this *despacho*, on inspiration, I asked Don Augustin to do a coca leaf divination about our meeting with the Hopi. I knew almost nothing about the Hopi people, but I had heard they were very reserved and quite suspicious of strangers and outsiders ... not surprising, given that their history for well over a century had been one of invasion, betrayal, and abuse. The coca leaves didn't tell much at first, but then they revealed that the meeting would go well, Don Augustin informed us. Very well.

We took off in our van for the Hopi Reservation, driving through the beautiful, barren wilderness of the open desert, with its scattered red rocks and high, flat-topped mesa that jutted out like ancient volcanoes under a vast canopy of blue sky. It felt as if it hadn't rained here in centuries. I didn't know that one of the major ceremonies performed by the Hopi was the rain dance.

Throughout the two-hour ride, Don Juan Pauqar kept playing the same haunting melody on his small Andean reed flute, over and over, until it began to acquire an incantatory power. At one point it sent tingles up my spine and I turned to look at him, certain that he was not just playing a song, but was rather ritually invoking something. I asked Juan to translate my question to Juan Pauqar. But when asked, Juan Pauqar only smiled and kept playing his eerie music.

Flute playing

At last, we arrived and installed ourselves in our Hopi Land Hotel, hoping to get a good night's rest before the next day's proceedings. We had a morning lecture scheduled at one of the reservation schools, and in the afternoon, our much anticipated meeting. I got out my camera and started to take a picture, when the Hotel clerks officially informed me that photographs were "not permitted in Hopi." I was duly warned, in fact, that if I took out my camera at one of the traditional sites, I ran the risk of having it forcibly taken from me, and possibly destroyed. After a quick dinner at the Hotel Café, we all hit the sack, dead tired.

The next morning we were escorted to the Hopi school where the teachers had assembled all the children in the gym. First came a talk by

Juan, after which the priests described their lives in their home villages. Then the kids asked them questions, and finally Juan Pauqar played an ancient Q'ero tune on his little flute. The children were enchanted and came up to touch Juan Pauqar, his Q'ero poncho, and his magic Andean flute.

After lunch it was time for our meeting with the Hopi Elders. We followed Barbara by a circuitous route to a little house at an undisclosed address. We might as well have been blindfolded–I couldn't find the place again if my life depended on it. We waited outside while she went in and made our presence known. After about fifteen minutes we were invited in.

As soon as we walked in the door, we were met with a cold blast of suspicion. The man of the house, an older white-haired man of medium stature with a large barrel chest, shook hands with us without looking at us directly or introducing himself, perhaps another Native North American custom. We entered into the living room of a small, tidy, one-story house, where we were invited to sit down. There was only the older gentleman, another man who we figured was his brother from their brief discussion of the old Ford parked out front, and someone whom we could not see but only heard, clanking around in the kitchen. We sat on a couch in the corner of the room, in a silence so thick you couldn't have cut it with a jungle machete. We waited in the frozen silence, while one by one, the others arrived from their various locations.

I went to use the bathroom down the hall and passed a washer and dryer in a corridor leading into a spacious bedroom. I couldn't help thinking how much better off the Hopi were than their Peruvian counterparts, at least materially speaking.

Finally, eight Hopi Elders had arrived and were assembled around a large conference-like table in middle of the room. The still nameless white-haired man of the house motioned for us to come and sit with them. After another incredibly long silence he spoke.

"We want to know why you are here. What do you want from us?" he asked, in an unfriendly manner. It sounded like a challenge. My heart sank, and the cat grabbed firm hold of my tongue. I felt it was not my place to speak. Juan, the natural spokesman of the group, rose to the occasion.

"We wanted only to bring your South American brothers here to greet you. We thought you might share some things in common. We have a prophecy about this time, about the joining of the Eagle and the Condor, among many other things. These Q'ero priests wanted to bring you their greeting and share with you their prophecy." The men at the table appeared unmoved, only eyeing us in silence with long, cold, hard stares.

Finally, they began to ask a series of very precise and serious questions as to the nature of the Inka prophecies. Juan, perhaps out of nervousness or hoping to expedite the conversation, answered most of the questions. Occasionally, he consulted the priests, and translated their answers to the Hopi who only grunted in reply and, after a while, asked another question, never offering anything in return.

Almost two hours passed in this way. It seemed our interview was going very badly. My body had grown stiff with tension and I felt sorry for my Q'ero friends whose natures, like their culture, were totally open and friendly. These two happy and playful characters responded to human warmth and laughter, not this kind of cold interrogation. I wondered how on earth Don Augustin's coca leaves could have said our meeting would go well.

Things were looking really black when suddenly, Don Juan Pauqar stood up and began to recite the story of his initiation by lightning in Quechua. Juan and I exchanged looks of concern. We had told Don Juan that, at various times on the trip, he would be asked to tell his initiation story. But we hadn't expected him to do so now. It seemed, under the circumstances, a misguided and certainly futile gesture. Not knowing what else to do, Juan simply translated exactly what Don Juan Pauqar was saying. His unexpected act had certainly captured everyone's attention, and he held our attention throughout the entire story, which he told with a moving simplicity and sweetness. It took him fifteen minutes to tell, while I worried the whole time about how these Hopi Elders would react. Finally Juan Pauqar finished and sat down again, a look of satisfaction on his face.

Suddenly, the nameless white-haired man sighed deeply and said, "Well, what do you know. The exact same thing happened to me!" He then stood up, arms outstretched toward Juan Pauqar and, to everyone's amazement, proclaimed "Brother!" Juan didn't miss a beat. No one had to translate a thing for him to understand what was going on. He went right up to the man (who, it turned out, was the leader of the Hopi Elders) and hugged him in a powerful embrace. Huge smiles lit the faces of all the Hopi sitting around the table, and the atmosphere of the room transformed at once from chilly aloofness into a warm, cozy, family ambience.

Out of nowhere, as if she had been waiting in the wings for her cue, the white-haired Elder's wife appeared, bearing large steaming trays of traditional Hopi foods. She placed them before us and we all began eating, talking, and laughing together as if we were old friends and nothing had ever been amiss!

The leader now held up his hand for everyone to be silent and asked Juan Pauqar a few more specific questions about how he had been cured after being struck by lightning. Juan told how he had gone to a sacred site to perform rituals, and was confined alone in a room for several weeks without eating salt or garlic. "Yup," the white-haired Elder confirmed, "that's exactly what the elders did to me too." Everyone laughed, and at that moment a huge clap of thunder sounded, and it began to rain. We didn't realize at the time what an unusual and auspicious event was rain in Hopi Land. It seemed nature too, was giving both confirmation and her stamp of approval to our meeting. I never knew for sure, but I had a strong suspicion that Juan Pauqar's flute had had something to do with the coming of that rain! Or who knows, perhaps it was the meeting and embrace of two lightning initiates.

The afternoon meeting lasted until long after nightfall. The Hopi elders, now eager to give of themselves, shared with us many stories, and told us of an ancient belief in their culture that their earliest ancestors had migrated across the continent from the South. After our encounter, they were more convinced than ever of its truth. By the end of the night I saw that Don Augustin's coca leaves had not lied. Indeed, our meeting with the Hopi Elders had been so successful that they invited us back the next day to eat with them again.

Knowing we had to drive to Phoenix to catch our plane to Northern California the next day, we scheduled our gathering for the early afternoon. The group picked up on the same note of friendship as the previous evening, and at the meeting's end, gifts were exchanged. The Hopi Elders presented the Q'ero priests with beautifully woven Hopi Corn Baskets. In exchange, the Q'ero gave the Hopi powerful Andean *khuyas*, ritual stones carved into small squares and inscribed with potent Inka symbols. The carved images included a farm—symbol of the earthly female generative power, the star—symbol of the divine guidance and masculine power, and the *tawantin*—the power of four—the symbol of stability upon which the *Tawantinsuyu*, or Inka Empire, was based, to name just a few.

The most humorous moment came when the Hopi actually got out THEIR cameras and asked to take pictures of US. They first took pictures of all of us, and then asked Juan and I to take pictures of them with their Inka brothers. We did so, of course, and then asked if we could get our cameras and take pictures with them. Although we were breaking all Hopi Land rules, they couldn't refuse. A hilarious photographic session ensued, that filled us all with a happy glow of comraderie. And on that sweet note, we parted company.

We made it to the Phoenix airport on time, and by late afternoon were on a plane bound for San Francisco. I felt proud and excited to be bringing these two delightful Q'ero priests and my teacher Juan, for the first time, to my home in Northern California. On the flight Juan shared with me some of his impressions of the USA.

"You know, Elizabeth, for a long time I thought of the United States as nothing more than a big business-minded country with only money money money and work work work on it's mind. Now, having come here, I see this is not totally true."

"No Juan? What do you think of us now?" I asked, very curious about his impressions of my country.

"I believe you have a very refined cultural code with only one problem." I waited as Juan paused for effect. "It is not grounded!" he pronounced. Although it seemed a curious way to express himself, I knew exactly what he meant. We had many lofty beliefs and values ... our country after all was based on the truly spiritually inspired vision of our forefathers. But these lofty beliefs and values did not always manage to bear fruit in our everyday reality. Even more to Juan's point, we had created a highly sophisticated culture that was completely disconnected from, and to a large extent set in opposition to, the natural world. In that way our culture was not grounded in the most primal of life forces—Nature herself!

We had no rituals for connecting to nature. And for the most part we did not even see the need for, or value of, such a sacred relationship to the earth on which we rested, and out of which we sprang. Perhaps not so curiously we were a people with little or no connection to "place" to our land. We had few, if any, potent cultural rituals by which to acknowledge and celebrate important life transitions. What rituals we had, often suffered from impoverished spiritual views of life, and were often marred by intrusive marketing hype and an absurd and predominant cultural denial of death. I wondered how we could change all that.

On our drive from the airport to my house, we passed the beautiful sight of Mount Tamalpais, Marin County's mountain sacred to the Bay Area Native Americans, and my local *Apu*! The priests immediately wanted to know the Mountain's name, and I told them.

"Why are they so interested in Mount Tamalpais, Juan?" I asked, curious as usual about the perceptions behind the questions of these Q'ero priests. We had passed many mountains on our trip so far and none had inspired such interest.

"They say they are seeing so many plants and animals and people here—so much life!" Juan translated. "They say they feel so much life force that this must be a very powerful *Apu*!"

I was delighted by their response. I knew that Marin County would be most receptive to the wisdom and blessing energy these two priests had come to give. And in fact, the largest response to the Q'ero's tour did occur here at home. That evening's lecture at the Marin Unity Church would be standing room only.

I was disappointed to hear from Jeanette upon our arrival, that CNN had cancelled our interview due to "late breaking news." No doubt it was bad news, I thought, that would send a pall of gloom over the airwaves, rather than the blessings that might have gone out from these representative of one of the oldest surviving spiritual traditions on the planet. Still, I knew that TV or no TV, these Priests would touch peoples lives here as much with their spiritual presence as with any words they might speak. The child-like wonder and joyous innocence they embodied and seemed to call forth in those they met were a potent reminder of what a gift it was to be alive here on this beautiful earth!

◆ ◆ ◆

That night after the introductions, Don Juan Pauqar had something very surprising to tell us. He stood on the stage before a crowd of several hundred people, looking stunning in his native garb; by now he appeared totally at home in front of the microphone. In a voice at once authoritative and simple, Juan revealed his own surprise as he spoke, eyes wide with wonder.

"Never, when I was living in Q'eros, did I dream of the possibility of coming here to your country! But strangely, now that I am here, I realize that I recognize this place from a dream. Three years ago I had a dream of a Mountain like this, with water at her feet. And I came to a large room like this, with many people…you people…and taught the knowledge God has given me. So tonight, I know that I am in the right place, doing the right thing, following my path as God has laid it out for me. And for this I am grateful!" He was almost in tears—he had spoken so sincerely from his heart. We were all deeply moved and surprised by this revelation.

Juan and I exchanged looks of wonder, "I will never cease to be amazed by the magic of this path," he murmured. I could only nod my reply.

The initiation stories of Juan Pauqar and Don Augustin were followed by the creation of a humongous collective *despacho*, during which everyone of the nearly three-hundred person audience came up before the priests both to be blessed by their *despacho* and to blow three times on the sacred offering, adding their living energy to this gift that honored our local mountain spirits. A representative of the Miwok, the original coastal people of the Bay Area, met the Q'ero and was invited on stage to help officiate. As with most ceremonial events, this took hours, but by the end of the evening more than two hundred people had signed up for the weekend workshop!

Yet this auspicious first night in Marin was offset by another drama that was now building behind the scenes. I had arrived at my home that afternoon with Juan and the Q'ero priests. Although Jacques and I lived in a small apartment, I had hoped and assumed that they would stay with us. Besides, Jacques was going to be out of town that weekend for yet another psychology conference. Unfortunately, I had been so absorbed in preparations for the tour that I hadn't thought to discuss the matter with Jacques, nor had he thought to ask. Of such communication breakdowns are train wrecks made.

Jacques came home from work that evening and saw three unfamiliar faces in his living room. He didn't need to say anything ... his expression told all. I knew there would have to be a change of plan. I guessed that he had begun to feel a little intruded upon with all the chaotic preparations, including Jeanette working in our living room over the past month. It was clear that he needed his privacy back.

So I called Kirby Ann, one of my Board of Directors. An absolutely golden-hearted Native American woman, Kirby was a social worker who had been my clinical supervisor during my psychotherapy internship. She had a large house not too far from us; her children were grown-up, and I knew she had room. A while ago she had offered her house to Juan and the priests during their visit. I now 'called in' on her offer and she happily agreed. I told Jacques that our guests would be staying with Kirby. She arrived at my door fifteen minutes later, delighted, and whisked them away. Later she told me having Juan and the Q'ero priests in her house felt wonderful, like being back on the reservation and hanging out with her numerous uncles!

The next morning Kirby brought them all back early and went off to work while I made breakfast. Jacques was leaving later that morning and this would be the only time for Juan and he to get acquainted. While I was cooking, I left the two men alone in the living room, and the priests went out in the backyard to inspect our local *Pachamama*. I was delighted that Juan and Jacques could finally talk, and they seemed to be hitting it off … I heard them talking, laughing, and carrying on. Then I suddenly heard Jacques's concerned voice. "Darling, what are these?"

I poked my head around the corner into the living room and saw Jacques clutching his chest, a stricken look on his face. In his left hand he held a bottle of aspirin, in his right hand a little packet of aluminum foil, and on the table in front of him sat a half-drunk glass of orange juice.

"What's wrong dear?" I was confused and worried by his panicked look.

"These," he waved the little packet of aluminum foil, "are the aspirin I took with me to Montreal. And this," he held up the aspirin bottle, "is the original bottle."

"So?" I asked, still puzzled.

"I'VE BEEN TAKING THESE!" he nearly shouted in rage, shaking the aspirin bottle. "But these are NOT aspirin!" He showed me the pills from the bottle, which were clearly different than those in the aluminum foil. "So WHAT have I been taking?" I was shocked at this uncharacteristic outburst. Jacques was typically calm and easy-going, but he suddenly seemed like a hysterical child. Juan glanced at me with a look of concern.

"Honey, I'm sure it's nothing." I tried to calm him down. "Remember when my Mom was here? She was probably cleaning up and…"

"Call her NOW and find out WHAT I have been taking!" he shrieked. His face was white with anger and something more … terror. I immediately called my mother. When she didn't answer, I left a worried message, vaguely feeling as if I had done something terrible. Meanwhile, Jacques paced the floor nearly wringing his hands. Maybe he was nervous about his presentation at the conference, I speculated. But his reaction was so extreme. I couldn't figure it out.

A few minutes later, the phone rang. Thank God! It was Mom calling back. She'd been in the shower. "Oh yes honey, you had a few vitamin C lying around in a huge bottle and I just put what was left it in that little white aspirin bottle. I hope it's not a problem."

"Vitamin C huh?" I said loudly, "No, no, Mom don't worry. I just wondered what it was. Thanks. Talk to you later." I hung up the phone and gave Jacques an unmistakable "I told you so" look. He seemed only a little embarrassed. But more, he seemed shaken … he was actually trembling slightly.

"Well," he said defensively, "tell her not to do that again. Jesus Christ!"

Juan broke the tension with a joke about how he thought vitamins were supposed to be good for you. We all laughed. Then Juan suggested the Inka priests perform an empowerment for Jacques with their *mesas*. Jacques agreed and went into the backyard to receive the two Q'ero *mesas* on top of his head. He appeared to feel better after that, and left for the airport with a smile on his face.

Still, I was puzzled by Jacques's reaction, and surprised by the intensity of his fear which seemed all out of proportion to the situation. Always an emotional person, he laughed and cried easily, and we had a strong emotional rapport and a very harmonious relationship. But I guessed he was under more stress at work and at home than he'd been willing to admit. For the past few months, our home and life had been the center of a tremendous storm of activity. For the most part, Jacques had been incredibly loving and supportive, helping out with errands here and there, and maintaining a very positive attitude toward my incredibly busy and unorthodox schedule. He had never complained about any of this. But perhaps he had been giving beyond his means.

But both the drama and my relentless schedule were far from over. After the priests' scheduled return to Peru, I had a week's respite. Then my dear friend Carol Adrienne and I were taking a group of twenty spiritual seekers to Peru to undergo the *Hatun Karpay* Initiation and work with Carol on the Nine Insights from the Celestine Prophecy.

Carol was also the keynote speaker at our first Wiraqocha Foundation Fundraising Dinner, a grand finale event scheduled for Saturday night after the workshop. Don Juan Nuñez, Don Juan Pauqar, and Don Augustin would also speak. Then there would be live Peruvian music, followed by a silent auction to raise money to cover tour expenses. As this was the first official project of the Wiraqocha Foundation on home turf, I wanted everything to be perfect. I was absolutely buried in details.

The first day of the workshop was fantastic! Saturday morning began with teachings on the principles and practices of the Inka tradition. Then we moved into action. Going outside to the little inlet of water beside the church, we offered our collective *despacho*, made on Friday evening, to the Spirit of San Francisco Bay. The *despacho* was the formal practice by which Andean priests entered into and maintained a harmony with nature, giving back love and gratitude for all of nature's gifts. Next Don Juan and Don Augustin performed the Inka equivalent of a kind of soul retrieval, or "calling in the spirit," invoking blessings and empowerment for each person in the workshop. This was similar, I discovered, to what Don Manuel had Done to cure Christina Grof's back problem in Manaus, but was a more general "spirit calling" ceremony to empower each persons unique bubble and bring back any stray or missing pieces of their energy field.

First the priests invoked the power of all their *Apus,* guides, and all the sacred beings of the *Hanak Pacha* (superior world) to which they had a direct personal relationship. Then they called on the power of all their teachers and all the *khuyas* in their mesa to help them and give them strength. Next they commanded any missing pieces of the living energy of the person who was kneeling before them—lost at any time during their lives—to come immediately into their mesa. Finally, they blew that living energy (and therefore a piece of that person's soul) back into their body where it belonged. They performed this ceremony, which lasted several hours outside under the mountain, with great heart, simple dignity, and incredible concentration.

The fundraising dinner turned into a spontaneous celebration of the unprecedented spiritual work that had been accomplished. For the first time, authentic Inka Priests had come to the USA and initiated modern Westerners into the ancient practices of their hitherto unknown mystic tradition. Carol gave an inspirational speech. Then Juan and the two priests gave a humorous account of their trials and tribulations in acquiring their Visas that had the crowd in stitches. Next Don Juan and Don Augustin expressed, with poignant emotion, their gratitude for being allowed to come and share their knowledge and tradition with the people of the West. Many were moved to tears. After that, a high-spirited Peruvian band playing traditional instruments turned the mood into one of uninhibited party revelry. Soon the crowd was on its feet, hand-clapping, foot-stomping, and dancing deep into the night. Both the wine and the spirit were flowing generously, as any good Peruvian celebration ought.

Sunday, the last workshop day, didn't start until noon. It began with Juan Nuñez's inspired lecture on the Inka prophecies, and culminated with a special ritual. Our group of nearly two hundred people formed a huge collective bubble by first focusing on and cleaning our individual bubbles, then visualizing our individual bubbles melting together into one giant collective field of living energy. Now that our individual bubbles had been empowered by the soul retrieval and connected to and harmonized with the bubbles of Mount Tamalpais and the San Francisco Bay Ñust'a, by our Friday evening *despacho* ceremony, our collective bubble power had become enormously potentiated. Next, we invoked the collaboration of these nature deities to help "eat" and spiritually "digest" the heavy energy of the whole group, thus making our collective bubble both clean and harmonized with the land on which we stood. Next, we used the power of collective energy field to pull down the highly refined living energy, or *sami,* from the *Hanak Pacha,* the superior world, and absorbed this into our group bubble. Finally, we sent this very fine energy to places all over the globe disturbed by war, disharmony, and unrest.

Using the collective intention of a large group to move energy was one of the most exciting parts of the practice for me. Its effects were powerful, at times to the point of exaltation. And the spiritual and ener-getic merging of a group seemed to me the highest purpose and expression of human community. Rather than striving for individual enlightenment or mystical experience, the Inka tradition valued collective work with en-ergy—eating *hoocha,* directing *sami,* using the potency of the community bubble—thus generating a spiritual power beyond the capacity of any one individual. Yet in the process, as many in our workshop would later attest, the individual was empowered by the practice, and moved significantly for-ward along their personal path to wholeness. Though there was no guaran-tee that moving toward real wholeness would be easy or painless.

With the workshop over, the two Inkan ambassadors of spiritual goodwill, and their spokesperson, Juan, now had two days to play tourist

[183]

before returning to their homeland. Luckily, in San Francisco, there was no shortage of exotic territory to explore. A group of us took them down to Fisherman's Wharf where they rode the cable cars, had Irish coffee's at the Buena Vista, and visited the chocolate factory at Ghirardelli Square. Then a Church member who was also a local pilot took them up in a private two-seater airplane. It was the perfect end to a magical tour, which had clearly been a high point in all our lives. Yet, little did I know that being significantly moved along my personal path to wholeness meant I would soon come face to face with one of my greatest and most difficult challenges yet.

 Disaster

and Despair

*S*everal days later I trundled Juan and the Q'ero Priests safely onto the airplane and back to Peru. Jacques and I began settling back into normal life. Then one evening he came home from work acting very odd. Normally extroverted and very talkative, he was strangely silent. I asked him several times what was wrong.

"Nothing," he told me, taciturn—a normal response for most males, but NOT Jacques.

"Sweetheart, tell me what's the matter. This isn't like you. Talk to me." I spoke as warmly and encouragingly as I could.

"I don't know, I guess I just haven't been happy lately," he said, looking like he was afraid to hurt my feelings. Jacques had never said anything like this to me in our nearly six years together. He often told me how extremely happy he was in our relationship, and said, "I love you," many times a day. We'd had our fights and disagreements like any couple, but we always made up right away. I felt we were a solid partnership, strengthened by storms weathered and adversities overcome together.

Now I took his words very seriously. Ordinarily Jacques easily articulated his emotions, and with his psychology background he even, at times, bordered on the clinical. So when he couldn't tell me exactly what was wrong, I got on the phone and began calling couple's therapists, begging for an emergency appointment. I had to leave for Peru in less than five days, and I wasn't about to leave this situation unattended. I found someone who could see us right away, and we went at five p.m. the next afternoon.

The therapist, recommended by Kirby Ann, my former supervisor, was a friendly young-looking man in his middle forties who had been married for fifteen years. The appointment went well. Jacques expressed feeling left out over the last few months while I had been so busy. I understood completely, apologized, and promised we would have *lots* of time together after I returned from Peru. It was my last scheduled trip of the year. I explained how this tour had been the culmination of a dream born, and of subsequent work begun eight years ago. I told Jacques how grateful I was to him for being so supportive and giving. At the end of the session things felt much better between us, and for the next few days leading up to my departure, our relationship felt almost completely back to its former loving normal.

The night before I left, Jacques and I made warm and passionate love. He drove me to the airport, where I met Carol. Before leaving, I promised Jacques I'd call him when I arrived, and after our usual mushy goodbye, I headed for the plane with Carol. I knew Jacques didn't like it when I was gone, but I assumed he was used to it by now. From the beginning of our relationship I had warned him that I wasn't like most women, and that I had a spiritual mission that was central to my life. It had never been a problem during our long-distance-romance days. For the first three months after Jacques moved in, I had tried to convince him that I would make a terrible long-term partner—always boarding airplanes, engaging in unorthodox practices, performing strange ceremonies, spending time in the company of unusual characters—and that he'd best cut his losses and run. But Jacques had persevered, and had instead convinced me that I *was* the one for him, and that he was the one for me. He'd pursued me, and wooed me beyond all my reasons "why not". He was so sweet and pure and kind-hearted that, in the end, I had given in to love.

I only had one moment of consternation ... just a few weeks after

Jacques and I met, I heard a very clear voice in my head say, "this man is not on your spiritual path!" I rationalized this to mean that he wasn't involved in the Andean Tradition, then convinced myself that it didn't matter. Besides, if I had to find someone on the Andean Path, it seemed I'd have to wait forever. In the two years I'd lived in Cuzco, I hadn't found one Peruvian man I even wanted to date, let alone an Andean Priest!

I'd always experienced an inner conflict between my spiritual longings and my yearning for a normal, conjugal life. A strong part of me was drawn toward a life of pure spiritual devotion and service—I felt as if I'd followed that path in many past lives, renouncing relationship and marriage. Our modern culture also seemed to dictate that to be a successful career woman one had to sacrifice family. I wanted a successful spiritual career AND to be married with a family! I actually believed (or hoped) that part of my learning in this life was to have both. And on my trip to Q'eros, I had seen a model for the kind of family I wanted. Now it seemed I was on my way, finally beginning to reconcile in my driven, chaotic life what had, until now, seemed two irreconcilable opposites.

But as independent as I was I finally admitted, as my book neared completion, that deep down I had a fear of being an author, and a public figure, alone and without the strength and support of a partner. And I had resolved to marry Jacques if our relationship survived this last test … the publication of my book.

I pondered on all this as the airplane took us in for our dramatic high-altitude landing at the Cuzco airport, flying amidst towering ice peaks into the rich and fertile green valley where the city lay, shaped by the Inkas into the form of a Jaguar.

The Peru trip, another fascinating educational experience, was laced with synchronistic events. It was an interesting and diverse group of about twenty people—from doctor to hippie to business person to house-wife—bonded together by a similar spiritual longing that had called them to Peru. Juan and I were challenged to our limits by the practical and logistical details. Carol, with her humor, intelligence, practical common sense, and nose for synchronicities, was both a delight and invaluable help.

There were also some difficult moments during the trip. Roughly a third of our group was doctors, and ironically, all of them suffered the worst bouts of altitude sickness. Juan and I ended up having to nurse them. And perhaps not surprisingly, they were terrible patients! It became humorous, as each commented privately to us, what terrible patients the others made. But, as tended to happen on these trips, both the rituals and adversities shared ultimately served to bond the group strongly together.

Each person had come with some stirring life question or issue that was central to the next step in his or her growth. Some were changing careers, getting married, divorced, or significantly altering patterns of interaction with others in their life. But all of it, without exception, involved facing fears—the true test of moving from the third to the fourth level—overcoming blocks to their life purpose and the true expression of their deeper selves, and moving toward new levels of happiness. Throughout the trip Carol, Juan, and I heard report after report from our group on how each had gotten some new insight, clue, and sometimes clear instructions, on how to proceed on their path. It was an honor to be allowed these intimate glimpses into the workings of each sacred human soul on our trip.

Even several husbands "merely accompanying" their wives broke through to new levels of personal and spiritual awareness. I thought of Jacques, wishing he would have come to Peru with me. I had invited him many times, but he was always "too busy". And I didn't want to push "my thing" on him.

Near the end of the trip, Carol and I were so exhausted by the ceaseless demands of the tour, and then by a sudden ambush of Montezuma's revenge, that we let Juan take the group out alone. While we were holed up in our hotel room, relaxing, recovering and enjoying ourselves before a roaring fire, a group of Q'ero came by looking for Juan. We took advantage of the opportunity to ask them for private coca leaf readings.

Earlier that afternoon I had tried to call Jacques—on my trips, we usually talked by phone at least every other day, depending on my location and the availability of modern luxuries … like telephones. First I called him at the University, but his secretary said he was home sick.

Concerned, I called home, but he didn't answer. I don't know why, but my stomach started churning, and it wasn't Montezuma. Jacques was almost never sick. And he never missed work!

I then called several of his friends and left worried messages. He finally called back hours later, very apologetic—he'd gone to visit a friend who was feeling depressed. It was so like Jacques, the perpetual giver, to be out helping a friend even though he himself was sick. I was just relieved that he was alright. I told him to get under the covers and rest, that I would be home in two days to take care of him, and that I loved him.

"I love you too," he said.

On the plane home I was exhausted, but filled with gratitude. How lucky I truly was! I had a loving partner, wonderful friends, a terrific career that fulfilled me body and soul, and my first book would soon be published and out in the world!

I had missed Jacques terribly on this trip and felt perhaps I was being too rigid about not wanting to get married until after my book was published. I resolved to talk seriously with him about this when I arrived home. I had even consulted the Q'ero in our coca leaf reading about our potential marriage and our having a baby together. The response was unclear. They seemed to say it would be problematic and that I would have one son, but not for quite a while. I had a feeling that they saw something they didn't want to tell me.

When we arrived back in California, Jacques was waiting for Carol and I at the airport, wearing his usual charming smile. Delighted to see him, I threw my arms around his neck and gave him a big hug and kiss. He gallantly took our bags and we all walked to the car together, chatting amiably about our trip.

Carol was still feeling a little sick and decided to stay in San Francisco with her son, Gunther, rather than go back to her house in Richmond. We dropped her off in the city and headed across the Golden Gate Bridge for home. Jacques and I didn't talk much in the car. When I told him how happy I was to be going home with him, he smiled but didn't say anything. I too, was still feeling a little sick—mostly exhausted from the last few months of ceaseless activities and demands—and was anxious to finally be able to relax at home. When we arrived, he took my bags into the house and asked me to sit down on the couch with him.

"Elizabeth, I have to tell you something," he said.

"Yes sweetheart, you can tell me anything." I replied, with a big smile, stretching like a kitten at home in her lair. "What is it?"

"I'm moving out."

◆ ◆ ◆

The next hours, days, weeks, and months were, without doubt, the most painful and horrific of my entire life. Suddenly, with no warning, and no real explanation, my lover and best friend of more than six years had left me. When I asked him why he was leaving he would only say, "I don't want to talk about it."

For weeks afterward, my mind went over and over the events of our lives over the past few months, searching for clues. Compulsively, like Lady Macbeth's hand-washings, I viewed and reviewed key scenes and incidents between us, feeling horrible guilt, certain that something I had done must have turned Jacques's heart from me and driven him away.

Was I simply too driven along my own path to be available to another to the degree required for a relationship to work? Or perhaps I wasn't cut out for any conventional relationship. Perhaps my dreams of marriage and a family were simply unrealistic, given who I was, what my life was about, and the chaotic, travel-bound maelstrom directed by unpredictable inner callings that seemed to be the defining feature of my life.

I had no answers to the questions flooding my mind. I was confused, in pain, and feeling completely powerless. All I knew was that Jacques was gone and I missed him terribly. I couldn't eat. I couldn't sleep. I couldn't work. For days, and longer, I just sat on my living room couch and cried. I kept wishing this would prove to be a case of temporary insanity, and that soon my lover would come back to me.

I wondered if he was having a nervous breakdown. And I half-feared I might be having one of my own. Yet somehow, in the midst of these painful events, a simple realization began to coalesce in my mind. Growth, I saw, was a choice; everyone was free to choose their own pace at which to grow. And some people chose to grow, while others did not.

I knew that the choice for growth was an essential part of my nature, and that this painful ordeal with Jacques was part of that process. I had decided in my youth that I was here on Earth to change and learn and grow, and that I would face any challenge and slay any dragons, inner or outer, to overcome the obstacles in my path. I had first gone to Peru seeking to directly encounter and learn about the shadow. It was almost an invocation to the universe.

The universe had obliged—in spades! I had met my first teacher Ricardo. A third-level Andean Priest, Ricardo practiced the thrilling and seductive arts of "spiritual" phenomena. In powerful ceremonies performed in his small, pitch-dark, dirt hut outside of Cuzco, he physically manifested the *Apus*. I personally heard them, invoked by Ricardo, explode out of the roof of his little tin-roof hut, manifesting in the form of condors flapping over our heads, and landing with very material thuds on his altar table to give their proclamations or cures for illness. Sometimes twenty or thirty materialized, all speaking at once in a babble of voices.

Witnessing such phenomena in more than a few ceremonies and locations over several months certainly served some purpose. First, it captured and held the attention of a logic-oriented Westerner like myself. And second, it presented my skeptical mind with evidence of an insoluble mystery that ruptured my materialist world view and opened my mind to the reality of the spiritual world.

Yet several things became clear over time. First, Ricardo's cures didn't seem to last. Also, in-fighting and conflict surrounded Ricardo and his group of initiates—and a "Spiritual Peyton Place" wasn't my cup of tea. These factors, along with the groups' willingness to project their own spiritual power and authority outside themselves onto spirits that appeared and spoke in the dark, seemed indicative of fundamentalist religious superstition, and symptomatic of the immature ego. The Andean path of Ricardo clearly had its share of shadow-driven practitioners interested in self-aggrandizement, fame, fortune, seduction, and power over others.

The Andean Path, I learned from Juan, saw this shadow-phase of powers and their seductions as a kind of adolescence in their spiritual developmental structure. They called it the "third-level." The fourth-level was the beginning of psycho-spiritual adulthood. My struggle to understand my experiences with Ricardo had led me to meet Juan. But the ultimate word on Ricardo and the path of powers and shadows he represented had come from the Master, Don Manuel Q'espi himself, when we were in Manaus. I had asked Don Manuel if there were priests like Ricardo in Q'eros, who worked with physical manifestations of the *Apus*.

"*Si,*" he confirmed to me, "*pero no sirven.*" Meaning simply, "Yes, but they are of no real use." Such was Don Manuel's simple, yet astute determination. Third-level powers were seductive and dramatic, but temporary, illusory, and potentially destructive, like the Bull that Don Augustin had so wisely renounced during his priestly initiation. But most importantly, the actions of the third-level priest did not truly benefit the community, and this was the true mark of the fourth-level practitioner.

I knew these abysses of the unconscious—issues of power, seduction, weakness and victimization—had to be encountered, understood, and mastered in order to enter what the Andean's called the fourth-level. If this work was not done, these inner forces might turn against us and manifest in destructive forms, in physical, emotional or psychological illness, or even in amoral acts and behaviors that might be called evil. I believed that mental illness could result from the simple yet persistent refusal to take responsibility for one's life and actions.

I knew that to become whole, one had to grab one's 'shadow' and wrestle it like Gabriel with the angel in order to channel one's life-force energies in beneficial directions. Yet my task remained to wrestle with my own shadow and to not fall into the victim role. This bitter ordeal offered the possibility of significant growth, and therefore required a deeper response on my part. While I knew all this, still, I was a mish-mosh of spiritual knowledge and flailing emotion. Another part of me still refused to believe the entire ordeal was even happening. My emotions needed time to catch up to my spiritual and psychology understanding. The pain and shock were still too great!

Not long after that, in a moment of despair, I called Juan in Peru. Sobbing hysterically, I told him everything that had happened over the last two months. "Elizabeth," Juan said in a voice of absolute calm. "I must tell you something. Do you remember the incident at your house, with Jacques and the vitamin C?"

"Yes," I said, not seeing what that to do with anything.

"In that moment I *saw* Jacques. Do you understand?"

"No Juan. What do you mean?" I asked, bewildered.

"In that moment, I saw into his soul. Jacques has a terrible fear of death. And someone with that kind of fear may choose not to change, not to advance to the fourth level."

"Ohh. Umm." I could only respond with sounds. But as the cold, objective light of what Juan was saying dawned as a reality in my mind, I began to calm down.

"If Jacques chooses fear over change he will not to advance to the fourth-level and therefore he cannot be a suitable life partner for you. You must pray a lot and ask if your relationship is bound together in the world of living energies, the *kausay pacha*. You must find out if he still has *sami* for you. If he does, he will come back. If not, you must tell him "thank you very much for the beautiful times," and like a good *Ñust'a*, you must let him go."

It was not at all what I wanted to hear. Yet I knew, deep in my heart, that Juan was right. The problem was, I was still unsure of the outcome. Maybe Jacques and the *kausay pacha* were too. Could Jacques overcome his fear, integrate his shadow, and come back to me? Would he choose to? How long could I wait? In the meantime, there was nothing I could do. Now I was forced to confront another deeply hidden aspect of my own shadow, powerlessness!

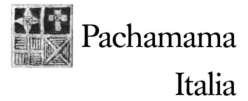

CHAPTER SIXTEEN

Pachamama
Italia

I thought and thought about what Juan had said, yet neither my Inka training nor my psychological sophistication could save me completely from getting caught up in the emotional drama of Jacques' leaving me, and now seeing him with a new girlfriend—the pain was too great. Even though I had asked him if there was someone else, he had refused to answer. But worse yet, it unnerved me that I, a trained psychotherapist and practicing Andean Priest, had not seen any of this coming.

Even now, I surprised myself....my feelings in general, and especially toward Jacques, were totally unstable. One minute I was in despair, and the next I wanted to kill him; one minute I pitied him, and the next I loved him and wanted him back again! What a mystery is the human psyche! Not to mention the human heart. Perhaps I, Miss Independence, had grown too dependent on Jacques and his love. Now his departure and betrayal of our friendship had pushed me over the edge, and I had fallen into unfamiliar, subterranean depths in my soul. This wasn't my first such encounter with betrayal which, it seemed, had some critical life lesson to teach me.

Each past experience of betrayal, after the pain subsided, had yielded profound spiritual fruits despite my sense of victimhood and my limited perspective. But my Inka training and practice had given me a larger perspective, and new tools. Now I had at least the notion that I could embrace consciously as an initiation, and transform as a priest, an experience I had formerly endured unconsciously as merely a personal injustice. Still, I would need time and distance to give me the strength to put my knowledge into practice.

And I had been both prepared and forewarned by Juan. He had told me long ago that when you work directly with living energy and increase the power and capacity of your bubble, other peoples' projections can no longer penetrate and infiltrate one in the same way as before. An empowered bubble becomes, Juan said, like spiritual Teflon, a non-stick surface that reflects directly back to the sender, energies we in psychology call "projections of the unconscious" or "the shadow."

To all of us who underwent the *Hatun Karpay*—the Great Inka Initiation—Juan had given a warning: a potential outcome of this ten-day ritual was that people in our lives might react to us very differently afterwards. Those functioning at a similar level of energy and integration would be very positively attracted to us. Those who were not might even be repelled!

But forewarned, I now discovered, was not necessarily forearmed. Nothing could have prepared me for the searing agony of this ordeal with Jacques. I began to resent...even hate the Andean tradition. What good was a spiritual path if it led to this much pain? At moments I wished I had never gone to Peru. Couldn't I have stayed home and led a normal life? What had made me pursue this alien path? Was it merely some egoistic need to feel different, special? Did I *have* to publish a book at the cost of a marriage and a possible family? Looking back in this way over the last decade of my life made me wonder ... had it really been worth it? Wasn't spiritual knowledge supposed to bring you peace? Bliss? Happiness? Did spiritual attainment ultimately lead to a place of aloneness?

I remembered Juan telling me how he had felt after Don Benito, who had been his spiritual father, died. Don Benito had led Juan by the hand from logic-bound anthropologist into the mystical world of an Andean priest. There Juan had discovered a new-found happiness previously unknown in his life. Like many Andean Masters, Don Benito knew beforehand when he was going to die. When his time came, he called all his students to come to his house to say goodbye, and to give away his most treasured possessions, his *mesas*. Due to a communication mix-up, Juan never got the message—disciple and Master never had a chance to say goodbye in the flesh. Devastated, Juan threw his *mesa* across the room and swore he would never go another step along the Path that had brought him to so much pain. That was *exactly* how I felt now!

In moments of clarity and insight, I knew these experiences were summoned by inner soul forces … they were an essential part of my human journey and *must* be encountered. In such moments I knew that all was happening for the best; this wound was ultimately medicine, healing to my soul, helping me grow in strength and self-mastery. Seeing things in this light gave my ordeal meaning, and gave me a fleeting sense of peace in the midst of chaos. And then, with seeming perversity, life would bring more salt to rub into my wounds and further insult to add to my injury, testing me to my absolute limits, and I would find myself "outraged by the injustice of it all" back in the mindset of the victim. And so I flip-flopped between third and fourth-level perspectives, trying desperately to find my balance.

It was my friends who saved me. Thank God for true friends! At this most devastating moment of my life, mine stepped forward with unbelievable love, support, and humor! They called me daily, invited me over for dinner, took me out to movies, lunches, on hikes. Without them, I might have shriveled up and died!

Slowly, slowly, I began to see and feel the great power in the pain of what was happening. I was living through my worst nightmare, surviving, growing, healing. Slowly I began, on a much deeper level, to trust that this was ultimately empowering for my soul.

Meanwhile, life kept on throwing me perverse curve balls. In the midst of the traumatic dissolution of my deepest relationship, when seeing couples kissing in the street made me nauseous, my dear friend Cyntha asked me to be an officiating priestess at her wedding. Now six months pregnant, she and Yahia had planned four weddings in four different countries for the sake of all their family and friends. They had already had weddings in Paris and Egypt (where, at Cynthia's insistence, the standard clause legally allowing the man to have four wives ended up on the cutting room floor). They now had two more countries to go: the United States and England.

The USA wedding would be in San Francisco. Dave, our gay South American "pimp" and dear friend, would co-conduct the ceremony with me, both of us being licensed priests who had performed weddings before. But I was not only to be a priest, but also the wedding organizer! Cake, flowers, wedding hall, music, rehearsal, dinner restaurant, and photographer all had to be chosen, arranged, rented or reserved well in advance. In the process, I rose not only to the occasion, but also back into a semi-functional life. In two short weeks I had arranged everything.

Finally, after all the physical and emotional preparations, on a gorgeous February afternoon, I invoked the local *Apus*, (mountain spirits) of Mount Tamalpais, Mount Diablo, and the female *Ñust'a* (water spirit) of San Francisco Bay. Then Dave had his turn, performing his own particular form of humor-tinged voodoo. The wedding was fabulous … even the weather was perfect! All of Cyntha's family came, and even some guests from England and Paris.

Happily, days after the wedding, I had a personal victory to celebrate. In early January I'd begun looking for a condo to buy. I'd been living in Jacques's and my former love-nest, which was now beyond my means and an unpleasant reminder of the past. Condo shopping provided both a pleasant distraction, and the necessary emotional hallucination that I was actually moving on with my life. Finally I found a great place at a great price—the mortgage payment would be two thirds of my current rent! Shortly after celebrating one of my dearest friend's wedding, the sale of my condo went through!

In early March I moved into my new home, but the celebration was bitter-sweet. I had always imagined buying my first home with my one true love. Now I was a woman of property, yet alone. Kindly, the universe once again sent reinforcements in the form of one Luis Carlos Machicao. Luis Carlos' parents, Señora Clemencia and Señor Juan, had virtually adopted me when I had lived in Peru, and Luis Carlos had been my little Peruvian brother. Now a famous fashion designer—the Peruvian equivalent of Giorgio Armani—Luis Carlos designed costumes for Peruvian television, theater, and opera, as well as personal clothing for Peru's First Family, and had served as an official image consultant to Keiko Sofia Fujimori, the President's daughter.

A mere thirty-two years old, famous, and devastatingly handsome, Luis Carlos was now in Canada, having gone there with bright hopes for a new love. Now, less than two weeks later, his romance abruptly shattered, he called me, desperate and too wounded to go straight home.

"Come here," I told him sympathetically. "We can drown our sorrows together!" A few days later I picked him up at the airport, and within hours we were getting toasted on champagne in my condo complex hot tub, laughing and crying and singing old Peruvian love songs together.

"If we must be miserable, we can at least be miserable in style!" Luis Carlos joked at one point, dousing me with the bottle of champagne. We understood each other. We shared creative and moody artistic temperaments. And thanks to an inspiration that appeared to us out of the ethers one golden Marin morning, his visit turned into an unexpected kind of blessing.

In a fit of muse-inspired brainstorming, we hatched a plan to design a line of super chic clothing, incorporating the magnificent Q'ero weavings into stylish upscale daywear that could give the Q'ero a significant income for performing their traditional work! Finding a way to help the Q'ero upgrade their lives without "westernizing" them and destroying their traditional culture was a long-standing dilemma. And this fashion idea seemed like a brilliant solution. It could be business run by the Wiraqocha Foundation. Although neither one of us had a good head for business, we resolved to try it. And before returning to his fashion designing duties in Lima, Luis Carlos planted another idea in my mind.

"Elizabeth, what happened to all that wonderful music you used to play when you were at my parent's house in Cuzco?" he asked me one day out of the blue. "They even sent me a tape of your singing. It was beautiful!"

"Oh, I don't know…I guess I just don't have time up here," I answered. "I don't know any musicians here either." It was an excuse. I loved writing and playing music more than anything, but lacked the confidence to pursue it.

"Why don't you come to Peru and record your music? I know everyone in the music industry. I can help you! You can stay with me at my apartment in Lima," he offered kindly. "Besides, you really need to get away, get a change of scenery." Luis Carlos was right. Everywhere I went, I was haunted by memories of my life with Jacques. And I ran the risk of running into him and his new girl-friend at any moment. I tried to use my Andean tools, eating not only my *hoocha*, but also Jacques' and his girlfriend's *hoocha*, everyday. It helped, but didn't bring the joy back into my life. I needed to make a positive, more creative step toward joy—and music, for me, was pure joy!

Exactly one month after Luis Carlos left, I called a musician friend, William Luna, in Cuzco. We had composed much music together and performed all over town. We had even made a professional tape in an outdated local recording studio. William's Aunt answered the phone and told me he was in Lima for several weeks recording some of his music. She gave me his number. The signs couldn't have been clearer. I called Luis Carlos and told him I was coming. I spent the next week putting my things in order, and soon after, I was on my way to Lima to record my first CD!

Through Luis Carlos' professional connections, we landed Pepe Ortega, the best musical producer in Peru. Pepe, a brilliant, quirky, slightly round musician with a little artistic chin stubble and small circular John Lennon glasses, was Peru's answer to Quincy Jones. He was one of the current managers of Peru's largest record company—Discos Hispanos. His day was spent making record deals, but his first and foremost love was playing music.

Pepe agreed to produce my CD, and even wrote all the musical arrangements and selected the musicians. Working from recordings I made for each song—just a tape of my voice and a guitar—Pepe created lovely musical arrangements using classical Andean wind and percussion instruments. Pepe was a gifted musician, and at my insistence, he himself played on the CD—a killer base, guitar, and the charrango, a little six stringed Peruvian guitar made from the body of an armadillo.

Pepe's sense of humor, which ranged from piercingly clever to obscenely bawdy jokes, started each recording session off on a note of warmth and laughter. It proved to be a crucial human element in what turned into a grueling musical marathon. Between writing all the arrangements, musicians' rehearsals, laying down all the instrumental tracks, vocals tracks, harmonies, and the mixing—we completed the entire project in eighteen days.

I had composed most of the songs on the CD during the years I had lived in Cuzco to give voice to my feelings, sensations, and perceptions of this magical Andean landscapes and culture, that I couldn't express in any other way. Many of the lyrics were about local people or places in or near Cuzco. But the first song seemed to have risen out of the bosom of the *Pachamama* herself during my first weeks in Cuzco. This song later became the title song of the whole CD...**Inka Spirit**.

William had a half-composed tune about a river, which in one afternoon we transformed into an ode to an encounter with the "Black Princess," the mystical feminine spirit of the Willkañust'a River, also known as the Urabamba, the Inka's most sacred river. Another song—not surprisingly about the pain of lost love—William and I composed on the spot. Its lyrics were in English and Spanish, with the refrain translated into a haunting Quechua that only Señora Clemenica, with her poetic understanding of the Inka language, could provide. With Luis Carlos as my Executive Producer, Mom on lyrics, and her husband (my Peruvian Dad) supplying the gorgeous watercolor for the CD cover, it had been family effort!

I was continually amazed how everything worked out for me when I was in Peru, as if I had entered a land where all the Gods were on my side. During our Initiation Training trips even Juan had been surprised at how I could bend plane reservationists and Hotel Managers to my will. In Peru, *I* was a queen of manifestation. Surprisingly, I never once called Juan on this trip—I think I needed a break from all things "spiritual." And for the first time ever, I didn't even go to Cuzco—a short one-hour plane ride away! This trip was uniquely and wholly focused on the artistic creation of my CD. (I didn't realize at the time that becoming permeable to the muses and making music was part and parcel of my mystical training.) For now, any contemplation of the spiritual path that seemed to have brought me so much suffering was far too painful. I was still licking my wounds.

Years later I learned that, during the making of my CD, I had spent nearly a month next to the Pachakamaq temple, the birthplace of the Inka philosophy of *Yanantin*—harmonious relationship between different things—and the Andean key to sacred partnership. According to the Inka Prophecy, Pachakamaq Temple just outside Lima was also the place of the prophesied arising of the first and only *couple* of fifth-level healer priests—the *Inka Mallku* and his *Ñust'a*! It was, so far as anyone knew, a prophecy yet to be fulfilled.

Each October, Pachakamaq Temple held the Festival of the Señor de los Milagros, (the Lord of Miracles), attended by more than one hundred thousand people. The temple thereby possessed a collective ritual bubble of enormous power. Unwittingly, I had placed myself in the direct vicinity of this Inka source of living energy for sacred partnership—exactly what my bubble required!

Before leaving Lima, Luis Carlos invited me to accompany him to a near Peruvian equivalent of a 'royal wedding.' It kept being postponed, due to the hostage crisis in the Japanese Embassy—one of the hostages was a relative of the marrying couple. Then one day we got the message that the wedding would take place that Friday, no problem.

During the next recording session, as I was in the middle of laying down the vocals on one of the last songs, I lost my concentration. Pepe looked at me, puzzled. I had an ominous feeling. I left the studio to go for a walk. "Well, go then Elizabeth," Pepe said. "Just make sure you come back. And don't go too far. It could be...you know...dangerous." Our recording studio was just four blocks from the Japanese Embassy. I walked through the streets feeling a tremendous inexplicable angst. The streets were eerily quiet.

Suddenly, I rounded a corner to find a throng of people crowded around a store window, eyes glued to a television hanging from a wall showing scenes of the Japanese Embassy. Apparently, there had been a complete turn-around in the hostage situation. President Fujimori's troops had made a daring, near-miraculous military intervention, rescuing all the hostages—and killing all the terrorists. Yet the Peruvian news reporter stated repeatedly that "no one was killed."

Apparently the terrorists, admittedly people who were threatening others' lives, no longer qualified as people. This was a shock to my naïve North American mind and heart. I, who had never lived under terrorism, was now getting a real-life education in it. Still, no matter who was right or wrong, I had personally experienced the suffering of those dying terrorists—even at four blocks away. That was the disturbance I had felt in my bubble!

I reported the event to my friends when I returned to the studio. They seemed greatly relieved, and a bit emotional themselves. Pepe added further clarity to my naïve perspective. "When you live under terrorism everyday," Pepe told me passionately, "when your friends' little eight-year-old sister gets killed by a car bomb because she was on the wrong street on the wrong day…you lose compassion for those bastards."

On Friday, the morning of the wedding, Luis Carlos had his beauticians stylishly cut and color my hair with a slight reddish tinge, pluck my eyebrows, and do my nails. Then he took me home and dressed me up in one of his most fabulous creations, a floor-length black satin evening gown with slits in the front that reached the tops of my thighs, and a beaded black bra that could have given a skeleton cleavage. But when he draped a mink stole over my shoulders and planted costume diamond drop earrings in my ears, I couldn't even recognize myself. I looked and felt like Cinderella, only with a young Latin male for a fairy-god-mother. Luis Carlos was an artist. And I was his Pygmalion!

The irony was that I had always been the epitome of the all-natural, granola-crunching, hiking-booted California girl who almost never dressed up or wore makeup. When we got to the wedding, Luis Carlos was swarmed by a flock of young beauty queens and models dying to be in his next fashion show. I had to laugh when several of them asked me, a bit nervously, if I was a model he'd brought back from the States—as if they feared I might steal a coveted spot in his next fashion show!

The reception dinner, littered with famous Peruvian artists and diplomats, was held in an enormous beachside home and art gallery of a famous Peruvian sculptor and painter. Not surprisingly after the Japanese Embassy incident, we had to pass three different security checks just to get in! On my previous trips I had moved and lived among Peru's "lowest" social castes—mostly among the materially impoverished, yet spiritually affluent Indians of the population. Now I had somehow stepped through a mirror and all was reversed ... I was seeing how the other half lived. But even the most expensive Gucci designs couldn't hide a bubble heavy with anger, jealousy, stupidity or greed. Not that there wasn't exquisite beauty here too, amongst the bubbles of the Limeño upper class. But if there were a Peruvian bubble beauty contest, the Indians would win hands downs!

We dined and danced outside on the beach cliffs under immense canopies of ivory colored silk, with tables covered in peach linens and fresh roses, lit by dozens upon dozens of silver candelabras! I had more offers for dates that night than I had had in my whole life. I actually enjoyed flirting, playing with the illusory power of my upgraded appearance. I felt like an anthropologist studying human mating rituals!

I learned another interesting and timely lesson that night as my fourth-level training enabled me to see past appearances—even my own! I now realized I could enter more easily into the hearts and minds of many different kinds of people, if I was willing to wear their costumes.

The Inkas had also used this knowledge. They would exchange clothing with the chief of a village they had conquered so the people would see and accept the Inka as one of them—and see their former chief as an Inka! The Inkas had similarly used fashion as a tool in expanding their empire and to facilitate the integration of diverse ethnic groups. This was key information I would find myself using in the next act of the unfolding mystery I had now come to know as "my life."

A few days later I received an urgent fax from my international agent; she had tracked me down in Lima. My book, just released in Italy, had hit the Italian National bestseller list in three days! I stared, dumbfounded, at the fax in my hands, with a copy of the list from an Italian newspaper. I scanned down the list, past several familiar names, among them Grishom, Critchon, and … yes! Jenkins, *Il Ritorno dell'Inka*, mistakenly listed as fiction, but in the number ten spot! The fax went on to say that my Italian Publishers, Sonzogno, had invited me to Italy for an all-expense paid publicity tour!

When I told Luis Carlos, he acted as if it was all perfectly natural.

"Of course. You see! All my work on you the other night was not in vain. Now you can look the part of a professional author. My friend Chayo can do your publicity photos—he was Claudia Schiffer's personal photographer when she came to Lima last week." He immediately got on the phone and began making the arrangements. I could only laugh in amazement.

I had always hated glamour, publicity, interviews, and photos. The last thing I wanted to think about was my "public personae." Now circumstances required that I embrace what I had formerly detested—and now, I found, it could even be fun! As Juan had predicted, the living energies of my bubble were shifting my fate. I seemed to be caught up in an irresistible flow of events, directed not by me but by the universe itself—events that were forcing me to move beyond old preconceptions and judgments that no longer served me, or that might hinder my higher purpose. All I needed to do was trust and let go.

◆ ◆ ◆

I gazed at the vast rolling countryside, stretching out beneath me, a multicolored patchwork of exquisitely textured beauty. The fields and trees had a soft, rounded, voluptuous quality. I unconsciously extended my energy bubble beyond the confines of the airplane, down toward the glorious Italian face of *Pachamama* speeding past beneath me. Suddenly, in my mind's eye, I saw a large, lovely, curvaceous, dark-eyed woman, at once elegant and jovial. I sensed her opening her arms to me in the most graceful and flowing gesture of love and salutation, to say, "Welcome to my house, daughter of mine. We are pleased beyond all telling that you have come to spend time with us."

Now, I saw her flanked on either side by a myriad of Nature Beings:

Italian *Apus*, *Ñust'as*, and many tiny fairies of the flowers and bushes, all distinctly classical, rounded and sensuous in appearance, like an Art Nouveau painting. My body was instantly flooded with warmth and a deep sense of security and care. I was about to land in the lap of the most nurturing mother in the world: *Pachamama* Italia!

"Now, let me tell you all about your Italian brothers and sisters..." she continued, and she began to explain to me, in great detail, the precise emotional and psychological state of her people. I experienced a rush of insights and intuitive perceptions—her offering to me—on how I should proceed with the interviews, on what her people needed in the spiritual arena and how I could help them, and on what approach to take in my lectures to best reach the hearts and minds of her Italian people.

One part of me was stunned by this communication, while to another part it seemed the most natural thing in the world. It was as if I had just returned from a long journey, and my grandmother was filling me in on all the family gossip, telling me how my aunts and uncles and cousins were doing, and what I could expect to encounter at the next family dinner.

By the time the plane landed at the Mal Pensa airport, just outside Milano, I no longer felt I was arriving in a foreign country, a place I'd never been before. I rather felt I was coming home to an old familiar house where I could relax in the presence of loving relatives and be cared for, fed, and well looked after.

"My God!" I murmured aloud, realizing that with the fourth-level initiation, there was now no place on our beautiful *Pachamama* that I could go and not feel totally at home. *The earth was my home.*

CHAPTER SEVENTEEN

Kaq'cha:
Blinded by the Light

My week in Italy whooshed by. To my surprise, I found that I enjoyed speaking about my Peruvian adventures and the wonders of the Andean Mystical Tradition to countless journalists wearing mystified expressions. As I spoke, my love and dedication for the Andean Tradition was naturally rekindled. Almost subliminally, the messages I delivered to countless interviewers fed back into my own deep unconscious like a healing balm.

"Yes," I heard myself saying, "I do believe it was my destiny to go to Peru and learn about the Inkas so that I could share their knowledge with you now." And the truth of my own words soothed my soul.

Although my interview schedule was jammed fuller than a can of sardines, often with eight to ten hour-long interviews each day, I was having a fabulous time. News and magazine reporters often seemed surprised to encounter an ordinary person discussing amazing mystical experiences with a down-to-earth, informal attitude. And my Andean tools definitely came in handy in critical moments.

One of my most favorite experiences in Italy, and best illustrations of the usefulness of the Inka tradition, occurred with an Italian taxi driver in Milan. I was lunching with my publisher, Ornella, an absolutely delightful, attractive, spitfire of an Italian woman, and Alexandra, the superb translator for my book, as the waiter brought dessert—real Italian tiramisu (a sweet, creamy cake laced with rum)—and cappuccino! We'd been lost in conversation when Ornella suddenly looked at her watch, buried amidst a large cluster of golden bracelets and ornate wrist bangles.

"You must go!" she commanded me. "You have a radio interview in fifteen minutes." I looked down at my first real tiramisu, heartbroken, well aware of the European cultural taboo against doggie bags … *.arive derci* tiramisu! But then I steeled my nerve and ordered the waiter to wrap it up for me! What a look he gave me! He whisked my tiramisu away, returned poste haste, and handed it to me, still in the bowl, now wearing a tin-foil hat, along with a stainless steel spoon and a napkin. I ran into the street toward Stefania, my guide, who had already hailed a cab.

As we leapt into the taxi, the driver, a rather pale yet handsome, dark-haired Italian man with a "Don Johnson" beard, informed me in loud Italian-English, "You not'a gonna eat'a THAT in'a MY taxi!" I immediately surrendered without a bite. Still huffing and puffing angrily, he took off like a bat out of hell at an anger-fuelled madcap pace that literally put me in fear for my life. I was considering ordering him to stop so that I could get another taxi when suddenly it occurred to me that I had another option. If I couldn't eat my tiramisu in his taxi, I might as well eat his heavy energy—his *hoocha*—instead.

Immediately, I visualized my *qosqo* (spiritual stomach) opening like a camera lens, and began willing his heavy energy to come to my center. Using *my qosqo* like a voracious spiritual vacuum cleaner, I pulled his anger, his fear, his upset into me, to be absorbed and digested by my spiritual stomach. I channeled the *hoocha* down my legs into *Pachamama* and felt the lighter aspects of the energy float upward toward my head. This separation of heavy and light energies was the sign by which I knew I was digesting properly.

It was always such a fascinating sensation, to consciously pull someone's heaviness toward you, rather than anxiously try to get away from it. Each time, the experience was literally energizing and empowering, and often changed the mood of the person or situation as well.

Within minutes, the driver had visibly calmed down and slowed his frenetic pace. He also kept turning to look at me every few minutes. He sensed that "something" was happening, but didn't know what to make of it.

"Had a bad day?" I offered.

"Yes," he replied, in his now charming accent, "I just'a had a terrible fight with'a my wife over our sixteen year-old daughter."

"Teenagers!" I harrumphed sympathetically. Soon we were laughing, talking about families and life. The former bat-out-of-hell was now all good-cheer and driving relatively safely—for an Italian taxi driver. Best of all, I was now allowed to eat my tiramisu in the forbidden zone of his passenger seat! How practical and useful these Andean tools were when one remembered to employ them!

I arrived at the radio station expecting a barrage of adversarial, logic-driven, paranormal-busting questions from my skeptical interviewer, to find instead a keen student of esoteric and spiritual knowledge. Mario, a tall, dark journalist with fiery eyes and a propensity for laughter, had even read my book, and in great detail. He asked excellent questions, skillfully and respectfully probing deeply into the spiritual philosophy of the Inkas. It turned out to be my best, most in-depth, and interesting interview in Italy!

I was rather surprised to find that many of the journalists I met were extremely interested in the spiritual experiences I had described in my book. Of course, there were the antagonistic few who believed anything other than the Catholic Church—even ancient traditions like the Inka, or Buddhism—to be a cult. But nearly all wanted to know what I thought of the "New-Age" movement and whether or not I fancied myself one of its gurus.

"First," I told them unequivocally, "this is a sixteen-thousand year-old spiritual tradition based in Nature. There is nothing new or "new-age" about it. Second, we don't believe in gurus. We are trying to create colleagues, not disciples, and to empower people, not make them dependent. This tradition seeks to uplift the collective, rather than to glorify the individual!" Some seemed disappointed that they couldn't easily find things to criticize in my position. Others were fascinated and wanted to know more.

Soon I realized that, as the Andean Path was based in direct, personal experience, the only way I could truly convey the tradition was to teach it right there and then. One morning I was being interviewed in the Hotel Lobby by a lovely, intelligent young woman who was clearly in conflict about her own spiritual beliefs, and experiencing pain in her life. I had been describing the practice of eating heavy energy, when I found that I had to stop talking right there and literally show her how to do it. Afterward, she was tremendously relieved and thankful, and the incident made me realize how much people needed the knowledge I now had to offer!

In one moment I knew my anger and pain—perhaps more like a temper tantrum—at the Andean Path was now sufficiently healed, and the proof was my own excitement and inspiration at the prospect of teaching. In fact, I was itching to share the spiritual tools I had learned, and get people moving along a new line of thinking. What if everyone knew how to eat *hoocha*, cleanse their bubble with *sami*, or tap into the natural resource of father sun's living energy, bringing it into their heart when they were sad or tired?

I finally convinced my publishers to get me a venue where I could present a free introductory workshop. As Juan's teacher, Don Benito, had told him, "Once you reach the fourth-level, there is only one way to proceed to the fifth. You must teach to others everything that you know. You must give away all your knowledge and power. Only then can you become empty to receive more."

I gave a lecture and a mini-workshop right there in the bookstore of my next engagement. I taught them the basic principles of Andean Mysticism and what I found to be one of the antidotes to the Western worldview: everything in the world is made of living energy—rocks, trees, humans, dogs, cars, plants, buildings—and there is NO SUCH THING AS POSITIVE OR NEGATIVE ENERGY. "Water is water," Don Benito used to say, "it may be clean or dirty, but it is not evil, it is just water. And so it is with living energy, it may be heavy or refined—but it is not negative or positive—it's just energy!"

We in Western culture were so programmed to categorize everything in terms of 'good' and 'bad'. But the Andeans followed nature and in Nature there were no "bad" plants, no "evil" animals—everything, even humans, had a purpose in the great, interdependent ecosystem of planetary life. So with living energy, some of it was heavier, some more refined, but it all served a purpose, and as an Andean Priest you were trained to work with it, to help order the world of living energies.

What the Italians liked best, however, was learning the practice of *hoocha miqjuy*, or "eating heavy energy." Of course in order to "eat" something, you have to first think of it as potentially delicious, rather than bad, icky, or negative. This was a practice that had to be taught in person, as it involved learning by energetic imitation, which was largely a non-mental process. We had found it worked best if students were in the presence of a trained spiritual stomach so that their *qosqo's* could naturally awaken and imitate its energetic action. The Italians were surprisingly good at *hoocha mijhuy* and activated their spiritual stomachs with ease and *gusto*!

As Juan had once explained to me, martial artists harnessed the basic drive of aggression, uplifting it to a spiritual path, while tantric yogis used the basic drive of sex. The Andean priests elevated the basic drive of eating to a spiritual art form, using this primal instinct to achieve a spiritual goal. No wonder the Italians, those artists of gastronomy, loved it!

Everyone was pleased with even this bare introduction to the Andean techniques, and several invited me to come back and teach a more complete workshop in their local towns. I had a feeling Italy was not going to be done with me after a mere week of publicity touring!

When the journalists asked me my opinion about the New Age movement in Italy, I told them truthfully that I knew nothing about it. But their question inspired me to ask one of my own. "What is the ancient tradition of magic or Nature Wisdom here in Italy?" I knew that every culture on earth, at one time or another, had a native, earth-based magical-spiritual or shamanic tradition.

"That would be the *stregge*," one of the women journalists told me with a look of distaste on her face. "A *stregga* is a witch," she said in answer to my confused expression. As I asked more and more of the Italians I met about this, I found that most equated the *stregge* with evil-doing; casting dark spells, the evil eye, putting curses on people, etc.

A very few people mentioned that the *stregge* were also the healers, herbalists, and trained midwives serving in childbirth. The very word *stregga* seemed to invoke fear or discomfort in the average Italian. I found this fascinating, and filed it away for future investigation.

At my next lecture, Daniele, the Milan publisher of the Italian Celestine Journal, was in attendance. When we chatted after the lecture, he mentioned he had been researching Pope Celestine the fifth, and had located his monastic retreat in Abruzzo, just East of Rome. In his late fifties, with a neatly trimmed beard, spectacles, and a quiet and refined demeanor, Daniele had the look of a scholar and a priest himself. He was going to the Abruzzo monastery for the weekend, and invited me, along with a couple of Italian journalists and friends, to accompany him. Since I had the weekend off, I accepted his offer, glad for the opportunity to become a simple tourist in Italy for a few days.

That Saturday morning, after exiting Milan, we drove for hours through beautiful mountainous landscapes graced by fields of wildflowers. Finally, we ascended through windy mountain passes until we entered a huge canyon surrounded on all sides by tall peaks. There, built right into the side of a mountain which rose to a towering snow-covered peak, was the monastery. The brick and stone used to construct the building was of nearly the same color as the mountainside herself, making the monastery blend into the natural landscape. Only the windows and towers gave away this ingenious architectural design as something more than nature alone. We were able to drive right up to a large, flat, park-like area with abundant trees in front of the monastery and park in an ample parking lot.

As we approached the old gray stone building, we saw a huge wooden door set into the stone wall. The door bore a large marble lintel on which the words *"Porta Celli,"* or Sky Door, were carved in enormous ancient letters. *Porta Celli* was the sanctuary of Pope Celestine the fifth—the only Pope ever to resign the papacy because he felt the church was too materialistic.

Immediately, I was pulled inside by a powerful and delicious force. Once inside I was drawn into the exact center of the entry room. I felt

Sky door

myself bathed in a huge column of highly refined living energy. My feet tingled as it coursed through my body and shot straight up through the ceiling of the room and into the sky. I felt my consciousness desiring to ascend. I literally wanted to climb into the sky.

"Daniele come here!" I called my guide. Daniele and the others were conversing with a curly-haired young man wearing a blue T-shirt, overalls, and sandals … he had appeared in the doorway shortly after we entered. Daniele came right over, with the young man close at his heels. "Feel this," I told him, pulling him into the center of the column of energy. I could almost see the hairs on the back of his neck rise, as he closed his eyes and his mouth curled into a little angelic smile. After a few moments he opened his eyes wide and looked at me.

"Wow!" was all he said. The young man at his side looked perturbed, almost agitated. "Oh, excuse me," Daniele said, also noticing the swirling energy field next to him. "Elizabeth, this is David. He is one of the monks who lives here. In fact, he is the only person here today. They are restoring the monastery and he has kindly offered to give us a tour."

"Pleased to meet you," I said, and shook his hand. "What an amazing place you live in! Can you tell me what this room was used for?" I asked, as the rest of our little group of journalists and friends trotted up.

"Yes," said David, "this is the place where Pope Celestine had his most important vision. You can see part of the painting representing this scene…there," he gestured upward. "We are in the process of restoring it." We looked up to see, in a dark corner near the ceiling, a painting of a man bathed in light with a few bits of angels and the profile of Jesus looking down on him from above.

"In his vision he saw the sky open right here, in this room," the Monk continued, "and Mary, Jesus, and all the saints descended to Earth to speak with him. They told him that sin was like a nail in the soul. Confession was like pulling out the nail, but forgiveness was what was needed to fill in the hole." This was a parallel, albeit Christian, description of releasing *hoocha* and refilling the space left with *sami*!

"Yes I'm sure. Can you feel this…here?" I asked him. He looked askance, avoided the question, and continued his rote tour-guide prattle on Pope Celestine and the history of the monastery. But the look on his face, were I to fill in words, told me, "Yes I feel something, though I'm really not supposed to. "

At that moment I was struck by a profound realization, as if a grain of sand that had been worrying my deep unconscious for days, finally produced its pearl. On the road trip to Abruzzo we had passed several monasteries. I had found myself reaching out with my bubble to taste the living energy of each one, and I had discovered, in each case, a similar sensation. I sensed that these monasteries were places, closed off to the public, where people went to follow a specific structured spiritual path, maintaining a series of rituals that led them to their own holy knowledge or personal experience of the divine. In the Andean tradition, the path itself was divided into two sides, and this would be called the Right Hand Side of the path.

For Andean priests the Right Hand Side was defined by a series of structured initiations and rituals that involved study, rigor, and discipline. Working on the Right Side petitioned the qualities of cold, rational logic, analytic and systematic thought, order, discipline, and structure

[213]

—functions we associate with the "left-brain." In Inka philosophy it was known as "the road to God" or *Wiraqocha*, and was related to mysticism. To me, these Italian monks and their monasteries' bubbles reeked of the Right Hand Side of the Path.

This perception led me to ask my friends how the monks interacted with the community. Did they share or teach their spiritual knowledge to the public? "No" was the answer I received. Some fed and clothed the poor, and of course they trained other monks—but that was the extent of it.

The Left Hand Side of the Inka Path required *application* of the divine knowledge acquired on the "road to God." The Left Hand Side of the Path was all about practical application, and involved things like magic, therapy, healing, and knowledge of herbs and plants. It was characterized by the spontaneous, chaotic, wild, creative, and wholistic aspect of the human being—what we call "right brain" functions. The Left Hand Side of the Path was all about applying divine knowledge to practical human situations that could serve the community. In Inka terms the Left Side related to the Magical Arts while the Right Side related to the Mystical Arts.

Applying my Inka knowledge to the modern Italian culture that I was currently observing, made me think perhaps the Italian psyche was split in two. The Catholic Church and the monks and monasteries represented the Right Hand Side of the Italian psyche. While the *stregge* with their cures, herbal remedies, and midwifery represented their Left Hand Side. These two necessary qualities, talents, and human capacities had been split-off, separated, and divided into Good (the Church) and Evil (the witches). But they were simply two sides of a single coin. Perhaps this was partly why my book was so popular in Italy—it was a healing balm, and served as a counter-balance to this unconscious division in the Italian psyche.

In the Andes, both the right and left hand sides of the path had to be developed in the training of the higher level Andean Priests. Both were honored and recognized as essential. Of course, black magic was a bane for any community—this was the Left Hand Side gone crazy. Yet rigid rules, empty rituals, and hollow judgmental dogmas were equally misguided—this was the Right Hand Side gone crazy. At the fourth-level, simultaneous development of the Right and Left Sides was vital. Then integration of these two natural human modes and capacities was possible through the philosophy of *yanantin*, harmonious relationship between different things. Wholeness required that a harmonious relationship be cultivated between these dual aspects within the human psyche.

I walked as I mused, and looked up only to find that our tour had ended and our little group had gathered outside the front door again. Our guide David, pointing down into the canyon, said, "There is the River of the Holy Spirit, named by Pope Celestine himself. It's dry now, but still it's quite lovely down there."

We thanked him profusely for our tour, and I immediately suggested we go down to the River and have a look. Curiously, according to the Inka Prophecy, the Age we had now entered, called the *Taripaypacha*, was also known as the "Age of the Holy Spirit." This was due to the influence of an Italian mystic, Joaquino di Fiore, or St. John of the Flowers, who had had a prophetic vision so similar to the Inka prophecy that it had been easily assimilated by the Andean Indians in the early sixteenth century.

In his vision, Joaquino di Fiore had seen time, like the Inkas, as passing in cycles. The first cycle he called the "Age of the Father" which was, for the Inkas, the time of their God Wiraqocha, before the Spanish conquest. The second cycle he called the "Age of the Son," defined in the Andes by the coming of the Son of God, Jesus Christ, and his ensuing adoption into their world view. We were now in the third cycle, the "Age of the Holy Spirit," predicted both by Joaquino and the Andean Priests to be a Golden Age of Humanity blessed by deep collaboration with Nature. Something about the synchronicity of the River possessing this name sent chills up my spine.

We crossed a lovely old stone bridge, went down to the rocky banks, and stood on pure white glistening stone that had been washed smooth long ago by water coursing through a now bone-dry river bed. I talked our little group through the Andean ritual of releasing our heavy energy to the spirit of the river and receiving the *sami*, the refined living energy, of the place itself.

I released my *hoocha* to the rocks beneath my feet and felt it coursing down my legs. Suddenly I saw a picture, like an X-ray of my bubble. I saw three distinct layers of deeply encrusted *hoocha* in the center of my bubble, that reminded me of a fancy three layer dessert; white chocolate, milk chocolate, and dark chocolate. The white chocolate made up the outer layer surrounding the central core of my body, the milk chocolate layer was next, closer into my spine, and finally the dark chocolate, a layer of thick, dark, dense *hoocha*, encased my entire spinal column, which now appeared as a shaft of pure

River of the Holy Spirit

light in the very center of my body. These layers of ancient *hoocha*—which felt like lifetimes of anger, heavy thoughts, and destructive acts—now seemed to explode outward from the shaft of light at my center and release down, out of my bubble to be absorbed into the rocks beneath me. Thinking of Pope Celestine I remembered to fill in the space in my bubble, now empty of deep *hoocha*, with forgiveness. In all my years of Andean practices I had never experienced anything like this!

Just then a holler from one of the Italian journalists brought us all running to where he was standing, a hundred feet or so down River. While meditating with eyes closed in the dry riverbed, he'd begun to hear trickling water. Opening his eyes, he had seen a tiny stream of water at his feet, and inadvertently shouted in surprise. The River of the Holy Spirit had begun to flow again!

◆ ◆ ◆

Curiously, and by mistake, or perhaps by the will of the Gods, the Italian edition of my book had been released in mid-May, well before the American publication. My North American book launch wasn't scheduled until August first, Inka New Year, a highly auspicious and appropriate date! Upon my return from Italy, at the end of June, I had a scant month to make all the necessary preparations, which included mass-producing and packaging two thousand of my CD's for sale!

Luis Carlos was still in Peru working madly on our fashion collection. I had sent him money and eight ponchos I had purchased during our "sacred shopping" experience in the Q'ero village of Choa Choa. In return, he had produced a one hundred and eighteen piece fashion collection ingeniously incorporating traditional Q'ero weaving patterns into high-fashion tailored men's and women's suits, jackets, dresses, and even evening gowns! He planned to bring the collection from Peru in time for the book launch.

At the book launch we would present the Wiraqocha Foundation, give an abbreviated fashion show to introduce this new collection, play my CD, and of course, launch my new book. And we would follow it all up with a champagne reception! It seemed like a lot to pull off in an evening, but it was all so interestingly interrelated. Over two hundred people were invited to the Book Passage event in Corte Madera, California, and I had been running around madly for weeks trying to find models for the show, ordering champagne, and organizing a fancy mailing to our now huge Wiraqocha Foundation mailing list. Then, after the launch I had a two-week West Coast book tour.

Miraculously, everything came together on time, and the launch came off without a hitch. It was standing room only, and the models— including none other than our own tall, beautiful, strawberry-blond Peru-initiate, Nina, and her sister—promenaded to the strains of authentic Peruvian music played over the store speakers. I then played my CD, which was very well received, and lectured on my experiences in the Andean tradition. That night we sold over fifty books, and at the end of my two-week book tour, I learned that my book had hit the San Francisco Chronicle's Bay Area bestseller list for a week, curiously enough number ten again!

For months I had done nothing but work, and work harder. Now it was paying off career wise. Yet on a personal level I was feeling more despondent and lonely than ever. Success was not so sweet with no one to share it. After my Jacques fiasco, I wondered if I could ever trust anyone, or my own judgment, again. I felt like a jaded, cynical, cranky, old maid. Finally I hit a rock bottom depression that, curiously, seemed to click some internal lever, catapulting me into another state of mind.

I had lived through all my worst relationship fears. And I had survived. "What more can anyone do to me?" I thought. Then I made a firm resolution … I was not going to live my life without love!

A few weeks later I heard a radio announcement for a "singles" moonlight cruise on the San Francisco Bay. I'd never been to a singles event in my life! But now I felt energetically pulled. As soon as I heard the announcement, I knew I would go, and go alone. A few days later, while having lunch with a group of friends, one of them shoved a clipping of a newspaper advertisement for the same Bay Singles Cruise into my hand and said, "I just think you should go on this!" The universe seemed to be telling me "All aboard!" I made my reservation that day.

Luis Carlos, who'd been staying with me since the book launch, was my wardrobe consultant and personal chauffeur … he picked me up from a workshop I was attending in Sausalito and drove me into the city. I changed into my fancy evening attire in the car while crossing the Golden Gate Bridge in rush-hour traffic, and we reached the dock as the boat was about to leave. I ran in my high-heels and leaped onto the gangway with not a moment to spare!

I soon found myself "alone" in a crowd of single people. That was when it dawned on me in horror … there was no way off! I was *marooned* on a boat for the next three hours *with four hundred singles!* This, no doubt, was precisely the evil design of the diabolical singles cruise planning committee!

Knowing the antidote for sheer panic, I took a deep, slow breath … and walked straight over to the bar for a glass of "complimentary champagne." Then, champagne in hand, I made my way over to the boat railing and gazed up at the moon—*Mama Killya*. As her tender light caressed my face I realized I was not really alone. I made a quick silent prayer to the Bay *Ñusta*, offering her some champagne, and as I tipped a few drops from my glass into the water, I told her fervently, *"I am going to have fun here and no one can stop me!"*

Normally, a crowd like this would be my idea of hell. But a potent combination of breathing, champagne, and prayer had shifted my perspective. I entertained myself by observing the bubbles of the participants playing hunt and chase games. There really was a lot of living energy on this boat, and I found it stimulating. I knew the best way for me to have fun was to dance like a banshee. So as soon as the music started I hit the dance floor and went through a series of partners until I was absolutely winded and had to sit down.

As I walked to the bar for a glass of water, a magnetic force made me look up. There, at the opposite end of the boat, was the most attractive man I had ever seen. He was tall, dark, and impeccably dressed in a soft cream-colored turtleneck sweater, black linen pants, and black snakeskin boots. He wore a pencil thin mustache above a brilliant smile, and his large brown eyes sparkled with warmth, intelligence and depth. He was lean and strong, and his bubble exuded vigor, health, *life force*, and a positively riveting male animal charisma.

I wasn't the only one who noticed him. I saw several women's heads turn as he walked over to a table and picked up his drink. Our eyes met, and a flicker of intense energy passed between us. Recognition? Attraction? Whatever! I immediately walked off in the other direction, intimidated by this gorgeous man with the shining eyes and an energy bubble I could feel across the room.

In fact, I fled all the way to the next floor, to a third deck with a dance floor and live music. I was just going to dance with as many men as possible and enjoy myself. It seemed unlikely that I would even find a date, let alone a romantic partner, on a single's boat. So I might as well have a good time. I danced for two more hours, changing decks, dance floors, music, and partners as the mood struck me. Several times I noticed the handsome stranger, who seemed also to notice me. We never talked, but seemed to be circling each other in a kind of archaic ritual mating dance for most of the night.

With one half-hour of the boat ride left, I went to the bar for yet another glass of water, steaming from physical exertion. A deep resonant voice right behind me made me turn around. There he was … Handsome himself. We had somehow ended up back to back at the bar. He also turned at the same time and our eyes met.

"Hi," he said.

"Hello," I said a bit nervously. He was there talking with his buddy. In that moment, some combination of nervousness and mischief caught hold of my tongue, and I said something completely uncharacteristic.

"I was wondering if you two guys were just going to talk to each other all night," I said cheekily, "or if you were actually planning to talk to some girls."

"Oohh, ouch! I think I've just been insulted," Handsome answered, smiling broadly. Apparently, this was my adult version of the old grade school approach where you punched the guy you liked in the shoulder to get his attention.

"Would you like to dance," Handsome responded.

"Sure," I said.

Magically, grade school tactics still worked! Not only was Handsome very handsome—but the man could dance! He swung me around the floor like a rag doll, his arms and body all raw muscular power, and not one ounce of anything extra on him. Handsome was also funny and inventive on the floor, making up moves to go with the music, surprising me at every turn. I had to work hard to keep up with him. But something else was happening. Our bodies and bubbles were connecting, communicating, interacting on some "other" level. I had danced with over a dozen guys that night, and nothing and no one had felt like this.

Finally we stopped dancing and went back to his table to catch our breaths and get our drinks. His friend was still there.

"What do you do?" Handsome asked me.

"Guess!" I commanded flirtatiously. His friend eyed me curiously.

"Well, actually my friend and I had just been commenting on you,"

Handsome replied. "I thought you were in the arts. Are you a writer?" I couldn't believe it. Bingo, on the first try.

"Yes, actually I am," I said, slightly unnerved. Clearly, Handsome had a wicked intuition. It was more than a little scary...and intriguing.

Meanwhile the boat was pulling back into the dock. The cruise was over. People were moving toward the door. Handsome took my hands, pulled me over and sat me down next to him.

"So," I said, "are you going to give me your number or what?" I couldn't believe *I* had asked *him!*

"Absolutely," Handsome said, and he wrote down his name, home phone, pager, and cell phone number on one of the ships cocktail napkins.

"Barney? Your name is Barney?" I teased, looking at the cocktail napkin.

"That's correct," he told me, in all dignity. "And your name is...?"

"Elizabeth," I said holding out my hand for him to shake in a mock gesture of politeness.

"Well, Ms. Elizabeth," he replied, taking my hand in his, completely undaunted, "my friends and I are going to a club called Harry Denton's. Would you like to come along?"

"Sure," I answered, completely charmed, and especially impressed by his resistance to teasing. He seemed truly confident, not cocky or arrogant, like many of the men on the boat. He also seemed to enjoy, and even to be down right attracted to, my bold character and cheeky impertinence. He gallantly took my hand and led me down the gangplank and onto the dock.

Once on the sidewalk, I reached down and plucked off my annoying, and by now painful, high-heeled shoes, slung them around one finger, and kept walking. Barney stopped in his tracks and stared at me.

"You're...REAL," he said, looking astonished and favorably impressed.

"You were expecting Parkay?" I answered, unstoppable.

◆ ◆ ◆

When we arrived at Harry Denton's, Barney paid my cover charge and we entered a world of throbbing drums, and bumping and grinding bodies of all races, shapes and sizes, celebrating the vitality of life force flowing through them. Normally a hermit who preferred the woods and almost never went downtown, tonight this raucous, lively, outrageous, pulsating nightclub was just the place I wanted to be. Finally, due to my Andean training, I felt capable of handling this amount of living energy.

We walked onto the dance floor and as soon as Barney's arm enfolded me, I literally lost all consciousness of where I was. There was no room, no people, and what had been eardrum puncturing music became a far-off murmuring in the night. All I could feel, all I could sense, was this strong, manly body holding me close, as we swayed gently back and forth, completely alone, under a bright light that seemed to be the moon shining down on us.

A while later I looked up, suddenly aware that time had passed. At the same moment, Barney came out of it too.

"What happened?" I asked, looking into his eyes, bewildered. He gazed deeply back at me, then answered.

"We went into a trance."

There were bodies pressed against us on every side, bumping to the outrageously loud music, which I only now could hear. When I looked at my watch, I saw that two hours had passed!

◆ ◆ ◆

"*Kaq'cha.* It's called *kaq'cha,*" Juan repeated the Quechua word to me as I struggled to understand. It was months later, and I was with Juan in Cuzco, describing to him the circumstances of my first meeting with Barney. "When the room disappears and you can see only that person … that's called *kaq'cha* in our tradition. It is like being blinded by the pure light of the other's soul. It's exactly what happened when I met my wife Lida. But it has to have happened to both of you, exactly the same." He continued, shaking a warning finger at me.

"It did. It did!" I confirmed.

"Excellent. In that case, your Barney has a very high chance of being your life partner, your *yanantin*. This coupling is blessed in the *kausay pacha*," Juan pronounced.

Juan's pronouncement rang through me like a bell. I was even somewhat frightened by it. The only thing I did know for sure about Barney and me—was that time would most certainly tell.

CHAPTER EIGHTEEN

The Spreading of the Prophecy

$\mathcal{S}$ince my return from Italy, I'd been getting dozens of requests by phone, letters, and email to come back and teach the tools of the Andean Tradition. Initially, I was afraid of responding, intimidated by the task. Then I thought of my dear friend and fellow initiate Don Juan Pauqar Espinoza, telling us so humbly that he must share the knowledge that God had given to him with everyone who came to ask for knowledge; share with everyone without distinction. Only after that did I begin to feel that it was right to go forward and teach what I knew.

When my dear friend Carol Adrienne and I were invited to speak at the same conference in the Italian Alps in a town called Arco di Trentino, I took it as a further sign of the blessings of the Gods upon my new vocation. Apparently, my book was also doing quite well in Holland. My Dutch publishers, upon hearing of my imminent return to Europe, arranged a publicity tour for me in Amsterdam. In no time at all I had lined up three weeks of teaching work in Europe.

Meanwhile, I discovered that what I'd felt that night on the boat for a handsome man by the name of Barney didn't evaporate, but grew stronger with time. Our mutual trance on the dance floor of Harry Denton's had been a kind of spiritual downloading of information between our energy bubbles. I somehow knew all kinds of things about him, without knowing how I knew. And it was the same for him with me.

At first, I was very wary of Barney, and especially of my overwhelming feelings for him. I felt a deep, instantaneous love for someone I barely knew. I became intoxicated in his presence. I thought about him continually. These were all warning signs to me of infatuation. But when Barney confessed with some bewilderment that he was experiencing the same overpowering feelings for me, I began to relax. "I think you put a spell on me!" He said. It was exactly how I felt!

Also, my Mountain Spirit—Lady Tamalpais—told me I could trust him. The two Bay Area Mountains sacred to the Miwok and other local Native Americans were Tamalpais and Mount Diablo. Tamalpais, "the sleeping lady," was my very powerful feminine local mountain deity. Barney lived in Contra Costa County under the very male Mount Diablo, to whom he had always felt a strong connection. Indian legend stated that these two mountains had been lovers, separated by a terrible fight— but one-day they would get back together. Now we both felt that through us, these two Mountain Spirits loved again!

Most importantly, my feelings for him, and my spontaneous knowledge about him, proved true rather than false over time. And I began to trust them, and him, more and more. He was a man in the fullest sense of the word, someone who believed anything was possible, and he never ever acted the victim! He was a sensitive, honest, wise, confident, athletic, dignified, powerful male, with a soul as deep as the ocean. He was even humble! And...best of all...he knew how to iron! By some magic, we had gazed beyond one another's external personalities, directly into each other's souls. And our souls fit like hand in glove. The inexorable flow of the energy world had brought us together. We had seen and loved from the fourth-level perspective—direct perception of living energy. Bubble attraction! And we were a *YANANTIN!* At long last, I was happy again. Once more I could trust my path and know with certainty that everything did indeed happen for the best.

◆ ◆ ◆

Three weeks later, I was on a plane headed for Europe. And soon, I was back in the arms of my beloved *Pachamama* Italiana! This time the little nature spirits of Lago di Garda, the lake beside the town of Arco, spoke to me on my arrival, inspiring me with ideas for my lecture. But even I was ill prepared for what came out of my mouth at my first large public lecture in the enormous banquet room of the hotel in Arco. Before dozens of Italian journalists and an audience of about five hundred good Italians, I began my lecture with ...

"Friends, I have some news for you ... *Original Sin is a lie!*" I had no idea when I opened my mouth that those words were going to come out. As soon as they did I nearly clamped my hand over my mouth in disbelief. Then I cringed and literally closed me eyes, waiting for someone to come and throw me off stage. Imagine my shock and surprise when I looked up to see five hundred Italians rewarding my imagined blasphemy with a standing ovation.

Encouraged, I continued, "In the High Andes many people have never even heard of Original Sin. In fact, they believe in *Original Virtue.* They believe in the basic goodness and deserved happiness of all people. If you think about it, we've created an entire science based on Original Sin, on looking for what is WRONG with us. Maybe you've heard of it. It's called Psychology!" More thunderous applause erupted from the crowd. "In our own DSM IV, our diagnostic and statistical manual, there isn't even a definition of mental health—only a litany of our ills! Isn't something wrong with this basic presumption?"

I spoke for twenty minutes and concluded my talk by saying, "If you remember nothing more from this lecture—**please remember this**! Find what makes you wildly, giddily, ecstatically, ridiculously happy, and do it with all your heart. Even if, and perhaps especially if, everyone tells you you're wrong. Because when you're happy, the bubble of living energy around your body is light and filled with *sami,* brimming with refined energy. And this is the best way you can help the world, and help fulfill the prophecy of the Inkas. The Prophecy that tells us we are standing at the door of a great opportunity for the human race—a potential golden era. We must, each and all together, choose to walk through that door.

And if we do choose, and start walking all together as a global community, surely there is nothing that can stop us!"

As I left the stage the crowd went wild. And I realized that in giving this very lecture, I was doing my part in the spreading of the Inka Prophecy, by putting this esoteric and prophetic vision of the ancient Inkas into plain language that ordinary people could comprehend and believe in.

People need hope, something positive to focus on, a sane alternative to the excesses of fundamentalism, to the gossip and violence that has become the evening news, or to the apocalyptic visions of fanatical, frightened or despairing so-called "spiritual" groups. THIS was my new job as I saw it—to help spread healing by sharing the ancient Inka vision of a positive future for the human race—a prophetic vision that included complete instructions on how to get there. I had found a task that made me wildly, ecstatically happy. And I was doing it!

There was a simple, grounded, human truth behind this ancient mystical vision, a universal principle more elegant and comprehensible than any in modern physics. What makes the human energy field lighter, healthier, and more refined? More resistant to stress and illness? More in harmony with its surroundings? More able to communicate? More open to necessary exchanges of living energies between all forms of life on the magnificent, sophisticated, and intelligent organism we call Earth? *HAPPINESS!* So finding the work, service, or truth that generated happiness, and following it with one's whole being, *was one's path.* In fact, in this stage of human evolution, it now became an imperative and urgent task!

My last trip to the Inka ruin of Machu Pikchu, and my most recent experiences with Don Manuel Q'espi, and our trip to Q'eros, had given me new and invaluable insights. *Nature and humans needed each other equally in order to achieve their supreme evolutionary purpose.* Machu Pikchu was just such a monument to the grand collaboration of human intelligence and nature intelligence. It was a place of highly refined living energy, but more refined than the *sami* humans or nature could produce on their own. Machu Pikchu was what happens when humans value, honor, and follow Nature, combining their highest artistry, intelligence, and creativity with Nature's own. It was a love-child and prodigy co-created by two different orders of intelligent life working together as one. The Inka culture understood what could be achieved by this greater collaboration and actively pursued it.

Slowly, surely, these glorious mysteries began to reveal themselves to me. On ordinary days, in ordinary ways, I began to know and see and feel God and the force of the Divine deeply intertwined in every aspect of my being, and in my everyday heartbeat. This was the plain and simple mystery of mysticism, that the very ordinariness of life was itself running absolutely rampant with magic. The magic of a human life infused with the force of higher consciousness is what makes us divine. This is the secret purpose of all mystical paths. And we humans **do** come with operating instructions—they are our highest dreams and visions for what our lives and what our world could be, should be, and must indeed become. The power of the heart and will together—what the Inkas call the power of *munay* (mooneye)—are all we need to manifest our visions, and grow into our divinity. To live this "path" makes us portals through which God's beauty, humor and compassion shine through, here on Earth. And the soul, a seed deep inside each of us, calls us to this.

Certainly the Inka prophecy and the Andean path pointed a way to this evolutionary destiny for individuals, for humanity, and for all planetary life. It was my calling to communicate that vision and offer those tools to anyone who wanted them. It was an offering of the ancients to a present generation searching for meaning, happiness, and a higher purpose. We could all commune with Nature, exchange living energies by spiritually breathing in and out through our energy bubbles, and give food back to the Gods to help prepare a receptive collective womb for the next step in human evolution—the Inka *Mallkus* and *Ñust'as*. These are the fifth-level healer priests who can fix all human ills with the simple touch of their human/Godly hands.

According to the Inka Prophecy, the first *Inka Mallku* would rise at the Qollorit'i Festival. He would rise out of the energetic collaboration between the giant, sacred energy bubble of human beings in prayer, and the *sami* of the great *Apu* of the sacred mountain, Sinak'ara. Humanity would achieve the fifth-level stage by collaborating at the highest level with Nature. And each of us, by our own personal communion, fulfilled our part in this plan.

Such were the insights flooding my consciousness as I traveled from country to country lecturing on the tradition and prophecy I had come to love so much. The Dutch *Pachamama* was kind and strong, and very methodical in her instruction of me. She taught me to give practical examples to her people in my lectures. The British *Pachamama* was refined, terribly well-mannered, and surgically precise about my giving a scientific and ecological flavor to my presentations, as this would best reach the ears of her people.

And while lecturing in Los Angeles, I had yet another incredible encounter with *Pachamama* Hollywood that once again turned my preconceptions upside down! One morning, shortly before dawn, she called me out of my Hotel room onto the street, and seemed to speak to me through some huge palm trees a hundred yards from Sunset Boulevard.

"Look at my vegetation!" she stated proudly, as I noticed the incredible pink, red, and orange bottle brush trees lining the street, the enormous, statuesque birds of paradise, and the immense palms, all giving me the feeling that I was standing on the set of fantasy land. "Why do you think this place is called the Dream Machine?" She gave a silvery laugh as she spoke. "It is because of us…we fire the imaginations of the people here. These plants bloom of my own most bold, audacious, and fantastic visions and dreams! *I, Pachamama* Hollywood, am the motor behind your *Dream Machine.*

"Look here, over here," she told me, as my body felt an urge to move down the street another fifty yards or so. There at the end of a tree branch, hanging just inches above a parked car, was a delicate hummingbird's nest filled with two small babies. "You see what I can do—even here! Even in smog?" She chanted and sang happily to me as I continued to sense the life force coming from the hummingbird nest. "They live with me, open to the air. Day and night they absorb my living energy." I wanted to run home and move my bed into the backyard!

"Yes, and if you ingest certain of my plants, we can change your chromosomes … your very DNA can be transmuted by a cellular collaboration with us. We have the power to cure your many ills if you would only learn to use our deeper knowledge! You have seen what happens here in your human population, when beauty merges with beauty and creative talent mixes genes with creative talent!" I was in awe, given an understanding of Hollywood different than any I could ever have imagined. "Come," she beckoned again. "Here. Over here. Look. Listen." She had coaxed me down the street right onto Sunset Boulevard just at the moment of the rising sun.

Suddenly I heard them, all singing together at once—the trees of Sunset Boulevard—stretching up their voices in a glorious chorus, an opus to the sky, greeting the dawn with wild rising voices of gold, silver and green beauty. Tears of joy and inspiration streamed down my face as an early jogger, carrying a lidded cup of Starbucks coffee in her hand, breezed pass me. Looking at my face, she smiled. After all, I was still in California. I couldn't believe this was happening in Hollywood. *Pachamama*, the parked cars, the traffic, the hummingbird nest, the smog, the jogger, the singing trees, and Starbucks! The sacred and the mundane fused together in one moment of impossible glory.

Still, I knew many of these larger insights came from yet another source. And as I raised my face up to the glowing morning sky, I felt the presence of my guiding star, who offered a perspective from which one could see the whole of the planetary system, and get at least a flash, a glimpse of its functioning. One of my favorite exercises, which I now taught to my groups, was to go outside under the night sky, pull into my bubble and absorb the living energy of the very stars. Doing this practice over time deepened my connection to my guiding star, whose presence now seemed to be constantly with me. I discovered that my own guiding star was the repository of my deepest dreams, the storehouse of my life purpose that revealed itself stage by stage as I carried out the next piece of the plan.

In training others in this practice I would tell them, "You instinctively know where your guiding star is in the sky. It doesn't matter whether or not you know its name, or to what constellation it belongs. Just feel its living energy. Let your bubble guide you to the highest, purest aspect of yourself, find your star, and absorb its living energy directly into your bubble, your mind, heart, and body."

This exercise invariably produced, in those who practiced it, a sublime intoxication on the free and living energy of nature.

Teaching the prophecy and techniques of the Inka tradition also gave me sublime satisfaction. And my book, spreading throughout the world, caused people to go and find Juan in Peru, a real flesh and blood teacher of an authentic living mystical tradition. Now through our efforts, hundreds of people around the world knew how to eat and digest heavy energy, and how to absorb into their bodies and bubbles the living natural energies of sun, wind, water, earth, *sami*, and the stars. They were also learning to connect and collaborate with their local *Apus* and *Ñust'as*— the male and female Nature Spirits in their own neighborhoods. One of my students in Alabama made such a powerful connection to the Earth Spirit of her street, that on that same day, after having lived in her house for eight years, she finally met and conversed with every one of the neighbors on her block for the first time!

Once one's energy bubble is grounded and strengthened in the forces of Nature, one is ready for intimate contact and connection with the highest aspect of one's guiding star. Now the living energy of the guiding star could inspire individuals to real actions in the world that would bear tangible, spiritual fruits!

The many examples of real life changes not only in Juan and myself, but in all our students, showed the results of what can happen when everyone connects to the living energies of Nature, and their own guiding stars. They became happier, and naturally attuned to their own unique, divinely inspired life-purpose. This gave me confidence that the fifth-level phase of human beings would indeed arrive.

I believed that we were moving collectively forward toward this real and attainable goal. I experienced examples of it daily. Many people were now finding their life purpose, creating their own happiness, and contributing their life force to the larger collective bubble. And as this occurred, our collective experience was moving more and more into the plane of personal and conscious awareness.

Years earlier, upon my first return from Peru, I had experienced a vivid vision of the Tiannamen Square massacre. My vision was confirmed months later, when I saw the exact images from my vision on T.V. when the massacre occurred. The same phenomena of spiritual sensitivity, in which the collective spontaneously manifested in personal awareness, had occurred in my experience during the Japanese Hostage Crisis in Peru. This made the spiritual truth "We are all one" a more tangible and visceral reality for me. Many of us were now feeling, seeing, even experiencing what happened to others, as if it were happening to us, whether we saw it with our physical eyes or not!

Years after my Tiannamen vision, I had the good fortune to dine with one of the student leaders of that movement. When I told him of my vision, he nodded and informed me that dozens and dozens, perhaps hundreds of people all over the world, had told him similar stories of visions and psychic impressions of being at Tiannamen Square. They had heard the tanks, felt the bullets, seen the blood, and experienced the pain, suffering, bewilderment and grief of the Chinese people. It seemed that many of us were there that day, on Tiannamen Square!

He also told me that he had never, before then, been involved in political rebellion. Coming out of his computer class, he saw students sitting in the auditorium in silent protest. There was an empty stage waiting, yet everyone was too afraid to go up to microphone and speak their truth for fear that they or their families would be persecuted. But in that moment, with no forewarning, the certainty came to him that this was his destiny. He knew that if he didn't go up, he would be going against everything inside him. He would be following the counsel of fear, just like the oppressors he sought to change.

So he walked up to the microphone and pronounced his name and address. He did not feel powerful, he told me; he did not feel like a hero. He just did what he felt he must do, what in that moment he knew he was born to do. He answered the call. Immediately, world attention was turned on him and his family in such a way that the Chinese government was rendered incapable of doing anything to them. He had followed his higher consciousness, and received a kind of divine protection that allowed him to carry out his mission.

His was one dramatic example of many more stories now occurring all over the world. People were waking up, listening to the voice within, and acting on their spiritual visions. They were answering the call, like hummingbirds drawn by the irresistible pull of flower nectar. And slowly, at times dramatically, but often quietly, the world was changing, just as the Inka prophecy foretold. People were coming home to a new and better vision for the future. And this was a vision as delicious to the Gods and the Nature Beings as it was to us humans.

For five hundred years the Q'ero, Keepers of the Spirit of the Inka, labored to keep this tradition alive. Now, warm, sweet, and nourishing, the Inka Prophecy was spreading like honey on hot home-baked bread—slowly, surely, deeply, organically embedding itself into the psyches of whomsoever it touched, filling cracks in the souls of the world with its warm nutritious nectar, spreading a sweetness that would make ants weep. As people are called and come to their Path, or this Path, or to Juan, or I, or the Q'ero, or others, and we all continue to give the knowledge that God has given us, and to live and teach and lecture and learn and train and initiate, we fill the world with sweetness, we fill the world with a new dream.

GLOSSARY

OF QUECHA TERMS

Alto Misayoq (alto-meez-eye-yoke) High Priest. An Andean Priest of the third level.

Apachiqta (ah-pah cheek-tah) An ancient prayer of thanks spoken upon arrival at the top of a mountain, meaning roughly, "lord surely you have carried me here."

Apachita (ah-pah chee-tah) A modern transliteration of apachekta, apachita now refers to the large stone houses often erected at the peaks of mountains to mark one's passing and honor the spirits.

Apu (ah-pooh) Lord. Mountain spirit. The tutelary nature deity of a village or region, inhabiting the peaks of the highest Mountain. Classically there are twelve tutelary mountain spirits of Cuzco city: APU AUSANGATE, APU SALKANTAY, MAMA SIMONA, APU PIKOL, APU MANUEL PINTA, APU WANAKAURI, APU PACHATUSAN, APU PIJCHU, APU SAQSAYWAMAN, APU WIRAQOCHAN, APU PUKIN, APU SENQ'A. Apus are generally considered male nature energies, except for a few aberrant females like Mama Simona in Cuzco, Veronica in the Sacred Valley, and Putukusi in Machu Pijchu.

Apu Sinak'ara (ah-pooh see-nak-ara) Tutelary Mountain Spirit of the Qollorit'i Festival.

Atawalpa (ah-ta-wal-pah) Twelfth ruler of the Inka Empire. Son of Wayna Qapaq and his Ecuadorian Queen. He waged war against his brother half brother,Waskar, and lost his Empire. Because he and Waskar inherited an Empire and did not return one to their children, they broke the law of *ayni,* therefore becoming full of heavy energy and sinking to the underworld. Myth states that he and Waskar are in the underworld now teaching *ayni* to the beings there until they can return to this world.

Ayllu (eye-lyoo) Family and/or spiritual community to which one belongs.

Ayllu kausay (eye-lyu cowz-eye) Collective energy.

[234]

Ayllu Apu (eye-lyu ah-pooh) A local tutelary mountain spirit who oversees a small village or community, related with the first level of the Andean path.

Ayni (eye-nee) Sacred reciprocity. If you give you will receive and if you receive you must give back. This is the one law of the Andean Mystical Tradition still often witnessed in small mountain villages today. A way of life founded by the Inkas upon which, in the high Andes, one's very survival depends.

Chontah (chon-tah) A dark and extremely hard wood from the jungle

Chullo (choo-lyo) A traditional Andean woven wool hat with earflaps, often sporting colorful tassles and intricate bead work.

Chumpi (Choom-peeh) Belt. In Andean mysticism this term also refers to the belts of living energy that surround the human body and make up the human 'bubble' or energy field.

Chumpi Paqo In Andean Mysticism this refers to a special designation of mystical priest initiated in the art of the chumpi's, or, opening the energy belts.

Chuño (choon-yo) A dry, hard, small black potatoe that has been freeze-dried Inka style.

Ch'uncho (choon-cho) A traditional hourglass design in Q'ero weaving, it is a symbol of the jungle dancer.

Despacho (des-pah-cho) A Spanish word popularly used to refer to the traditional Andean offering of thanks or supplication sent to the Nature Spirits. Despachos can contain up to 200 different ingredients and are made in a ceremony performed by Andean Priests. This offering is traditionally burned, buried, or sunk in a lake or other body of water depending on the meaning and purpose of the offering. HAYWARISQA is the actual Quechua term.

Haika (hi-kah) A Quechua bartering term that means "how much?"

Haku (ha-koo) Means "come on" or "let's go."

Hanpiq (hom-pek) To cure.

Hanpiq Runa (hom-pek roo-nah) Curandero. Healer.

Hanpuy (hon-pwee) Command form of the verb 'to come' used by Andean Priests to call the spirit of a person, God, teacher, or a Nature Being. COME!

Hanak Pacha (hah-nak pah-cha) The upper or superior world, defined by it's abundance of super-refined energy or *sami*.

Hapu (ha-pooh) Sacred couple-finest form of Yanantin. A sacred couple who have both reached full development of the three human powers: mind, heart, and body.

Hatun (hah-toon) Great, big, or high. See Hatun Karapy and/or Hatun Q'eros

Hatun Karpay (hah-toon kar-pie) The Great or High Initiation or Transmission.

Hatun Q'eros (hah-toon keros) High Q'eros. This town serves as the ceremonial center, umbilicus or *qosqo* of the Q'ero Nation.

Haywarisqa (hi-wa-ree-ska) Traditional Andean offering to the Gods, *despacho*.

Hoocha (hoo-chah) Heavy energy. Mistranslated by the Spanish as "sin."

Hoocha Mikhuy (hoo-chah meekh-hwee) To eat and digest heavy energy with the spiritual stomach. This is the central spiritual practice of the Andean Priest.

Huanka (wahn-kah) Sacred Song. Also spelled Wanka. The *Señor de Wanka* or "Lord of the Sacred Song" is an important healing sanctuary in the Cuzco area.

Huinioch Rumi (ween-yoke roo-meeh) Growing rock. Refers to the living energy and changing nature of rock.

Illia (ee-lee-ya) Lightning, also enlightenment.

Illiasca (ee-lee-ya-ska) An illumned person.

Inka (in-kah) A ruling class of people inhabiting the Cuzco valley in the late 1100's to 1532 A. D. Possibly comes from ancient word *enqa* which means "black hole" or one who can absorb all the living energies.

Inka Mallku (in-kah mal-koo) A male initiate of the fifth-level. One who can heal every illness, every time, with only a single touch. The female counterpart is *Ñust'a*. *Mallku* comes from the root word meaning tree, thus Inka *Mallky* also means "one connected to the spiritual geneaology of the Inkas."

Inti (in-tee) The living being we call the Sun.

Inti Tayta (in-teeh ti-tah) Father Sun.

Itu Apu (eeh-too ah-pooh) Masculine spirit of one's place of birth, also known as the "guiding star." Don Benito spent hours scrying in a cosmic plate to communicate with his guiding star. It makes you part of a larger cosmic system.

K'intu (keen-too) Sacred coca leaves, generally a bundle of three perfect coca leaves, chosen as an offering to the Nature Spirits. *K'intu* are generally used in multiples of three when making *despachos*.

Kamasqa (kah-mas-kah) Unique type of fourth-level priest who receives *kurak akulleq* initiation (fourth level) directly from God or *Wiraqocha*.

Karpay (kar-pie) Initiation or Transmission. See *Hatun Karpay*.

Kaq'cha (kak-chah) The state of being blinded or stupefied by a brilliant light. In mystical terms this light usually refers to the light or living energy of another' soul.

Kausay (cowz-eye) Living energy.

Kausay Pacha (cowz-eye pah-chah) The world of living energies. The energy universe.

Kausay Poq'po (cowz-eye poke-poh) The bubble of living energy around a human, plant, animal, town, mountain, or nature being.

Kay Pacha (kai pah-cha) The world of material consciousness. The "middle" world, filled with both heavy and refined living energies, typically symbolized by the Puma.

Khipu (key-pooh) Series of knotted cords used by the ancient Inkas for accounting.

Khuya (koo-yah) Impassioned love. Power object.

Khuya Rumi (koo-yah roo-mee) Gift stone from teacher or Nature Being to disciple.

Khuyay (koo-yaiy) To love Passionately.

K'intu (k'een- tooh) A bundle of three perfect coca leaves used to make an offering to the Nature Spirits. *K'intu* are a central element in the *despacho* and are generally used in multiples of three.

Kurak Akulleq (koo-rock akool-yek) Great chewer of coca leaves. This term refers to a fourth-level priest.

Llanqay (lyon-kai) The power of the body, industriousness. The power of physical work.

Llaqta Apu (lyak-tah ah-pooh) This is a medium-sized tutelary Mountain Spirit related with the second level of the Andean Path.

Lliklla (lyeek-lyuh) A small rectangular cloth woven from alpaca and used to to wrap the Andean Priests collection of power objects (the *mesa*).

Lloque (lyo-kay) Left Hand Side of the Path. Relates to the magical knowledge or application of spiritual knowledge in the physical world. Healing, magic, therapy, and remedies are all considered gifts of the left-hand side of the path. The complement is pana, or right–hand knowledge (see pana)

Mama Qocha (mama-ko-chah) Female spirit of the great ocean, water, mother of all waters.

Masintin (mahs-een-teen) Harmonious relationship between similar things, homolgous.

Masy (mass-eeh) Equal.

Masachakuy (mah-sa-cha-kwee) The act of joining two similar energy bubbles. (See Yanachakuy)

Mesa (may-suh) A Spanish word signifying the collection of *khuyas* or power objects given by the teacher or Nature Spirits to the *paqo* (initiate). The *mesa* is a physical extension of the Andean priests power and is used in almost all ceremonies.

Mikhuy (meekh-wee) To eat and digest living energy. *Hoocha* Mikhuy is the practice of eating and digesting heavy energy.

Miskayani (mees-kai-ya-nee) The mythical city inhabited by highly evolved and extremely beautiful spiritual women, revealed in Q'ero mythology. The female counterpart to the myth of Paititi.

Muju (moo-hoo) Seed. Can be a literal seed for planting, or the spiritual seed within each person. The *Hatun Karpay* provides the living energy necessary to germinate the seed.

Mullu Khuya (mool-yoo koo-yah) A specific set of five stones, progressively carved with one to five humps, used to open the human energy belts. These are the tools of the *chumpi paqo*.

Munay (moo-nai) The power of love and will together.

Ñust'a (nyu-stah) Female nature spirit, Inka princess, female of 5th level.

Pachakuti (pah-cha-koo-tee) Literally world turned upside down. In Inka history this terms refers to a cosmic transmutation occuring between one era and the next.

Pachakuteq (pah-cha koo-tek) Ninth Inka Ruler attributed with building most of the Inka Empire.

Pachakamaq (pa-cha-ka-mak) Creator. He who puts order in the world. A temple outside of Lima where the philosophy of *yanantin* was born.

Pachamama (pa-cha-mah-mah) Mother Earth.

Paititi (pie-tee-tee) The Mythical "City of Gold" or El Dorado spoken of in many historical writings on the Inkas. The Spanish were searching to plunder "El Dorado" but more than likely misunderstood the spiritual significance of "gold" to the Inka.

Pampa Misayoq (pahm-pah mee-sigh-yoke) An Andean priest who specializes in rituals such as performing *despachos* or coca leaf readings.

Panaka (pah-nah-kah) In Inka times this word refers to the twelve royal lineages of Inka families that competed in Wiraqocha Temple to become the next *Sapa* Inka or ruler of the Empire.

Paqarina (pah-ka-ree-nah) Female nature spirit who is the guardian of one's birthplace. Most prominent feminine aspect of the natural geography at one's birth site. Female counterpart of the *Itu Apu*.

Paqo (pah-ko) Initiate or student of the Andean Path.

Pana (pa-nya) Right Hand Side of the Path, relating to mystical knowledge. The cold, rational, objective and structured side of the path governing initiation and ritual. Known as "the road to God."

Phausi Runa (pah-see roo-nah) Water Vapor Spirits. Little nature deities inhabiting running water: streams, creeks, and waterfalls.

Phutuy (pooh-tooh-ee) Flowering of a plant or of the spiritual seed of the initiate.

Poq'po (poke-poh) Literally means "bubble" and refers to the field of living energy surrounding the human body.

Pukllay (poohk-ly-eye) The play of children, lovers, or the playing out of a ritual.

Putukusi (pooh-tooh-kooh-see) The name of the female mountain just at the entrance to the ruins of Machu Pijchu. Her name means "Flowering Joy."

Qawaq (cow-wak) Clairvoyant, or "seer of living energy."

Qayqa (kay-kah) A psychic or energetic knot of energy released through healing, ritual or intiation work, often causing the initiate or patient to choke or dry heave.

Qochamoqo (ko-cha-mo-koh) Literally mountain lake. This is the name of one of the highest altitude Q'ero villages.

Qollana (koy-ya-na) Excellence. In mystical training this refers to the student who keeps the teacher honest by continually pointing out inconsistencies or contradictions in their teaching. Teacher's Pet Inka style!

Qorimoqo (ko-ree-mo-koh) Golden Mountain. This is the *Apu* that watches over Hatun Q'eros.

Qollorit'i (kol-yo-ree-tee) An ancient festival in the high Andes attended by more than eighty-thousand indigenous people. Literally the word means "white as snow," or "purity."

Qosqo (kos-koh) Spiritual Stomach. Also the ancient name for the Inka capital, meaning "navel of the world." In mystical terms *qosqo* refers to the energy center located near the physical navel. It's function is to eat and digest living energy.

Qoya (koy-yah) Queen. Female or Priestess of the sixth level.

Quillya (keel-yah) Moon, or the female living energy or consciousness of the moon, oftened referred to as Mama Quillya, Mother Moon.

Ranti (ran-teeh) Equivalent.

Rumi (roo-mee) Stone.

Runa (roo-nah) Man, human, or being.

Runa Simi (rooh-nah see-mee) The tongue of man, the language of the Inkas.

Saiwa (sigh-wah) A tall column of stones built by an Andean Priest to represent his/her power, or a column of living energy.

Sami (sah-mee) Refined energy

Saminchakuy Practice of receiving refined energy into the top of one's bubble from the Hanak Pacha and releasing heavy energy from the bottom of one's bubble to Pachamama.

Saminchaska Practice of empowering another paqo's bubble with sami.

Sapa (sah-pah) Unique, the one and only.

Sapa Inka (sah-pah een-kah) The Supreme Inka (i.e.,the high king).

Seqe (say-kay) Line of living energy running through the earth, or between two ritual sites.

Seqe Rumi (say-kay room-ee) Stone of living energy lines. A sacred shrine in Hatun Q'eros.

Simi (see-mee) Tongue or language.

Sinak'ara (see-nah-ke-ara) The overlighting mountain deity of the Q'ollorit'i Festival.

Soq'a (sohk-hah) Twisted female nature spirit. More accurately, a third level initiates vision of a powerful female nature spirit. When fear is conquered, the frightening *Soq'a* transforms into a beautiful *Ñust'a*.

Suyu Apu (soo-yoo ah-pooh) A large-sized tutelary Mountain Spirit overseeing an entire region, related with the third-level of the Andean Path.

Taki Ongoy (tah-kee on-goy) Collective delirium brought about by singing. In Inka history the Taki Ongoy refers to the National Inka Movement of the 1700's that nearly overthrew the Spanish.

Taripaypacha (tah-ree-pie-pah-cha) Literally meaning "encounter with the universe," in Andean Prophecy this word refers to a new golden era in the human experience. It is known as the "age of meeting ourselves again"—and heralds coming together again of the Andean people, and the recreation of a new and better Inka Empire.

Taytacha (tie-tah-cha) Father, Lord.

Taytacha Temblores (tie-tah-cha tem-blo-rayz) Lord of the Earthquakes. This refers to an icon (statue) of the black Christ given to the city of Cuzco by Charles the fifth of Spain. It was paraded around Cuzco during a terrible earthquake and is considered by the people to have the power to stop earthquakes. This is a powerful guiding star for many Andean Priests.

Taytanchis Ranti (tie-than-chees rahn-tee) Equivalent to God on Earth. This term refers to the powers and capacity of the seventh level initiate in the Andean system of psychospiritual development. According to Inka prophecy the seventh level priest will be capable of ressurecting their own physical bodies after death.

Tawantin (tah-wahn-teen) Four.

Tawantinsuyu (tah-wahn-tin soo-yoo) Four corners, or four regions. The ancient Quechua name of the Inka Empire.

Taqe (tah-kay) To join forces, or join energy bubbles. To bring together in harmony.

Tinkuy (teen-kwee) Encounter, meeting.

Tukuy (too-kwee) Complete, fully developed.

Tukuymunayniyoq (too-kwee-moo-nie-nee-yoke) The fully developed power of the heart.

Tukuyyachayniyoq (too-kwee-ya-chai-nee-yoke) The fully developed power of the mind.

Tukuyllanqayniyoq (too-kwee-lyonk-eye-nee-yoke) The fully developed power of the body.

Tukuy Hanpiq (too-kwee hon-peek) The fully developed or complete healing power. Refers to the fifth level of psycho-spiritual development and the healing abilities of the Inka Mallku.

Tupay (too-pie) Conflict. Spiritual sparring of two Andean priests.

Tupaq (too-pok) Challenge. As a title, "One who challenges."

Ukhu Pacha (oohk-hoo pah-cha) Interior world, lower world, underworld, unconscious, or inside of the planet. The world within, traditionally symbolized by the serpent.

Ukuku (ooh-kooh-koo) The bear men or spiritual warriors of the *taripaypacha*, or new era. The "police" or keepers of order at the Qollorit'i Festival.

Unkhu (oohn-khoo) Traditional black Inka ceremonial shirt with a red seam made of alpaca and woven left-handed for spiritual power.

Unu Kausay (ooh-noo cowz-eye) The living energy of water. Water spirit.

Wacho (wah-cho) Lineage. Row of earth dug to plant seeds. The waking spiritual seed in people.

Waka (wah-kah) Sacred. Often spelled "huaca" this also refers to any sacred object or place of the Inkas.

Wanka (whan-kah) Sacred song. The Señor de Wanka (Huanca) is an important sanctuary for healing outside the city of Cuzco.

Warmi (wahr-mee) Woman.

Waskar (wah-skar) The son of Huayna Qapaq and the last "officially selected" ruler of the Inka Empire.

Wanu (wah-noo) Death, or life after life.

Wayra Kausay (why-rha cowz-eye) The living energy or spirit of the wind.

Winay (win-yay) Germination. Again this refers to plant germination as well as the spiritual germination of the initiates "seed."

Willka (veel-kah) Sacred and dangerous.

Willka Ñust'a (veel-kah nyoo-stah) Princess of the black light. Ancient name of the Urubamba River.

Wiraqocha (wee-rah-ko-cha) Lord. God. Creator. Title of respect. The Q'ero use this term to refer to one another meaning something like "good sir."

Yachay (yah-chai) The power of the mind.

Yanachakuy (yah-nah-cha-kwee) The Andean ritual for joining together two different energy bubbles.

Yanantin (yah-nahn-teen) Harmonious relationship between different things. What we usually conceive as opposites the Inkas conceive as complements, i.e., male and female, light and dark, right and left.

AUTHOR   BIOGRAPHY

IN THE LATE 1980's, Elizabeth Jenkins first traveled to
Peru on a much-needed vacation, to visit a girl fiend and take a little side
trip to investigate indigenous healing practices. What she found was a
land so compelling and a mysterious inner calling so profound, that she
returned home to San Francisco, left her PhD. program in Psychology,
fiancée, sold everything, and went back to live in Cuzco, Peru without a
single rational explanation why. Upon her return to Peru she found that
following her spiritual impulses at last bore fruit when she was taken on
an unprecedented journey deep into the mysteries and shadows of the
high Andes. Finally, persevering through the first set of hair-raising challenges and spiritual 'obstacles' with her 3rd level teacher, she was able to
enter the higher level of the Inka wisdom and under the guidance of a 4th
level Andean Priest, receive the Inka's Great Initiation of *Hatun Karpay*.
Over the course of fifteen years, she has traveled back and forth, studying,
participating, and leading others into the mystical traditions of the ancient Inkas.

Her internationally bestselling first book, *The Return of the Inka*, reveals the story of her travels both inner and outer, her spiritual trials, and ultimately describes in detail the Great Initiation known as "*Hatun Karpay*," a ten-day ritual into one of the oldest and most sacred traditions in the world. Now in this sequel, Elizabeth takes the reader deeper into this ancient mystical tradition as she travels to the home of the Q'ero Indians of Peru, the modern day descendants of the Inkas. Adventures abound in the high Andean Villages of the original Inkas, and continue when she brings her teachers to visit the USA. The Q'eros, who today number fewer than 600, are the Keepers of Spirit of the Inka. Theirs is a philosophy based on principles of nature's fundamental unity. Their prophecies proclaim that in 1993 humanity entered a period, due to end in 2012, with auspicious possibilities for collective spiritual evolution.

Today Elizabeth lives on an organic orchard in Hawaii with her husband and two sons. From there, she heads the Wiraqocha Foundation, with chapters also in Europe, Peru, and California. She regularly travels the world to teach, leads groups to Peru, and is creating a retreat center on the Big Island of Hawaii. To order her books, music CD "Inka Spirit", or learn more about programs for the preservation of indigenous wisdom, visit www.inka-online.com or contact (808) 929-8785. Or you may write the Wiraqocha Foundation at P.O. Box 500, Naalehu, HI. 96772 USA.

ORDER FORM

Make checks payable to
Elizabeth Jenkins c/o Wiraqocha Foundation:

Pu'umaka'a Press
PO Box 500
Naalehu, Hawaii 96772 USA

AVAILABLE TITLES:	QTY	PRICE
The Return of the Inka		$18.95
Journey to Q'eros: Golden Cradle of the Inka		$18.95
Add Shipping & Handling each book $5.00 priority shipping within USA $9.00 priority for Europe		$
	TOTAL	

Ship to:

_____

NAME

_____

STREET

_____

CITY   STATE   ZIP

20% of all book proceeds go to
Wiraqocha Foundation for the Preservation of Indigenous Wisdom.
For more information see **www. inka-online.com**

Wiraqocha Foundation is a 501(C)3 not-for-profit corporation.
Tax deductible donations may be mailed directly to
PO Box 500, Naalehu, Hawaii, 96772